"HE'S ALL MAN"

"HE'S ALL MAN"

Learning Masculinity, Gayness, and Love from American Movies

JOHN M. CLUM

Withdrawn

palgrave

First published 2002 by

PALGRAVE™

175 Fifth Avenue, New York, N.Y. 10010 and

Houndmills, Basingstoke, Hampshire RG21 6XS.

Companies and representatives throughout the world.

PALGRAVE™ is the new global publishing imprint of St. Martin's Press LLC Scholarly and Reference Division and Palgrave Publishers Ltd (formerly Macmillan Press Ltd).

ISBN 0–312–24035-X hardback

Library of Congress Cataloging-in-Publication Data

"He's all man" : learning masculinity, gayness, and love from American movies / John M. Clum.

p.   cm.

Includes bibliographical references and index.

ISBN 0-312-24035-X

1. Men in motion pictures.   2. Machismo in motion pictures.
3. Homosexuality in motion pictures.   4. Homosexuality and motion pictures.
I. Title.

PN1995.9.M46 C49   2002

791.43'652041—dc21

2002016935

Design by Letra Libre, Inc.

First edition: April 2002

10   9   8   7   6   5   4   3   2   1

Printed in the United States of America

121169001

For Jean and Jan

CONTENTS

Ten pages of illustrations appear between pages 96 and 97.

ACKNOWLEDGMENTS

Thanks first of all to Michael Flamini, my editor at Palgrave, for his faith in me and my work, and for his friendship. And to all the other wonderful folks at Palgrave, particularly Production Editor Alan Bradshaw and his terrific staff. They make it all easy.

Thanks to Michael Schwartz, with whom I co-taught film courses at Duke University for a number of years and from whom I learned a great deal about film. To Jane Gaines, another co-teacher and mentor. And to the pioneers in the field: the late Vito Russo and the brilliant Richard Dyer.

Thanks to Richard Riddell, chair of Duke's Department of Theater Studies, for giving me the time to write this, and to my colleagues at Duke, particularly Dale and Phyllis Randall.

To my dear friends who offered moral and intellectual support and great acts of kindness during the writing of this book, particularly Bob West, Eric Thornton, and Marcia Cohen.

Thanks to the folks at the terrific video stores that made my research possible, particularly Video Americain in Baltimore and Movies Worth Seeing in Atlanta.

And thanks, as always, to my partner, my muse, and my filmgoing companion, Walter Melion.

Foreword

RONALD REAGAN, AUDIE MURPHY, AND I

A Saturday Matinee Education into Manhood

"He's All Man" is an investigation of images of masculinity that Hollywood and, to some extent, Broadway, the source of many classic films I discuss here, have given us. As a gay man of a certain age, I am interested in what these works, many of which I have seen or read many times and at different points in my life, say about where I fit into American myths of masculinity. I am particularly interested in the homoeroticism and anxiety that circulate around films that define and maintain conventional masculine roles. I also want to show how gay filmmakers try, often uncritically, to find a place for gay men within traditional scenarios of male bonding and testing. I will explore how we are allowed to prove ourselves as at least "straight-looking and -acting," and, in a society in which marriage, an on-going structured domestic pattern, is the norm for heterosexual men (and women), how our writers and filmmakers offer an ambivalent picture of gay "marriage." A major theme of this book will be the ways in which gay artists have been influenced by the mixed messages on masculinity that Hollywood has been sending over the past century. Can one really be both hard and soft? Can one love a man without feeling any desire for him? Does male-male love fit within the paradigm of marriage, and can that paradigm work without the concept of patriarchal authority?

"HE'S ALL MAN—WE MADE SURE OF THAT."

The title of this book comes from a statement by Ronald Reagan, whom critic Susan Jeffords describes as "the premiere masculine archetype for the 1980s, embodying both national and individual images of manliness that came to underlie the nation's identity during his eight years in office."[1] I, however, remember Reagan from my growing up in the 1950s as the man who shared the screen with a chimp in *Bedtime for Bonzo* (1950) and the bland guy who hosted *General Electric Theatre* on television. I could see Reagan neither as a masculine hero, a John Wayne type—though his and Wayne's politics are similar—nor as a masculine figure I could admire or eroticize. He was another remote father figure—all of Reagan's biographers emphasize his remoteness, which for some was a sign of masculine strength—sure of his simplistic beliefs, cold, lacking in compassion, and devoid of irony, which gay men of my generation think essential to survival. Only a man without irony could order the invasion of Grenada! I don't think like a social conservative, so I couldn't believe in Reagan's ability "to portray himself as both a 'real man' and a 'real president,' as both a father and a king."[2] He was just a dull, ordinary guy, much like my father and the fathers of my friends—in other words, what I desperately fought against becoming. The Ronald Reagan cult comprises folks nostalgic for the 1950s, people for whom the 1960s were a time of destruction of the best of our culture. I'm not a great fan of Robert Bly, but I like his description of Reagan as an example of "the Fifties male":

> This sort of man didn't see women's souls well, but he admired their bodies; and his view of culture and America's part in it was boyish and optimistic. Many of his qualities were strong and positive, but underneath the charm and bluff there was, and there remains, much isolation, deprivation, and passivity. Unless he has an enemy, he isn't sure he is alive.
>
> The Fifties man was supposed to like football, be aggressive, stick up for the United States, never cry, and always provide . . .
>
> The Fifties male had a clear vision of what a man was, and what male responsibilities were, but the isolation and one-sidedness of his vision were dangerous.[3]

Reagan at least *seemed* to be benign. The new incarnations of this "Fifties male" now dominate our political landscape, fiercer because they have to defend attitudes they think are above question, but adept at sheathing their claws, particularly during political campaigns and Senate confirmation hearings.

I would assert that this character whom Bly calls the "Fifties male" is a distillation of the male that Hollywood has given us since World War II and that our national literature had given us, in more complex forms, for a century before that. The bluff, powerful exterior encasing "isolation, deprivation, and passivity" is central to narratives of American manhood. Our classic male protagonist tends to be a split personality with a passive, reflective narrator recording and desiring a more powerful, if woefully incomplete alter ego—Ishmael and Ahab, Nick Carraway and Jay Gatsby, Sal Paradise and Dean Moriarty. In our classic drama we see the split depicted most powerfully in father-son clashes, like that of Miller's Willy Loman and his son, Biff, or Williams's Big Daddy and Brick. In film, we see it in the conflict between Rico Bandello and his beloved Joe in *Little Caesar*, the crypto-gay protagonists of Alfred Hitchcock's *Rope*, and particularly in some of the fraught depictions of masculinity of the past three decades, most vividly in films of the 1970s like *Deliverance* and more recent films like *Fight Club*. What complicates this split are the currents of desire that circulate between the two incomplete parts.

Ronald Reagan seemed powerful because he seemed coherent, though one can never forget that he was an actor who learned, during the forties and fifties in Hollywood, what America wanted to see in a man. He adapted his own image to those Hollywood models of masculine coherence, the western heroes of John Ford, Howard Hawks, and their imitators, particularly the heroes played by "all man" John Wayne.

During his first presidential campaign, this idol of the right wing, the man who wasn't a cowboy but who had played one in movies and on television (actually he hosted and did the commercials for 20 Mule Team Borax on *Death Valley Days*), had a slight embarrassment, a son who was a ballet dancer, which raised rumors of those things most dreaded by right-wing men: artiness, effeminacy, and homosexuality—which they equate. Defenders of American manhood could say that Ronald Reagan had sired a sissy, which would cast aspersions on his own manhood. When asked at a press conference about the rumors circulating about young Ron, Reagan's answer was "He's all man—we made sure of that."[4] Good parents like Ronald and Nancy would ensure that their son was reared to be properly and completely masculine and that his masculinity would be policed. What greater duty did a parent of the time have than to make sure his or her child received proper gender education? But what does "he's all man" mean? Anyone who had seen Ron Jr. in his ballet tights could vouch for the fact that he certainly was, shall we say, well equipped with the appropriate male appendages.[5] However, Ronald Reagan was responding to rumors that young Ron was gay. "He's all man" meant "he's all heterosexual." To support Dad's claim that his son was "all man," Ron, Jr. got married and moved from ballet to television, a more manly aspect of showbusiness.

Reagan's "he's all man" assertion puzzled and fascinated me. I had heard variants of it in my own childhood and knew it was a concept that excluded me. Somehow hearing it from Ronald Reagan epitomized its vagueness. Was Ronald Reagan, who loved to be photographed on horseback at his California ranch, really America's idea of "all man"? Was this hero of social conservatives, who was divorced and notoriously distant from his children, really a proper arbiter of gender? If anything, Ronald Reagan's use of the term "all man" only serves to show how problematic a concept manhood is. Only a Hollywood product like Reagan could evoke it so uncritically, unreflectively, unironically. Hollywood, after all, has devoted a great deal of energy to upholding the gender order and traditional definitions of masculinity.

Thrice cursed by being arty, intellectual, and gay, I have been puzzled and fascinated by the world of those who are considered "all man," particularly the heroes popular culture has offered me as role models. I cannot, for instance, fathom how a majority of American men can identify with or want to be led by George W. Bush. There's a whole world out there that speaks a language I cannot totally decipher: men, total strangers, bonding on buses, trains, and planes by talking about last night's football game, men who found Ronald Reagan particularly manly. Literature tells me that I am not the only man who feels out of the loop. Toward the end of Bret Easton Ellis's *American Psycho,* his mad, murderous yuppie protagonist observes of a friend who has just gotten a big promotion: "As he leaves I'm wondering and not wondering what happens in the world of Tim Price, which is really the world of most of us: big ideas, guy stuff, boy meets world, boy gets it."[6] "Guy stuff" is "getting it" in the sense of grasping the brass ring of success, but also in the sense of understanding the rules of masculinity. While I can't say I identify with Ellis's homicidal hero, I do understand his feeling left out of the "guy stuff," even as he convincingly performs it. In his eloquent memoir *Firebird,* gay poet Mark Doty recalls the moment in childhood when he realized that he was different from most boys, who seem already possessed of forms of knowledge opaque to me, things they grasp and I do not: baseball gloves, for instance, the inflation of rubber balls, marbles, the choosing of teams, names of models of cars. Where they got this knowledge I don't know; already I have a dawning sense that either it is too late for me to ask the questions or that questioning is not the way such understandings are gained.[7]

I know that it is essentialist and stereotypical to assert that all gay men feel the way Doty and I do. Many gay men "got" the knowledge of guy stuff and have found ways of being gay without feeling left outside of the masculine loop. Some of these are the guys proud of being "straight-looking and -acting" and of seeking friends and partners who are the same. The very use of the term "straight-looking and -acting" connotes that masculine appearance and behavior are intrinsically heterosexual—something a gay man can act but never be. Gender theorists like Judith Butler have consoled us with the knowledge that straight men are as separate from the ideal masculinity they may try to enact as we are, a notion gay-created plays and films constantly affirm. Mark Doty learned that being a boy—being masculine—was a Kafkaesque nightmare of learning rules that didn't really exist, so as not to get caught by those who police the rules:

> "You're a boy" means *I'm policing you now, we've got your number, we see your deviant ways. You must be vigilant, impossibly vigilant, because you could slip anytime, you could make so many mistakes, you don't even know what the mistakes are, since you don't understand what it is you're supposed to be.*"[8]

And everybody seems to be doing the policing: parents, teachers, peers most brutally. Most of the policing is done by other males. As sociologist Michael Kimmel points out, "American men define their masculinity not so much in relation to women, but in relation to each other. Masculinity is largely a homosocial enactment."[9] For many of us, masculinity is like the actor's nightmare of finding oneself in a play without knowing the script, without even knowing what play one is in. One thing we do know is that masculinity is, if not a script, at least, like commedia dell'arte, a series of learned routines one masters. Kimmel observes, "Over our two centuries of history, American manhood became less and less about an inner sense of self, and more and more about a possession that needed to be acquired."[10] Where does one get it? Gold's Gym? The Home Depot? And is it something one has to have?

The central assumption of this book is that we get manhood not only from modeling ourselves on those around us that we see as "all man" but also from the fantasies Hollywood offers us, fantasies starring the likes of Ronald Reagan. Like the real models for manhood that we see, Hollywood's models are more often than not complex and contradictory.

HARD OR SOFT

There never seemed to be any conflict between Ronald Reagan and his son Ron, who simply got married, packed up his dance belt, and moved on. According to his father's biographers, young Ron was an ardent and loyal supporter of his father who did what a good son should do. Symbolically, however, the difference between son—"the apple of his mother's eye," according to one Reagan biographer—and father demonstrates a formula we see in a lot of plays and films written after World War II: that of the hard, patriarchal figure and the softer, more feminized son. We see it in canonical plays like Tennessee Williams's *Cat on a Hot Tin Roof;* we see it more in the symbolic father-son battles played out in classic westerns and war films, particularly those starring the prototypical hard man, John Wayne. And we note its absence: The problem for the troubled teens in Nicholas Ray's *Rebel Without a Cause* (1955) is that there is no hard man for Jim (James Dean) and Plato (Sal Mineo) to emulate or battle on their way to sensitive manhood, which entails finding the proper combination of hard and soft.

After World War II American men were given a mixed message. On the one hand, they were to remain tough, the sort of men who fought and defeated the Axis powers. On the other hand, they were to be benign, domesticated figures like Ozzie Nelson (*The Adventures of Ozzie and Harriet*) and Jim Anderson (*Father Knows Best*), always gentle, loving, emotionally open. No work defined the postwar hard-soft confusion more clearly than Robert Anderson's hit play *Tea and Sympathy* (1953), later adapted into a successful film (1956) with its Broadway stars, Deborah Kerr and John Kerr (no relation). In a New England prep school, a sensitive, guitar-playing adolescent is suspected of being homosexual (though the word is never spoken). The real, if "latent" (a central word in 1950s psychiatric jargon) homosexual turns out to be the stern, homophobic, married headmaster who would rather take field trips with his boys than be a proper husband to his new wife. The hard man, "large and strong with a tendency to be gruff,"[11] is no longer "all man," capable of the settled domestic life of family and consumption. He might even like the boys too much. The young man can be as sensitive as he wants, provided he proves he is heterosexual. Here, as in many cultural productions of the 1950s, is an attempt, not totally successful, to separate sensitivity from homosexuality. Can "he-men" be sensitive, as well as capable of courageous action? As we shall see, though John Wayne was the most popular male star of the 1950s, he was always balanced by a "soft" young man who could be domesticated.

Though in the postwar period the soft son usually represented an essential compromise between the masculine values of the frontier and the domestic values of mid-twentieth-century America, the father was a strong, necessary symbolic presence. Yet by the 1970s, the era of liberation movements in American culture, all of which had a profound, unsettling effect on American masculinity, men seemed to be lost without models of masculinity. As I shall discuss in chapter 4, films like *Deliverance* and *The Deer Hunter,* films about men without father figures, without stable, successful models of masculinity, offer deeply troubled narratives of men in crisis for whom homoeroticism is a primary anxiety. By the Reagan era, in television dramas like *An Early Frost* (1985) or *Consenting Adult* (1985), the soft son was definitely gay and in conflict with his stern, homophobic, macho patriarch. Real men, hard men, were straight and intent on policing homosexuality. Soft was out—in more ways than one. Susan Jeffords wrote a superb book, *Hard Bodies,* about Hollywood's celebration of manhood in the Reagan era,[12] the heyday of Rambo and Schwarzenegger. Susan Bordo's end-of-the-century study, *The Male Body,* still proclaimed, "To be exposed as 'soft' at the core is one of the worst things a man can suffer in this culture."[13] Nonetheless, in 1999, a highly praised, popular film, *American Beauty,* which depicted a middle-class suburban man in crisis, also included a brutally homophobic, closeted queen Marine officer (a far cry from John Wayne's Sergeant Stryker in *Sands of Iwo Jima* [1949]) and portrayed a sensitive, straight, but gay-friendly young man as the ideal. In other words, we're not far from *Tea and Sympathy,* except that in *American Beauty,* there are real homosexuals in the neighborhood, and behind the scenes, an openly homosexual screenwriter.

MAKE ROOM FOR DADDY

As we are well into another Republican faux-macho presidency, masculinity is a hot topic in academic circles, but popular culture, now the most important teacher of gender, still offers a mixed message. Kids enjoy the clear, unambiguous message of rap—macho swagger, anger, misogyny, and homophobia to a heavy beat—but the same MTV that offers teenagers the latest pop-music heroes also devotes hours of commercial-free programming to combat the very violence against women and gay people celebrated in the lyrics of Eminem and the black rappers he imitates. The first season of the hit show *Survivor* (2000) offered as its toughest, cleverest, most ruthless desert island castaway an openly gay man—sissies no more! In that same year's hit film, *Traffic* (2000; screenplay, Simon Moore and Stephen Gaghan; direction, Steven Soderbergh), a teenage boy advises Robert (Michael Douglas), our expert in playing men whose masculinity is embattled, "Don't do this vigilante thing, OK?" as Douglas seeks his drug addict daughter in the inner city. Later, Douglas gives up a powerful position as the nation's drug czar to attend sensitivity sessions with his wife and daughter. "I'm just here to listen," he says. What would the Charles Bronson of *Death Wish* (1974) make of that? We accept the resolution of *Traffic,* however, because Hollywood has taught us since the end of World War II that a man's primary role is as husband and father. But what is marriage in the twenty-first century?

Which leads to a second Ronald Reagan memory that came to mind as I planned this book. During the 1984 Republican National Convention, the night before President Reagan was nominated by his party to run for a second term, Nancy Reagan appeared on the platform to a tumultuous reception. Here was a steely first lady who wielded a lot of power, but always in defense of and service to her husband. Petite, tidy, chilly Nancy mounted the podium to the wild cheers of an audience who saw her as the Ideal Wife; behind her, on a giant screen, appeared a televised image of Ronald Reagan in his hotel room. Nancy faced the screen, waved, and blew kisses. Here was a moment conservatives could love: a wife paying homage to a giant picture of her husband, who was in reality in another place altogether, apart from and above his spouse, to say nothing of the rest of us. Whatever the reality of Ronald and Nancy Reagan's marriage, which seemed from afar to be truly loving, this televised moment was for me a vivid image of a traditional patriarchal marriage short on real connection.

One major theme of this book is the ways in which masculinity and domesticity intertwine in Hollywood's myth of manhood. Even the macho heroes outside the family structure, like Alan Ladd's Shane (*Shane,* 1953) and John Wayne's Ethan Edwards in *The Searchers* devote themselves to saving families. Maximus in Ridley Scott's *Gladiator* (2000) seeks vengeance less for the injustices done to him than for the death of his wife and son. This Charles Bronson of ancient Rome is both super-hero and devoted family man. His nemesis, kinky Emperor Commodus, is neither. According to Virginia Wright Wexman's *Creating the Couple: Love, Marriage, and Hollywood Performance,* every aspect of Hollywood narrative cinema, from the scenario to the star system, exists to teach and reinforce concepts of heterosexual romance and marriage. This is why Ronald and Nancy Reagan, a B-movie actor and his B-movie actress wife, could portray an image of conventional marital love more successfully than just about any president and first lady in our history. What else had Hollywood taught them to play?

Hollywood's insistence on marriage and the nuclear family is not as potent now as it was in the 1950s, though Hollywood still expects its stars to be married, if for no other reason than to stave off rumors of homosexuality. Though film and television are less inclined to unquestioningly celebrate heterosexual marriage and the nuclear family, failure at marriage is yet seen as both a personal and cultural failure. Still, one understands the roles allowed lesbians and gay men (bisexuals, who present a greater challenge to traditional notions of monogamy and domesticity, don't exist) in movies best when one sees that gay men are constantly seen, positively and negatively, against the paradigm of marriage. Though many gay men are coupled, for the most part the entertainment industry offers us only the vain, immature, solipsistic creatures who inhabit shows like *Will & Grace* and *Queer as Folk.* What I want to suggest here is that this is in great part because masculinity and heterosexuality have been defined as that which is not homosexual, not as a set of positive qualities that stand on their own. And the point at which intense male-male relationships become a threat to that homo-hetero boundary becomes a place of extreme anxiety. Why else do conservative men argue that homosexual marriage devalues marriage for heterosexuals? If the Hollywood studios and network television are still skittish about gay men being sexual, much less romantic, unless they die at the end, independent gay cinema focuses on the possibility of romance. But as we shall see in chapter 7, the controversy within the gay community surrounding gay "marriage" is reflected in our films in the ambivalence toward "till death do us part."

"He's All Man" is structured as a series of related essays on masculine images and the ways in which homoeroticism and homosexuality have been part of dramatic and cinematic narratives of masculinity.

Part I, "Learning Masculinity," examines the ways in which certain genres—domestic melodrama, the western, the war film, the buddy film—offered models for masculine behavior and the way in which these models broke down in the Vietnam era. Chapter 1, "Dicks and Testosterone," is a preliminary exploration of works that focus on what are supposed to be a man's defining feature and characteristic: his penis and his aggression. I look at films in which the penis itself is at stake in defining relationships, then at recent celebrations of masculine aggression that focus on men doing battle, not against a clearly defined enemy, as in the war film or the western, but against an emasculating society.

In order to understand the primacy of the male couple in classic American drama and film, it is important to look at the ways in which the conventional gender order is presented. Chapter 2, "Father Knows Best," investigates films that examine the "proper" role of women in the domestic space. The central action of these works is the silencing of the woman and the triumph of the masculine voice. I will show that recent gay-created films aren't any more enlightened on gender equality than their predecessors.

Chapter 3, "Fathers and Cowboys," discusses fathers and surrogate fathers and their mentoring relationships with young men as displayed particularly in the postwar western. Here the conflict is between the idealized "hard man," the classic American loner hero, and the "soft" young man who has to learn some of the hardness of his mentor but is, because of his softness, able to fit into the domestic space so valorized in the postwar period.

Chapter 4, "Manhood Unraveling," looks at two "straight" films, set primarily outdoors, in which anxiety about homosexuality on the part of white heterosexual men is dramatized via bodily mutilation and violent death, and a gay film that echoes some of these same motifs.

Part II, "Learning Gayness?" analyzes some of the bizarre role models Hollywood has offered gay men and the link Hollywood has reinforced between homosexuality and criminality.

Chapter 5, "Gay Killers," examines the homoerotic element in plays and films about killers, focusing particularly on three works based on the Leopold-Loeb murder case.

Chapter 6, "Sex and the City," offers a discussion of films about violence as a punishment for transgressive sex in urban settings in which one can observe a transformation of the gay character from psychopathic killer to avenging lover.

Part III, "Learning Love," explores paradigms for male-male love in gay-created film. In Chapter 7, "In the Shadow of Cary Grant: Gay Romance," I examine the relationship of gay romantic comedy and classic "straight" romantic comedy. I also consider the ambivalent view of committed relationships one finds in gay-created films.

In the final chapter, "Black and White: Ennobling Love," I look briefly at race, gayness, and male-male love in a 1950s mainstream film, *The Defiant Ones,* and in two recent gay-created films.

While this is primarily a book on film, conceived of as a companion piece to my book, *Still Acting Gay: Male Homosexuality in Modern Drama* (St. Martin's Press, 2000), I do discuss the work of a few significant playwrights whose work is as much a part of Hollywood as the legitimate theater. All of the plays I discuss have been made into successful films. Though Hollywood is the primary purveyor of gender ideology (known in some circles as "family values"), I am interested in how mainstream American theater and film coalesce ideologically. While there are queer elements in many classic films, it is also the case that Hollywood often attempted to "dequeer" hit plays that dared to speak the name of homosexual desire. Hollywood's ideological machinery could remold a potentially transgressive work like Tennessee Williams's *Cat on a Hot Tin Roof* into a commercial for the traditional nuclear family.

I devote much of this book to mainstream works created before sexual and gay liberation took hold because I am fascinated by their complex, confused messages about manhood in general and homosexuality in particular. Queer-culture theorist Alexander Doty is spot on when he observes that "the coding of classic or otherwise 'mainstream' texts and personalities can often yield a wider range of non-straight readings because certain sexual things could not be stated baldly—and still cannot or will not in most mainstream products—thus often making it more difficult to categorize the erotics of a film or a star."[14] I don't think I'm queering *Little Caesar* when I point out the homoerotic relationship of the title character and his sidekick, Otero. It is already queered. My own sexuality does make me more interested in what Jeffrey Hunter's Martin Pawley is up to in *The Searchers* than in Ethan Edwards's much discussed monomania. There's a lot of homoeroticism in classic films that is hidden and countered by the dominant structure of the patriarchal, heterosexual nuclear family.

The book is not meant to be exhaustive. I don't discuss the comedy teams of the nineteen-forties and nineteen-fifties, particularly Bob Hope

and Bing Crosby and Dean Martin and Jerry Lewis. Other critics have
dealt brilliantly with them, particularly Steven Cohan on the Hope-
Crosby road pictures.[15] Nor do I deal with the more obvious "buddy
films" of the 1960s and 1970s, films like *Butch Cassidy and the Sundance
Kid* and *Thunderbolt and Lightfoot.* Some, like Susan Jeffords, have offered comprehensive studies of action films of the 1980s and '90s. I am
particularly interested in what might be called plays and films of masculine education and on the ways in which these works, while asserting
men's—and women's—appropriate place in a vertical, patriarchal gender
order, contain relationships that a gay audience member can identify
with. Once in a while I discuss a British film readily available on video,
for British filmmakers seem to be much more interested in breaking
down conventional categories of gender and sexuality than their American counterparts.

In the introduction to *Out Takes: Essays on Queer Theory and Film,*
Ellis Hanson notes:

> On the question of homosexuality in particular, the literature tends to
> shuffle between three influential and equally problematic models: first,
> a moralistic *politics of representation* that seeks to liberate us from dam-
> aging stereotypes; second, a *descriptive style of cultural studies* that takes
> for granted certain political and historical paradigms, usually Marxist,
> to define the meanings of a text through a surprisingly uncritical
> process of "contextualization"; and finally a *psychoanalysis of the cine-
> matic gaze* that occasionally addresses the phenomenon of same-sex de-
> sire, though usually in the rather dated and mechanical theoretical
> framework established by Freud and his most recent adherents.[16]

While my early work on gay drama fits more or less into Hanson's first
category, the politics of representation, I have moved to a more subjective
approach, part critical analysis, part memoir, which seems necessary when
describing what might be called gay viewership. There is no monolithic
gay viewership. I see films through my cultural education, which is different from that of someone younger or differently educated (I received
my formal education Before Theory), for instance.

Patrick E. Horrigan writes in his analysis of the effect certain films
had on him as an emerging gay child and adolescent, *Widescreen Dreams:
Growing Up Gay at the Movies,* "We as gay people find ourselves enmeshed in a culture that studiously ignores us or radically misrepresents
us; thus, in order to compensate for what the culture withholds from us,

we appropriate it (in fantasy, in subculture) and make it say what we need it to say."[17] Sometimes we're not making the film do anything: The queer connection we see is there—ignored, perhaps, by heterosexuals, but read, not read into, by gay critics. Beyond this introduction, this book is not the sort of memoir Horrigan offers, though how can a book based on a lifetime of watching films and plays not be somewhat subjective? Indeed, I have attempted in all my critical work to mix analysis with autobiography, criticism with personal enthusiasm. In his book *Flaming Classics: Queering the Film Canon,* Alexander Doty discusses the problem of the scholarly critic who is also a fan of the work he/she writes on:

> The result of a couple of decades of ignoring or hiding personal and cultural investments in our (post-contemporary theory) academic writing, however, has been to squeeze much of the life out of it in many senses, often relegating our investments in, and enthusiasms for, popular culture to the realm of hidden pleasures. It's as if showing too much interest in what we are writing about somehow undermines our credibility as intellectuals.[18]

Plays and movies are pleasurable experiences, writing and reading about them should reflect that pleasure.

SATURDAY CLASSES WITH AUDIE MURPHY

To present something of a subjective prelude to what will follow, I want to begin with a moment when movies and my life coalesced somewhat—with a B-western called *Walk the Proud Land* (1956; screenplay Gil Doud and Jack Sher; direction Jesse Hibbs)—and how a much older me now looks at that moment of education in manhood.

I grew up in an era of absolute heroes. World War II hero Dwight Eisenhower was president during much of my boyhood and adolescence. Baseball stars like Joe DiMaggio and Jackie Robinson were worshiped by my peers. My father took me to some Yankees, Giants, and Dodgers games, but I didn't see what the fuss was about. I don't think my father, who never watched sports on television, did either. I was taken by my parents to see John Wayne films like *She Wore a Yellow Ribbon*. Early television was a steady diet of formulaic B-westerns. I was also at the tail-end of the generation that was educated by the Saturday matinee marathon: a cartoon, an episode of an old Buster Crabbe serial (Buster was one of my first crushes) chronicling the heroic adventures of Flash Gordon or Buck Rogers, a half-hour live talent show broadcast on the local radio station, and a double feature. Like many boys who would become gay, I had a more complex reaction to these films than my straight peers did. I saw, in the westerns and fifties' monster movies, examples of heroism I was supposed to emulate, but I also realized I was turned on by some of the actors.

The Saturday matinee marathon in my hometown—almost four hours of entertainment for twenty cents (fifteen cents more for the glasses when one of the movies was in 3-D), plus another dime for candy—was at the Park Theatre, which featured B-movie double bills that changed twice a week. Though the Park double features were kiddie heaven, the theater had a more sinister side. Our mothers told us to avoid going to the bathroom alone because there were dirty old men in the Park Theatre who would ask a boy to do "bad things." Our mothers were right, and the sinister denizens of the Park gave me my first, scary impression of homosexuality.

As the local B-movie palace, the Park featured the kind of genre films kids love: science fiction, horror films, and low-rent westerns. Classy westerns with John Wayne and Technicolor MGM musicals went to the fancy Community Theatre. The mainstay of Park Theatre B-westerns was Universal-International's Audie Murphy. Though he is probably twirling in his grave at the thought, I did have a bit of a childhood crush on cute Audie Murphy, particularly when he played a character named John Clum in the low-budget epic *Walk the Proud Land.*

Audie Murphy is the only Hollywood star I know of who appeared in his own autobiography: *To Hell and Back* (1955; screenplay, Gil Doud; direction, Jesse Hibbs), based on his best-selling book. Murphy, a poor Texas farm boy, was the most decorated soldier in World War II. Unlike John Wayne, who never wore a real uniform, or Ronald Reagan, who confused his roles in war movies with his life, Audie Murphy was a real hero. When director John Huston chose Murphy to play the lead in a film of Stephen Crane's *The Red Badge of Courage* (1951), he called him: "this little, gentle-eyed creature," but then added, "Why, in the war he'd literally go out of his way to find Germans to kill."[19] Small and baby-faced, Murphy looked like someone who would have hung around with Mickey Rooney's Andy Hardy, yet this little guy was our fiercest killer in the war, reportedly single-handedly responsible for the deaths of scores of Germans. After the war, Murphy became the Army's poster boy for the returning soldier, and a famous *Life* magazine cover ensured his celebrity. Don Graham, Murphy's biographer, notes:

> Publicly the baby face was an ideal mask. The freckles and sunny smile could fool anybody if you saw him only in photographs, not up close, where the face more often than not revealed a certain tautness, a flickering tension that expressed itself in every part of his being, a terrible restlessness and, sometimes, an absent-spiritedness as though he weren't really there, but somewhere else, in a darker, bloodier place where men were dying.[20]

And, one might add, where little Audie Murphy was doing the killing. Restless and bored, Murphy went to Hollywood, looking more for excitement than for fame and fortune. Peter Biskind observes that within a few years, he "joined John Wayne as the ideal conservative hero of the fifties, precisely because he was so ordinary; he was the boy-next-door who could go out and slaughter Germans by the handful one minute and come back with his innocence intact."[21] Like Wayne, he wasn't really an actor. He had none of the mannerisms of the Method-trained actors who specialized in Sensitive Young Men. But if he was sometimes wooden and clearly amateur on screen, Murphy's real-life heroism provided a unique authenticity.

Boyishly cute Murphy would certainly qualify as "all man," but he was also a basket case. Susan Faludi writes: "He was haunted by what he had *made* happen: his personal body count, much trumpeted by the postwar press, of 240 Germans."[22] For Faludi and for Murphy's biographer, Don Graham, he was an example of the military's callous treatment of veterans, men who were sent back to normal civilian life without counseling. Graham quotes Murphy as saying, "They took Army dogs and rehabilitated them for civilian life. But they turned soldiers into civilians immediately and let 'em sink or swim."[23] For a decade and a half, Murphy did pretty well, until westerns lost their popularity and his baby face started to show the ravages of his personal problems. Murphy was haunted, "insomniac, secretive, suspicious, paranoid, a tireless pursuer of women, a man in touch with the dark underside of America."[24]

In a way, Murphy personifies the paradoxes in defining "all man." Historian of sexuality Angus McLaren notes that

> "Manly," which in the eighteenth century was primarily used to mean the opposite of the boyish or childish, was in the Victorian age increasingly

employed as the antonym of the feminine or effeminate. The nineteenth-century bourgeoisie were so concerned that the "naturally" different genders of men and women not be confused that they demarcated as sharply as possible the lines splitting the female from the male world; the home from the workplace; the private from the public.[25]

Like many American heroes, Murphy was manly in the sense of his being "not effeminate," but he was definitely boyish. Unlike patriarchal John Wayne, he emphasized the kid's daydream at the heart of the western and war film. In the genre films that were part of my education, the fantasy of men outside the conventional bonds of maturity—job, home, wife, kids—was always there in space, in battle and in submarines, on the open range, among the gangsters, and particularly in the adventures of those sexless, but nevertheless queer, couples that dominated cheap comedies—Laurel and Hardy, Abbott and Costello, Martin and Lewis. Though genre-film heroes are supposed to be heterosexual, they stand outside the nuclear family. In other words, by the measure of postwar America, at least as it was presented in Park Theatre double features, heroes weren't mature. They didn't support families or rear children, though they made the world safe for those who did.

In his book *Masked Men: Masculinity and Movies in the Fifties,* Steven Cohan quotes a 1956 article from the *Women's Home Companion* on the proper behavior of the middle-class man who has experienced the freedom and adventure of war:

> There are certain deep and perfectly normal masculine drives that were "permitted" during a war as they are not permitted in a suburban back yard. They are an inborn attraction to violence and obscenity and polygamy, an inborn love of change, an inborn need to be different from the others and to rebel against them, a strong need for the occasional company of men only and an occasional need for solitude and privacy.
>
> Certainly all men do not feel these drives to the same degree, and certainly these drives shouldn't all be permitted in that clean, green, happy back yard. But if they are always and completely inhibited—the man in the grey flannel suit will stop being a man.[26]

This article demonstrates vividly the paradoxes of masculinity in the fifties, an era of rigid gender definitions conceived of as "natural." Men are "naturally" violent, obscene, and promiscuous, yet must conform to the behavior appropriate in a "suburban back yard." Movies were one place men could see their "natural" selves played out, though, as we shall see, even the western often pitted the lone hero against a more domesticated, younger man who would embrace the home and family the hero had rejected. At the Park Theatre, boys could see the fun of being "all man" without the responsibility of the domesticity they would be tamed into as adults. The ideal boys' world, particularly for boys who would grow up gay, was a world in which guys eternally enjoyed adventures together. When the obligatory, but usually brief, love stuff arrived onscreen, we all retired to the candy stand for a refuel, or conversed until it was over and the fun began again.

In his heyday, Audie Murphy looked like a boy playing a man's role, the perfect genre-film hero for a kid, but in real life poor Audie Murphy, battle-marked (in a brief, shirtless moment in *Walk the Proud Land,* you can see the scar on his back), missing part of a buttock (that anatomical quirk fueled my childhood imagination), known to shoot up the mirrors in his home with the gun he kept under his pillow, represented darker aspects of masculinity. He was living proof that war wasn't simply kid's stuff, and that some men, no matter how hard they tried, would never fit in the "suburban back yard."

I didn't know much about Murphy when I saw his films in the 1950s. He seemed benign and unthreatening, even when he was killing scores of Germans or shooting up the bad guy. If he killed in *To Hell and Back,* it was because his buddies had been killed. This, after all, was the sweet, gentle soul who left school at twelve to support his brothers and sisters, who went into the Army because it paid better than his farm job and who sent most of his Army pay home for the support of his siblings. However young he looked, this was a guy who had to grow up fast. Early in *To Hell and Back,* twelve-year-old Audie tells his ailing mother that he's going to quit school and work to support their fatherless family. Mother tells Audie's younger siblings, "We just decided who the head of the family is." While Audie's fellow soldiers got into barroom brawls on leave in Naples, Audie was invited to dinner by an Italian family as thanks for his being kind to their young boy. He gives up a promotion because he doesn't want to leave his buddies. We never see what people who knew him saw: the menace, the "cold, almost deadly" eyes colleagues noticed, according to biographer Don Graham. At the end of the film, poor Audie's war wounds keep him from his real ambition: to go to West Point and have a lifelong career as an Army officer. Shucks, he only got to be a Hollywood star.

Did I identify with the Audie Murphy of *To Hell and Back?* Not really, but all that male bonding was interesting—there are more scenes of good-looking guys joshing and hugging (there's just enough female presence in the film to establish the characters' heterosexual credentials) than battle scenes—and Audie was cute, despite his dreadful hairstyle. A kid who hadn't read Murphy's book would have been shocked to learn that the memoir is a classic of "war is hell" literature, a frightening picture of a killer who is aware and troubled that he feels nothing when he kills: "Now I have shed my first blood. I feel no qualms; no pride; no remorse. There is only a weary indifference that will follow me throughout the war."[27]

When I see *To Hell and Back* now, I see a pretty bad film in which every locale looks like Southern California and all the scenes of comradeship and horseplay are tiresome. Compared with great war films like Stanley Kubrick's *Full Metal Jacket* (1987) or both versions of *The Thin Red Line* (1964, 1998), this is definitely B-movie stuff, though, unlike them, a giant box-office hit. Murphy's book, faithfully treated, would have made a great film, not this mediocre example of Hollywood white-washing. But in 1955 this was a film an adolescent boy could identify with—a film about a kid who's the wrong size (I was always self-conscious about my height), who is at first rejected by all the groups he wants to join (I was the last chosen for every team in gym class—for good reason), but becomes loved and respected by all his peers. Even a gay teen could buy that fantasy, particularly as the film's version of Murphy attains popularity without engaging in the rowdy heterosexual rites (bar fights, competing for women) of his peers.

Walk the Proud Land, the fictionalized version of the saga of my namesake John Clum among the Apaches, was more interesting to me. My grandfather regaled me with stories of my great-granduncle John P. Clum, who as an Indian agent captured Geronimo. It was interesting to have the same name as a western character and cool to hear my name from a movie theater's speakers, even though John P. Clum was more a pacifist than a gunslinger. He had, after all, left divinity school and gone west because of his asthma! This was hardly the sort of character John Wayne would play. I remember going to the premiere of *Walk the Proud Land* and thinking that Audie Murphy had made my great-granduncle not only interesting (to me, at least) but, as well as I understood such things at age fifteen or so, downright sexy.

Walk the Proud Land is an odd sort of western. Clum is sent as a representative of the Department of the Interior to the San Carlos Reservation, near Tucson, Arizona, to solve the Apache problem, something the Cavalry has not been able to do. The first man he encounters in Tucson is proudly displaying the scalps of six Apaches. Murphy's Clum, dressed in eastern clothes (later, the Apaches make him a new wardrobe), is horrified (see fig. 1). When he arrives at the reservation, he finds the Apache men in chains. He orders the chains removed, sends the Cavalry away, and gives authority to the chief. An armed Apache police force is established, and with that force, Clum is able to bring the renegade chief Geronimo back to the reservation. Unfortunately, Washington is not impressed with Clum's liberal treatment of the Indians, even though it is working, and restores the authority of the Cavalry and its racist tactics (actually, though this is not mentioned in the film, the Army resented losing the profits from selling food and supplies on the reservation). John Clum in *Walk the Proud Land* may not be the shoot-'em-up hero of the traditional western, but he exemplifies what film historian Peter Biskind sees as the key masculine traits of the 1950s: "realism, compromise, accommodation, flexibility."[28] The villain here is the inflexible military, forcing rigid, outmoded principles where compassion is appropriate. Even Geronimo must be made to respect the new order and conform to the kinder, gentler life Clum envisions for the Apaches.

Though a number of the Apaches are played by badly made up non-Indians, *Walk the Proud Land* is, for its time, a very liberal film on Native American issues, a counter to the common, violent cowboys-and-Indians movie. It shows the Apaches as having a culture (in the film as in life, Clum organizes a performing group of Apaches to tour the country, educating Americans about Indian culture and raising money for the reservation), coherent social structure, and strong ethos. Geronimo's hatred of the white man is seen as justified by the latter's racism. However liberal the film may be on racial issues, though, it is doctrinaire on issues of domestic morality. When a grateful Apache chief sends Clum a lovely Indian widow (played by the Italian-American Anne Bancroft) to take care of him and his household, it is made quite clear that noble Clum does not have sex with her, though he does become a surrogate father to her son. When Clum's white fiancée arrives on the reservation, and the Indian widow assumes she can stay in the household, Clum asserts, "Sometimes it is difficult for these people to realize how a man can want only one woman for all time," a line randy Audie Murphy must have gagged on. Monogamy is upheld, though the Apache woman must nevertheless instruct Clum's new wife on her proper domestic role: "For such a man there should be warmth from a woman. She should bend to his will the way a tree bends with the wind." When Clum goes off to capture Geronimo, his wife threatens to leave him, but when he returns she is faithfully there, her Apache mentor standing behind her, smiling proudly. The woman's duty is to love, honor, and obey—and allow her husband time for his adventures in the wilderness. The message of many fifties' genre films was that a wife was necessary for a man, but that she would also have to accept his exciting life outside the home. This message of B-westerns like *Walk the Proud Land* was consonant with the post–World War II American message of domesticity, as Steven Cohan expresses it:

> Home was supposed to provide married couples with a buffer against the hostile outside world, functioning to protect its inhabitants much as the nation itself did when holding the communist empire at bay. . . . In reinforcing Cold War domestic ideology, the national obsession with the heterosexual couple further helped to contain male and female sexuality within a relatively new form of social union, "eroticized marriage." As the only legitimate site for finding emotional and sexual fulfillment, the representation of marriage in such highly idealized terms—the companionate couple finding their unity in a mutual orgasm—served as an effective means of sexual regulation.[29]

While television presented this doctrine in shows like *Father Knows Best,* movies still offered an escape back into a world of boys' shared adventure. The girlfriend, mistress, or wife was there to assure audiences that a man who would rather be with his male friends was nevertheless heterosexual.

Walk the Proud Land was not the hit Murphy had had the previous year playing himself in *To Hell and Back.* After all, the film presented a liberal who defended the Apaches against the policies of his own government and whose domestic arrangements hinted at miscegenation and bigamy. Murphy's Clum, who loses one fistfight and seldom fires a gun, believes that the Indian, the traditional menace in many westerns, has a culture to be respected equally to the white man's. I doubt that the real John Clum was as charming and self-effacing as Audie Murphy's version, but here was a hero I could identify with: intelligent, politically different, an underdog who is right. And I am sure that on some level I also noticed the loving looks the cuter Apaches give Audie's John Clum, particularly Tommy Rall's Taglito, who kills his brother to protect Clum, then chooses Clum to be his blood brother.

The real Clum was a master at reinventing himself and was, for a time, owner and editor of the Tombstone, Arizona, newspaper, the *Epitaph*, as well as mayor, postmaster, and head of the local school board. He was also a crony of Wyatt Earp and his brothers, witnessing and reporting the shootout at the OK Corral and helping the Earps in their battles against cattle rustlers and other outlaws. What we know about the famous gunfight at the OK Corral is greatly from Clum's writing.[30] He was also active in establishing amateur theatricals in Tombstone and Tucson and, according to historian Douglas Firth Anderson, "defended the stage in print in response to some of his religious compatriots who questioned its moral justification."[31] In films about Tombstone, Clum plays a decidedly supporting role. He's a silent guy with a rifle in *Gunfight at the O.K. Corral* (1957; screenplay, Leon M. Uris; direction, John Sturges), in which the relationship between Burt Lancaster's Wyatt Earp and Kirk Douglas's Doc Holliday is one of the most intense male bonds in postwar westerns. When Holliday's mistress helps the evil Clantons in their plot to kill Earp, she tells Doc, "I thought if Wyatt was out of the way, you'd come back to me." What was a fifteen-year-old in repressed 1957 to make of moments like that? Clum is also a character in director Sturges's *O.K. Corral* sequel, *Hour of the Gun* (1967), and in Frank Perry's *Doc* (1971).

Clum eventually traveled further west as an assistant editor for the San Francisco *Examiner*, but he left that job for the more exciting life of a frontier postal inspector. This was hardly the bureaucratic plum it would be now: Clum had to investigate mail thefts and track down robbers. His success led to his being named chief of the division of postal inspectors, but he stepped down, in the midst of the Alaska Gold Rush, to become postal inspector for the Territory of Alaska. He died in Los Angeles in 1932.

Though never fully celebrated in film, John Philip Clum is a fascinating example of rugged American masculinity and enterprise. But perhaps what fascinates me most is the theatrical side of this courageous character: the impresario who took the Apaches on a barnstorming tour, the singer, actor, and defender of drama. Those activities also took courage in the manly West. If I have any old-fashioned ideal of masculinity, it probably stems from the stories of this frontier renaissance man whose life was far more complex and, to some extent, more mysterious than Hollywood's presentation of it.

So in 1956, John Philip Clum and Audie Murphy, two versions of American masculinity and heroism, merged in an unsuccessful B-western, *Walk the Proud Land,* that premiered in Clum's birthplace: Hudson, New York. And this fifteen-year-old, whose name is also John Clum, was spurred onto all sorts of reflections on manhood and impossible adolescent fantasies. And, yes, back there the first seeds of this book were sown.

I

LEARNING MASCULINITY

Chapter One

DICKS AND TESTOSTERONE

What Little Boys Are Made Of

"DROP TO YOUR KNEES, PUSSY BOY."

In one episode of the American version of the British television series *Queer as Folk,* fey, willowy Emmett (Peter Paige), who is ashamed of being a "nelly bottom," fantasizes that his Internet sex chat-room persona, a beefy brute with a 9" x 6" (6" circumference, I imagine) dick, comes to life and teaches him how to become a "top." This entails becoming rough, assertive, ordering other men to kneel down and worship his penis, which he at least believes is gigantic. At the urging of his Internet alter ego, Emmett goes to the apartment of "usemyhole27," who, on the Internet, has been playing submissive fantasy bottom to Emmett's top, and finds, to his surprise, a "straight-looking and -acting" guy built like a linebacker—butchness is, after all, a state of mind, not body. For the first time in his non-Internet life, Emmett orders a man to his knees and feels newly empowered. Here is a gay version of attaining conventional manhood, linking the magic of a large penis to masculine force. In this chapter, I want to look at recent films that emphasize the real and mythical defining features of manhood: a penis and a propensity toward aggression.

"A LITTLE THING WOULD MAKE ME TELL THEM HOW MUCH I LACK OF A MAN."

Once, when I was three, my mother caught me comparing peepees in the backyard with a neighbor boy my age. While punishing me for this heinous act, she informed me that "they're all the same anyway." This piece of misinformation is one of the few things I remember from that time in my childhood. (I'm sure a psychiatrist would make something of that.) I know that my mother's assertion did not deter my curiosity. Like many contemporary critics, though, I have become more interested in what peepees *mean,* particularly what they mean in American film and theater, where, as elsewhere, discussion of and display of the penis is linked to patriarchy and family values.

In Shakespeare's *Twelfth Night,* Viola, trapped into fighting a duel with Sir Andrew Aguecheek, expresses her knowledge that, however convincing her male drag, a "little thing" keeps her from being a man. Viola is speaking of biological sex, not gender, which is a cultural construction. In Shakespeare's comedies, putting on men's clothes is all it takes for a woman to gain the power and privilege of a man. (Since, in Shakespeare's theater, the woman was played by a boy, femininity, not masculinity, was the disguise, and the idea of a woman so easily achieving masculine privilege was defused.) Shakespeare could be both simple and poetic in saying what gender theorists discuss in labored prose: that masculinity is in great part a matter of costume and acting. Biological maleness, however, depends on that "little thing," which in the real world is "much" in defining the gender order as well as biological gender. Without it, one's claim to masculine privilege depends on maintaining the disguise; with it, one is obligated to "act like a man" or be relegated to gender limbo, neither masculine nor truly feminine.

Viola is actually posing not as a man but as a eunuch, a castrato. (Castrati were castrated before puberty so they would retain their soprano voices, and as men they often had underdeveloped, nonworking penises. A man castrated after puberty, however, has a functioning penis.) In *Castration: An Abbreviated History of Western Manhood,* Gary Taylor asserts that the modern enlightened woman wants a eunuch: "When I say that woman-qua-sexual-being wants a eunuch for a lover, I mean *eunuch* absolutely precisely; she wants a sterile human being with a penis,"[1] which will allow her sex without any threat of pregnancy. Taylor adds, "This is the specter that has haunted men for centuries: the fear that manhood will become, or has already become, obsolete, superfluous, ridiculous, at best quaint, at worst disgusting."[2] In Taylor's nightmare scenario, men become mere sexual performers to be used by women. Robbed of sperm, they lose their phallic power.

In Pedro Almodóvar's film *All About My Mother* (1999), Agrado, a former prostitute who is what Americans call "a chick with a dick," delivers an autobiographical monologue on authenticity in place of a canceled performance of Tennessee Williams's meditation on gender *A Streetcar Named Desire*. After cataloging what she paid for each of her body parts, Agrado proclaims, "You are more authentic the more you resemble what you dream you are." Gender authenticity, altering one's body to match one's mind, can be bought. In Almodóvar's film, the men who seek prostitutes on the outskirts of Barcelona are attracted to men who are "pneumatic and well hung," equipped with breasts and cocks. Even in female drag and with all the curves and contours of a woman, a penis is Agrado's meal ticket. While women do most of the film's loving and nurturing, the men seem primarily concerned with their cocks. When protagonist Manuela jokes to her teenage son that he may have to take to the streets to help support them, he responds, "You have to have a big dick for that." Mario, the movie's Stanley Kowalski, tells Agrado he needs his cock sucked to alleviate tension—he will be happy to suck hers in return. Manuela laments of her ex-husband, Lola, another "chick with a dick," "How could someone be so macho with such tits?" Even Huma Rojo, Manuela's lesbian employer, observes that it has been a long time since she "sucked cock." Cocks seem to be on everyone's mind.

Whether or not one buys Jaques Lacan's theory of the phallus, the first defining feature of a man's body is his penis. (Another defining attribute of masculinity is the penis's disproportionate importance to a man's thought process; hence that wonderful epithet "dickhead.") Even a gay man, considered to be not "all man," has one, though the low place assigned to gay men on the masculinity scale has less to do with what we do with our own penises than with what we enjoy doing with the organs of our fellow men. In many cultures, a man can put his penis anywhere on or into another man and still not be considered gay. It's when one allows another man to put his penis on or into him that he is perceived as "less than a man." A number of recent films analyze the role of the penis in assessing and critiquing masculinity.

BLINDED BY THE FULL MONTY

Perhaps one can best discuss the power and anxiety surrounding the penis, and the association of the penis with gayness, by looking at Terrence McNally's book for the musical version of *The Full Monty*, a work literally about its display.

The Broadway musical version of *The Full Monty* (2000; book, Terrence McNally; music and lyrics David Yazbek), adapted from the 1997 British film (screenplay, Simon Beaufoy; direction, Peter Cattaneo), ends with six men triumphantly doing a strip act that provides them with needed income and, more important, with the self-respect they haven't found in other masculine arenas. Professionally, these unemployed working class men are "scrap;" domestically, the married ones suffer the domestic indignity of being turned into house husbands by their working wives. What is at stake for the straight men in *The Full Monty* is reasserting their "proper" role in their domestic lives. Gaz (Jerry in the musical) wants the money so that he can see his son. His wife and her new boyfriend are trying to take away his visitation rights because he can't afford to pay child support. Dave, with his weight problem, is ashamed to have sex with his wife. Gerald doesn't have the courage to tell his spendthrift wife that he is out of work. One of the film's two gay men is a Mama's boy who finally gets a partner of his own after his mother's death (Mother dies because he has found a lover), thus fitting into the conventional domestic pattern. Only the black character's domestic arrangements are not an issue in the narrative (we know only that he has a niece). The women have the jobs and economic power. They even, at the beginning of the film, invade the men's room at the nightclub where male strippers are performing. Gaz, hiding in a stall, is particularly horrified to see one of the women standing at the urinal: "When women start pissing like us, we're finished." Doing "the full Monty," ripping off their G-strings and showing their penises to the cheering audience, will supposedly give these men back their manhood.

When the Big Moment comes in the Eugene O'Neill Theatre, the six men whip off their red G-strings, as blinding lights are shone in the real audience's eyes. The fictional audience may see the full Monty, but the paying customers don't see it—them (in the film, we only saw the men from behind). Is an invisible Full Monty a Full Monty? Why must it be invisible? If I were to wax Lacanian, I would say that *The Full Monty*'s saga of regained manhood isn't about display of the penis; it's about trying to gain that symbolic version of the penis, the phallus, the imaginary site of masculine power. As Susan Bordo describes it:

> The phallus stands not for the superior fitness of an individual male over other men, but for *generic* male superiority—not only over females but also over other species. And . . . the phallus stands for a superiority

that is not just biological, but partakes of an authority beyond (and often in contest with) the power, needs, desires of the body.[3]

The penis means sex, irrationality, the libido, while the phallus, a cultural icon, denotes, as Bordo asserts, "not the superior virility of the individual male or the sexual/generativity of the race but the divinely bestowed fitness of *men* to rule the earth."[4] The blinding light at the exposure of the phallus is symbolically appropriate.

Paradoxically, we live in a society that worships the power and authority symbolized by the phallus but which thinks it shameful, literally "indecent," to display the penis, not out of any particular puritanical mandate but, as critic Peter Lehman puts it, "the awe surrounding the penis in a patriarchal culture depends on either keeping it hidden from sight (as we see, for example, the classical cinema does) or carefully regulating its representation (as the pornographic film does),"[5] because "it is precisely when the penis-phallus is hidden from view in patriarchy that it is most centered."[6] To Lehmann, then, the hiding of the penis maintains patriarchy by insisting on the mystique of the phallus. The anxiety surrounding the display of the penis in *The Full Monty* supports the idea that such display threatens patriarchy, as oppressive to gay men as it is to women.

Art historian Margaret Walters notes that "To see another person naked can reassure or alarm, satisfy curiosity or provoke guilt, arouse desire or disgust and often both together." The Full Monty is also invisible because the visible penis might cause anxiety in some members of the audience. Who is bothered by the display of the penis? Not the women wildly cheering on the men at the performance I saw of *The Full Monty*— though what the women in the audience and on stage are cheering is the empowerment they feel at making men the object of their gaze, being in the specular position men have traditionally enjoyed. Susan Bordo writes that in the film *The Full Monty*, the naked penis is "a symbol for male exposure, vulnerability to an evaluation and judgment that women— clothed or naked—experience all the time."[7] Neither are the gay men in the theater bothered—the most successful gay plays have been those with nude scenes. It's the poor straight men who are uncomfortable because they are made to look at what they are not supposed to look at for fear that they might enjoy it. While Susan Bordo may be right that "the ones really fascinated by the penis and its dimensions are men,"[8] being caught looking at another man's penis raises questions about one's heterosexual credentials—about one's manhood. When, in the British film comedy

Virtual Sexuality (1999; screenplay, Nick Fisher; direction, Nick Hurran), high schooler Chas has to explain the rules of the locker room to Justine, who, due to a malfunction of a virtual reality machine, finds herself in a boy's body, he admonishes, "If you want to avoid trouble, don't look, don't point, and don't say anything about other boys' bits" (typical of British films, less inhibited than American movies, we are given glimpses of the boys' "bits").

In the oddest scene in both the film and stage versions of *The Full Monty*, "auditions" for the strip show involved men displaying their penises to the male judges. In the musical, a female character is added, an ex-vaudevillian turned accompanist, to "normalize" the scene somewhat, but the sight of a group of straight men (we don't know at that point that one of the auditioners is gay) watching other men and commenting on their genitalia is humorous because it is so out of character. Their only audible reaction is to the enormous penis of one of the men: "Gentlemen, the lunchbox has landed," says Robert Carlyle's Gaz in the film, of Ethan's endowment. Is it significant that the largest penis belongs to one of the gay men? In both play and musical the black stripper known as "Horse" worries that his penis will not "measure up" to the stereotype of the "Big Black Man," but the stereotypical hypersexuality, symbolically associated with a large penis, often associated with Black men, has been transferred in *The Full Monty* to a gay man.

Anxiety surrounds the potential unveiling of the penis because stripping is first presented in *The Full Monty* as a gay activity. The stripper the women are cheering at the beginning of the musical is openly gay. In the film, Gaz constantly refers to the professional male strippers as "poofs." Engaging in the strip routine, however empowering it turns out to be, connects him and his sexually threatened compatriots to a homosexual activity. It is because women will pay "ten quid and all to watch some poof get his kit off," that Gaz decides to make money stripping, thus heterosexualizing what seems to him to be a lucrative homosexual activity, though he and his friends will go further, baring it all. Looking at the poster for the strippers, Gaz observes, "He's got no willy, for starters," as if gay men who partially expose themselves for money aren't anatomically correct. Yet the largest "willy" belongs to one of the gay men in Gaz's group.

Throughout *The Full Monty*, homophobic canards are disproved. The gay Mama's boy begins as a stereotype, a man with no friends and no life who can't even manage to commit suicide properly, but he ends up happily partnered with the troupe's dumb bunny, who is also the best-looking and best-endowed. Meanwhile, their straight colleagues are in fraught relationships. In the musical, Keno, the gay stripper who enthralls the women of Buffalo, is far more together about his career and life than the straight men who look down on him. However progressive this might be in a Broadway musical, both the film and musical shy away from any display that would frighten or repulse their mostly straight audiences, in part because display of the penis has been equated with gayness. To keep heterosexual, the characters in *The Full Monty* must keep covered.

The musical is as timid about showing its male lovers kissing as it is about male nudity. When I saw the film, the moment when the two gay men were about to kiss got a nervous laugh from the audience. At the performance I attended of the musical, male and female members of the audience audibly cried "Don't" when the men were about to kiss, as if a real sign of affection and physical desire between the lovers would spoil the show. Both film and musical, in their bid for mass appeal, acknowledged and supported the audience's homophobia by settling for having the men hold hands. The skittishness about a male-male kiss is of a piece with the fear of display of the penis. Both would queer the musical, which would limit its popular appeal. It's all right to offer Broadway audiences cartoon queers, as the highly successful *The Producers* does, but not to present nudity or less stylized signs of male-male affection and desire.

Three months into its New York run, the *Full Monty* musical, which was doing a respectable, but not sellout business, despite rave reviews, changed its ad campaign. The first ad, which also serves as the cover art for the original cast recording, focused on the strip with a side-view drawing of the naked men shown from the waist down with police caps covering their genitalia and buttocks, a parody of the traditional ads featuring leggy chorines used to lure straight men to the theater. Indeed, there is something slightly androgynous about the photograph. Who's legs are these? The ad is more suggestive than it was probably intended to be. In the original ad, the pose, with nude men closely placed one behind the other, the genitalia of one man close to the posterior of the other, suggests a sexual intimacy the musical shies away from depicting, even for its gay characters. Like the musical, the ad's attempt to erase the penis and any queerness associated with its display only causes queerness to pop up everywhere, from the ironic appearance of police caps to the androgyny, to the sexual suggestiveness of the pose, to the aura of camp the ad communicates. Or did the producers want the ad to have a queer reading, to play to both straight and gay audiences, like a number of current television ads (What is the relationship of those two men in the Volkswagen ads?)? The ad was replaced by one with a photo of the performers fully clothed in police uniforms, with quotes from critics praising the show as a "feel-good" musical. The actors' goofy expressions and ungainly poses defuse any threat the show might offer straight men.

In a time when the Broadway musical is well on its way to becoming high-budget children's theater, an adult musical that sells itself on male nudity may be a bit too radical. Still, what we don't see in *The Full Monty* is testament to the penis's continued power to unsettle. *Naked Boys Singing* might play well to the gay clientele in a small theater downtown, but a Broadway musical aiming for a mass audience can't afford to frighten anyone off. Terrence McNally shows in *The Full Monty,* as he did in *Kiss of the Spider Woman,* that he knows how to balance musicals' intrinsic appeal to gay audiences and the need to attract and please homophobes as well.

"SO YOU'RE A BOY. NOW WHAT?"

In the first sequence of director Kimberly Peirce's 1999 film, *Boys Don't Cry* (screenplay, Peirce and Andy Bienen), a fascinating, if harrowing story of a transgendered person trying to find a place for herself, we see Teena Brandon (Hilary Swank) donning male drag for a blind date at a Lincoln, Nebraska, roller rink. Her gay cousin Lonny (Matt McGrath), who has just cut her hair, is amused and appalled at the sock Teena has stuffed in her jeans: "That is the most horrifying thing I've ever seen in my life. It's a deformity." Teena removes the sock, but later acquires a more realistic prosthetic. While Lonny sees his cousin as "just a dyke," Teena sees herself as Brandon, a male, and dreams of the day she can find the money to have a sex change operation to make "her" body fit "his" self-image.

Notably, *Boys Don't Cry* is not set in the usual bourgeois world of American drama, film, and television. Teena and Lonny are what middle-class folk refer to as "trailer trash." There's no money for fancy operations and hormone treatments. Teena Brandon/Brandon Teena's dilemma shows how arbitrary gender is, determined as it is by body, mind, and the prevailing culture. Is Teena looking for a means of empowerment in a society that grants women none? Is she a butch lesbian justifying her desire and self-image by imagining a biological imperative? Or is she really a man trapped in a woman's body? A gay clerk at the Atlanta video store where I bought the film said to me, "She should have just come to Atlanta. She'd have been fine here." But I think that Teena (or Brandon, as she would become) would have seen Atlanta's very open gay society as alien. To Brandon, sexual desire defines gender. "If you was a guy," Lonny says, "I might even want to fuck you." Brandon rejoins, "If *you* was a guy, I might even want to fuck you." To Brandon, gay Lonny is not a "guy." Yet Brandon cannot totally accept his own attempts to look and act masculine.* When he first stuffs a dildo into his briefs, he looks in the mirror and says, "I'm an asshole," expressing the sort of rebuke society might offer. When his biological sex is discovered, he says that he is a hermaphorodite with "both boy and girl parts," which is untrue. Later he admits to sexual confusion, more mental than physical.

To avoid an assault by young men who see him as a threat to their precarious sense of masculinity, who see him as "faggot" or "dyke," Brandon is happy to be spirited away to Falls City, a place even less enlightened than Lincoln. ("They hang faggots down there," Lonny claims.) But for a while, Brandon finds an accepting community of peers in which he is accepted as "all man." What he doesn't see is that this little tribe of outsiders has its own gender order, headed by two sociopaths: John (Peter Sarsgaard), who has problems with "impulse control," and his pal Tom (Brendon Sexton III). In this little community, John rules the roost. "This is my house," he says of the place where Brandon's girlfriend, Lana (Chloë Sevigny), and her alcoholic mother (Jeanetta Arnette) live, and people toe the line because John is a time bomb. This is also a society in which the women hold down legitimate jobs while the men support themselves through criminal activity. Yet the women, usually drunk, are miserably unhappy, lacking any power. Even Lana's mother seems in thrall to John, who presents his brutal power as benevolence: "You know," he says, "I just want to protect you." John and Tom are prone to shout "Shut up" in their most violent moments: Silencing alternative discourse is their way of staying on top. Lana, her mother, and Lana's friend Candace (Alicia Goranson) usually try to survive by saying only what the men want to hear.

---

* For the sake of political correctness, I will reluctantly refer to Brandon as "he," though biologically Teena is a "she."

Throughout, Brandon is the most verbal, articulate character, spinning fictions about himself, a sister who is a model in Hollywood (an ideal of femininity), a family in Memphis, a fiancée, an illegitimate child. With no visible means of support, Brandon lives as a guest of the women who dote on him, first Candace, then Lana, making himself particularly vulnerable to John's fits of possessiveness and jealousy. At first, though, Brandon is accepted by John and Tom because he passes their violent tests of manhood: dangerous car chases with the police and "bumper skiing." If this violent, reckless behavior is what it takes to be accepted as a man, he'll do it ("I just thought that's what guys do around here"), and he looks proudly in the mirror at the bruises and scars that make his face less feminine.

Brandon endangers his position by falling in love with Lana, who sees him as the only source of tenderness and affection in her world and as someone with whom she can escape from John's little kingdom. Lana doesn't care whether Brandon is biologically male or female. He has given her the best sex she has ever had, and proven himself a better model of masculinity than the biological males she knows. On their last night together, Brandon and Lana devise a plan to return together to Lincoln, where Brandon fantasizes they will be accepted by his mother and cousin Lonny, but such a conventional notion of marriage and family is not really possible—we have already seen the young men of Lincoln try to attack Brandon.

When Brandon's true biological gender is revealed, he becomes to John and Tom "a disease," a threat. They do what they think needs to be done to restore their sense of the gender order: They rape and beat Brandon and make him swear that he will not tell anyone. The exhilaration with which John and Tom whoop and cheer after the assault demonstrates, as if it needed to be demonstrated, how powerless men see asserting their dominance in the gender order as their only means of attaining control and power. (Even more powerful, though, is an earlier scene in which John and Tom rip off Brandon's clothing to expose his lack of a penis, stripping him of the power and privilege that comes with a penis.) Finally, Brandon is shot by John and stabbed by Tom in another of their vicious male-bonding rituals. Brandon's death, like his rape, offers the two men the opportunity to bond in the only way they can—through violence. More than any other film I have seen, *Boys Don't Cry* shows the potential sickness of male bonding and its attendant protective homophobia.

It is difficult for some of us to understand Brandon's attraction to these sociopaths—the same sort of guys who murdered Matthew Shepard—to the sense of belonging they offer, if only temporarily. But *Boys Don't Cry* depicts a strictly enforced gender order in which men, gay and straight, define and police those who don't conform to the binaries: male/female, gay/straight. The old order of heterosexual marriage is gone in *Boys Don't Cry,* but straight men still rule. No wonder Teena Brandon chooses not to see herself as a female. But without that "little thing," Brandon Teena's power is a dangerous illusion.

"NOW YOU KNOW WHAT IT'S LIKE TO BE CONFUSED ABOUT YOUR COCK."

In the first scene of the British love story *Different for Girls* (1996; screenplay, Tony Marchant; direction, Richard Spence), Karl, an adolescent boy, is alone in a schoolhouse shower, standing with his legs crossed so that his penis is hidden. His classmates discover him, taunting him mercilessly for trying to look like a girl, but they are stopped by Paul Prentice, who is obviously "man enough" to take on his peers. Paul puts his school blazer around his friend's shoulders and walks him through the crowd of jeering boys. It is clear that Paul loves Karl, and that in some schoolboy way that love has been expressed sexually.

Cut to seventeen years later: Karl is now Kim (Steven Mackintosh), a postoperative transsexual riding in a taxi that runs into Prentice (Rupert Graves), who now works as a motorcycle courier. Kim and Prentice become a kind of odd couple. Prentice is all testosterone, living a chaotic life, jumping from job to job and regularly getting into trouble. Kim has assiduously avoided trouble, fearing another violent reaction to her uncommon position in the gender order. Her life is tidy and timid. Yet once again, Prentice and Kim are drawn together.

Kim's re-entrance into Prentice's life throws him into sexual and gender confusion. "I'm straight, you know," Prentice says to Kim on their first evening out together. "So am I," Kim answers. Yet we see that Prentice's attraction to Kim happened long before her sex change: Prentice is shown looking at an old class photograph. While everyone else in the picture stares forward, Prentice joyfully smiles at Karl, standing beside him. However, in Prentice's "straight" adulthood, it is Kim's new biological gender, her vagina—which is, after all, her penis inverted—that allows their relationship to revive. He is fascinated with her anatomical changes to the point of reading up on transsexual surgery. He even gives a lecture on the biology of gender to his girlfriend: "We're all basically female," he tells her. "Maleness is just something added on." One night over a candlelight dinner in her apartment, Kim, at Prentice's insistence, describes the changes to her body that have taken place because of the hormone therapy. Prentice, sexually aroused, runs outside, and proceeds to unzip his pants and pull out his penis. "I don't know what the fuss is about, do you," Prentice shouts, "It just gets in the bloody way." Prentice is arrested for "indecent exposure" for waving his willy at Kim's neighbors.

At this moment in the film, we in the audience get a shot of Rupert Graves's large penis. Graves, like Scottish actor Ewan McGregor, has unabashedly shared his penis with audiences in a number of films over the past fifteen years. Beautiful, well-endowed British actors seem to feel empowered by such display. That exposure is crucial to *Different for Girls* because it is indeed the penis that is at stake in a film that spends a lot of time focusing on a character who eagerly gave his/hers up. "I never wanted it," Kim says. "It was just a growth." For Karl/Kim, becoming a woman was as much about getting rid of the penis as it was gaining the physical attributes of a woman. Prentice, confused about everything, questions even his penis until he finds that "it fits" in Kim's vagina. Though he certainly expresses a lot of masculine aggression, Prentice does not display the traits of authority associated with the phallus. Our last view of Prentice and Kim reveals them both out in gender-neutral clothing, identical leather outfits, on their new motorcycle. Kim is driving and Prentice is in the position usually occupied by a biker's girlfriend.

TESTOSTERONE

If the penis is the defining physical characteristic of masculinity, then behaviors associated with testosterone—aggression, violence—are often offered as the defining behavioral characteristics. The question Hollywood has grappled with since World War II is how men can assert their testosterone in peacetime.

In the early days of television, when professional wrestling was a staple of the fledgling networks, the most famous wrestler was a gentleman by the name of Gorgeous George (real name: George Wagner), also known as "The Human Orchid." Some say that Gorgeous George singlehandedly made wrestling popular television fare. Before his appearances, an attendant would spray perfume around the ring. George would enter, to the jeers of the crowd, in a flashy, feminine robe. His curly, bleached-blond hair was done up as if he were a lady going out for the night. When he finally doffed his robe, George was in pink briefs. "The consummate villain, George would cheat at every possible opportunity, infuriating fans to the point of rioting on several occasions."[9] Crowds flocked to see Gorgeous George, and millions watched him on television, but most viewers wanted this flamboyantly effeminate man to lose. Jeering him was jeering some violation of the rigid postwar sex-gender order—though besides the platinum blond hair, Gorgeous George looked like any overweight mid-dle-aged man. He certainly wasn't more flamboyant than the supposedly macho wrestlers now appearing on television. However gruff and menac-ing they sound, their hair is often long and bleached, their wardrobes like Nashville nightmares. Are these guys jeered? One of them was even elected governor of Minnesota! Gorgeous George worked up the crowds by portraying himself as a sissy man invading a guy thing, a highly the-atrical, apparently violent, utterly fake conflict—not as bloody as boxing or as tough as football, but still a guy thing. He got away with it because everyone knew it was a showbiz gimmick. Men could unleash their ha-tred for and anxiety concerning men who were not "all man" without having to leave a masculine environment. And Gorgeous George could make a fortune by being both nelly and violent.

In his provocative study of masculine violence, psychiatrist James Gilligan writes: "It is men who are expected to be violent, and who are honored for doing so and dishonored for being unwilling to be vio-lent."[10] Boys are supposed to like guns, not dolls. They are supposed to like to make noise and to fight, or at least be able to defend themselves. And according to Hollywood, war is the ultimate guy thing, where men are tested, where they can bond. Gilligan theorizes that shame, "the ab-sence or deficiency of self-love,"[11] is at the heart of the American man's impulse toward violence, and "The relation between shame and genitals is so close and inextricable that the words for the two are identical in most languages."[12] Playwright Sam Shepard, much of whose work fo-cuses on male violence, agrees: "There's some hidden, deeply rooted thing in the Anglo male American that has to do with inferiority, that has to do with not being a man, and always, continually, having to act out some idea of manhood that invariably is violent."[13] Our classic films of manhood tested take place in the past, as if one should feel nostalgia only for a time when one could *actually* attain manhood, or at least feel as if one had attained manhood. Certainly the violent responses to violations of the gender order chronicled in films like *Boys Don't Cry* and the telefilm about Matthew Shepard's murder, *Anatomy of a Hate Crime* (2000; teleplay, Max Ember; direction, Tim Hunter), suggest that the only power the assailants have is the power to defend their heterosexuality, which they feel is threatened by the existence of a homosexual or transsexual. These, films, however, are also about young men who are at the bottom of the class system.

How can a middle-class guy prove his manhood in a world where wars are fought by computers and missiles? Cut to a high-rise condo in a large American city at the beginning of the twenty-first century, the home of a prosperous gay couple. In one room, mats are spread out for a fight between one of the apartment's occupants and an opponent he has contacted via an Internet website for fighters. Why are these guys fighting? My friend, an investment banker, tells me: "My job is full of competition and aggression, but it's all mental and verbal. I just need a way to act it out physically." So he sets up fights with strangers in his home and, when he travels, in other guys' homes. There's a nationwide network of such men. For some gay men, part of the attraction of wrestling is that it connects them to manliness. One gay wrestling website entitled A New Breed of Gay Men explains, "Homosexual men have often been berated for being timid and lacking aggression, and even for being spineless." The solution is participation in contact sports like wrestling, "a valuable way of expressing one's anger safely."[14] Of course, for many gay guys, wrestling has an erotic component. The website called The Gay Site of Amateur Wrestling comforts young men who feel they are the only ones who get turned on by wrestling with other guys. Even straight guys, the site explains, are into "grappling and wrestling when they're on a beach or by a poolside. Yeah . . . this must be the thrill of the body contact—although no hetero would ever admit it."[15] Such sites also offer message boards and chat rooms so that gay wrestlers can contact one another. Sex and violence together in the manly sport of wrestling—what more could one ask?

A number of highly successful recent films address the difficulty of attaining manhood in a bureaucratic world that allows no outlet for expressing masculine aggression. Two of the best of these, *Fight Club* and *The Matrix*, offer narratives of timid, insomniac white-collar workers attaining heroic status through pain and suffering as much as through violent action. Heroism, in these films, means destroying the world that is robbing its men of their manhood and moral sense. Both films delineate male-dominated, male-centered worlds in which the protagonist has a special relationship with a male mentor figure. Both end with a barely credible, formulaic, heterosexual resolution.

"IT REALLY HURTS. HIT ME AGAIN."

My friend with the wrestling mats tells me that he was sexually aroused while watching the film of Chuck Palahniuk's novel *Fight Club* (1999; screenplay, Jim Uhls; direction, David Fincher). I don't think he got the message. The multiple-personality protagonist of *Fight Club* is punching himself.

Fight Club begins with an image of its nameless protagonist (Edward Norton) with the barrel of a gun in his mouth as his voice tells us: "You know the old saying, 'You always hurt the one you love'? Well, it works both ways." Phallic displacement is a major theme of this film, as is desire for an ideal male figure, all linked to ambivalence toward women. It ends, appropriately, with the picture of a penis. In between we have as vivid a depiction of masculinity in crisis as Hollywood has ever produced.

Our nebbishy narrator's job is to assess whether deadly automobile accidents were caused by a mechanical malfunction and, if so, whether the manufacturer can avoid the expense of having similar cars recalled. This is the sort of corrupt enterprise bureaucrats have to engage in to afford the luxuries of a consumer economy. Like most thirtysomethings, our protagonist is an avid consumer, even telephone-shopping from the comfort of his toilet. His condo, in a high-rise "filing cabinet for widows and young professionals," is an IKEA catalog picture in three dimensions. For a gay viewer who remembers that IKEA was once one of the first companies to target gay men in its television advertising, our narrator's choice of furnishings is the first of many clues that he might be gay. He says he is unattached because he knows he is a "thirty-year-old boy," and he does not seem to have any social life beyond the "single-serving friends" he speaks to on airplanes. He is a perfect example of contemporary anomie—and he cannot sleep.

The only cure for our protagonist's insomnia is the comfort he gets from visits to support groups filled with dying people: victims of tuberculosis, breast cancer, testicular cancer, kidney disease, parasites. At the testicular-cancer support group, he is paired up with Bob (Meat Loaf), a giant former bodybuilder and heavy steroid user who has not only lost his testicles but grown enormous breasts. Nestled against Bob's breasts, our hero can weep and, later, as a result, have a decent night's sleep. The cure for anomie, the solace in an impersonal, corrupt, meaningless world, is a castrated male maternal figure: "Being pressed against his tits, ready to cry—that was my vacation." But when Marla Singer (Helena Bonham Carter) invades the support groups (for the free coffee), they cease to provide comfort for our hero. Why is this woman such an intrusion, such a threat?

Enter Tyler Durden (Brad Pitt), our hero's alter ego. Unlike our soft protagonist, who looks as if he's never seen the inside of a gym, Tyler has a lithe, sinewy body (like a surrogate phallus), and his torso is often exposed almost to the groin. He is constantly in motion, but most of his energy is directed toward sex with Marla, with whom he will not speak, or destruction. Tyler is a phallic agent of chaos: He is a projectionist who splices subliminal images of cocks into family films, a waiter who urinates into the soup he serves. Sex for him is detached from any relationship: "We're a generation of men raised by women. I'm wondering if another woman is really the answer we need." This is also a generation of men without fathers as role models. "Our fathers were our models for God," Tyler says in one of his Robert Bly moments, "If our fathers bailed, what does that say about God?" In this godless, meaningless urban world in which men have been raised to be wimps, the answer to masculine salvation is structured, ritualized violence, the fight club. On their first evening together, Tyler dares our hero into a fight and fighting becomes his new addiction, "After fighting, everything else in your life got the volume turned down."

In writing about the plays of Sam Shepard, David Savran observes:

> Male subjectivity in Shepard is founded—masochistically—on a split between a passive and humiliated self and an active and violent self. Desire then circulates between the two, with the self longing for its other, which may be located either inside or outside the self—it makes little difference which. . . . Significantly, though, it is usually marked less by eroticism than by *violence,* by a longing to dominate and consume the other. For is it not the violence that circulates between self and other the very mark of desire, the sign by which desire becomes visible? And does not this closed system—joining self with other, humiliation with exultation, pain with pleasure—precisely mark the masochistic economy of desire?[16]

This formula perfectly fits *Fight Club*. In their first fight, Tyler asks the narrator to hit him, to regain his manhood by starting a fight. As in Sam Shepard's play *True West*, in which the warring brother-opposites may also be read as a man and his doppelgänger, our protagonist desires, imitates, ritually battles his ideal violent self. Soon large numbers of men have joined him and Tyler in nightly fight sessions that have the power of religion: "We all felt saved." Here is one view of an ideal man's world: shirtless men beating each other up in a sadomasochistic ritual supposedly devoid of any homosexual overtones—violence as male bonding—black eyes and bloody mouths as signs of empowerment. The Fight Club becomes like a secret religious order. One gives up one's worldly possessions for salvation through hopelessness and violence.

At the center of the film is a romantic triangle. Our protagonist lives with and for Tyler Durden in a dilapidated, remote house: "Most of the week we were Ozzie and Harriet." Only Marla, who has regular noisy sex with Tyler, threatens their relationship: "She invaded my support groups. Now she invaded my home." When I first saw *Fight Club*, I hadn't yet read the novel and was able to see the film as a classic example of homosexual desire expressed through violence. If the men thought it unthinkable to fuck, they could get their kicks by beating each other senseless. Our hero lying unhappily in bed listening to his beloved Tyler banging Marla seemed a typical example of unrequited gay love. But when Tyler informed the protagonist that the two of them were the same person, two aspects of a single personality, I felt cheated. Edward Norton didn't have a crush on Brad Pitt after all. Edward Norton *was* Brad Pitt, and they were both Tyler Durden. Tyler Durden is not only our protagonist's alter ego but his ideal: "I look like you want to look. I fuck like you want to fuck." While this split personality is convincing in the novel, in the film it seems a desperate, unconvincing ploy to erase the obvious sexual desire that holds the two men together.

At the end of the novel, the reader knows that most of what he has read is the imaginings of the narrator. But film is more literal and more formulaic. At the end of *Fight Club* the movie, our protagonist is holding hands with Marla, with whom he has finally established his own relationship, watching the spectacular explosions he and other members of the Fight Club have set off. Are we to believe that he has created a nationwide network of violence? Has he really been miraculously cured of Tyler and of his sexual confusion? If Tyler is a figment of his imagination, what isn't? While the novel has given us a picture of urban madness akin to that in Bret Easton Ellis's *American Psycho,* the film's final explosions echo the finales of masculine fantasies like *Die Hard* and *The Terminator.* The film wants us to see the violence as Tyler sees it, as revenge against an alienating society, as healthy masculine expression. The unconvincing heterosexual resolution eliminates any anxieties about homosexuality the narrative may evoke. Then there's the final shot of a penis, the taboo object in most Hollywood films. Though it is probably meant only as one of the film's many cute self-referential jokes, it can also be read as a sign that the entire film is a celebration of the basic, primal masculinity Edward Norton's character desired and created, the phallic man. Yet Norton's character is also the ultimate masochist, proudly showing his bloody toothless mouth, his acid-burned hand, his gunshot wounds. Masculinity here is based less in the pain one can cause than in the pain one can endure. "It really hurts. Hit me again," the protagonist says to Tyler after their first bout. In the one fight we see in graphic detail, Tyler is beaten to a pulp but continues to mock and provoke his assailant. The real issue is how well a man can "take it." Critic David Savran notes that the phrase "taking it like a man" "seems tacitly to acknowledge that masculinity is a function not of social or cultural mastery but of the act of being subjected, abused, even tortured. It implies that masculinity is not an achieved state but a process, a trial through which one passes."[17] Yet Tyler Durden has actually been viciously punching himself—even his masochism lacks a real connection to another person.

The Brad Pitt half of Tyler Durden is merely an exaggerated version of the odd combination of anarchy and order, homoeroticism and compulsory heterosexuality, expressed through violence we see in John and Tom in *Boys Don't Cry,* another violent male couple, or in Paul Prentice, in *Different for Girls,* who ends up with a biologically acceptable version of the boy he once loved.

"YOU ARE THE ONE, NEO. I HAVE SPENT MY ENTIRE LIFE WAITING FOR YOU."

A bright graduate student once declared that the difference between the straight male body and the gay male body is that the gay body is permeable—things are put into it. The idea of such permeability is terrifying to straight men. If this is so, what is done to beautiful Keanu Reeve's body in *The Matrix* (1999; screenplay and direction, Andy and Larry Wachowski), must be a source of some anxiety for heterosexuals in the audience and perhaps a source of pleasure to some of us gay viewers. During the course of this film, the body of Reeves's character, Neo, is subjected to all sorts of invasions and insults. Not only is he chased, hit, and shot at, but his body is repeatedly invaded by tubes. One can perhaps see Neo's wounds as those of a saint, like the arrows piercing the body of Sebastian.

If *Fight Club* presents a mental world in which reality and fantasy have become totally blurred, *The Matrix* presents a world in which the imagination is everything. In the film's notion of the future, humans are merely a power source for the artificial life forms they once created but who now rule. The world people think they occupy is merely a virtual reality they are fed while living in suspended animation, wired and connected to giant dynamos. Empowerment comes from gaining control of one's mind, but doing that requires imagining grand kung fu duels that are physically impossible. A group of rebels who have discovered the truth of the Matrix and are trying to destroy it to free mankind from their bondage are seeking their savior, The One, who will, through extraordinary feats of strength, courage, and endurance of pain, save them. Essentially, what the rebels seek is a place where tubes, wires, and cables won't be placed in their bodies, where they won't be violated by their rulers. Attaining manhood is resisting and overcoming sexual passivity through violence. While there are women among the rebels, all the agents of the Matrix are male, though their gender is an illusion, a trick of disguise.

The One turns out to be, like Tyler Durden, a man who leads a double life. By day he is Thomas Anderson, a programmer at a software firm, working out of a cubicle in a giant office building. By night he is Neo, a computer hacker trying to find his way into the Matrix and illegally selling narcotic computer programs from his apartment. The rebels find him and bring him to their leader, Morpheus (Laurence Fishburne), who enlightens Neo about the Matrix and prepares him for battle against the powerful, ruthless agents of the ruling artificial intelligences. When Morpheus tells Neo that "I have spent my whole life waiting for you," it is not the statement of a lover, but of a believer. His bonding with Neo takes the form of a spectacular kung fu duel. In other words, *The Matrix* builds on common masculine myths. Men hold knowledge; their devotion is shown through violence.

Through his alliance with Morpheus and the rebels, Reeve's Neo is transformed from a passive creature connected against his will to a dominating system to a powerful, phallic presence. In one notable scene, Neo, dressed in a terrific black designer overcoat and sporting cool shades, invades an office building with what seems to be an inexhaustible supply of guns. His companion in this invasion is Trinity (Carrie-Ann Moss), a woman equally good with guns and kung fu. "I thought you were a guy," Neo says when he first meets her. "Most men do," she responds. Like Demi Moore's G.I. Jane (in the 1997 Ridley Scott film), Trinity is an example of the new "phallic woman," "claiming space with [her] legs and groin in a challenging and confident way."[18] Only a woman like Trinity is a fit partner for The One and, in the final reel, just enough of a romance is established between them to assure the straight guys in the audience that even though Neo has had stuff plugged into him, he's also straight. His shoot-'em-up scene with Trinity is, however, more convincing than their love scene. In the old westerns, men bonded through violent action; Indian battles, gunfights, saloon brawls. In *The Matrix* a man and a woman bond through violence. Aside from this hint of romance, *The Matrix* is a pure testosterone movie, made all the more interesting because the hero isn't played by a ridiculously inflated creature like Arnold Schwarzenegger or Sylvester Stallone but by lean, beautiful, sweet Keanu Reeves. The real man at the turn of the twenty-first century is both action figure and gentle object of the gaze.

What The One is fighting for is "a world without rules and controls, borders and boundaries, a world where anything is possible." His goal is a libertarian paradise and *The Matrix,* like *Fight Club,* can easily be read as a masculine fantasy of a boy's world of freedom: no bureaucratic job, no boss, no impersonal apartment. His colleagues, even his girlfriend, are constantly engaged in exciting adventures, violent battles in which the hero endures all sorts of pain to defeat the bad guys and can even stop bullets. And the system that makes us grow up into "rules and controls" can be destroyed. At the film's end, Keanu's Neo is standing on a city street in our time (the Matrix's virtual reality has its slaves thinking they're in 1999). He has come to save us from a world that pacifies us, stores us in compartments and, worst of all, sticks things into us, as he has come to avenge his penetration.

At the same time, though, throughout these battles Neo is sitting in a chair imagining his duels in some alternative reality. In our television-Internet-Nintendo-dominated world, the line between real action and imagination is impossible to locate and no longer matters. We can battle the rules and controls and be manly in our minds without any of the real pain. Is this masculinity for the twenty-first century?

Chapter Two

FATHER KNOWS BEST

Picturing the Gender Order

"I will be both husband and father."

—*Don Ottavio, in Mozart's* Don Giovanni

In her chronicle of American men in crisis, *Stiffed,* Susan Faludi describes a man she met at a meeting concerning alternatives to violence:

> When he married for the first time he told his wife, without a trace of irony, "It'll be just like Father Knows Best!" In retrospect, he said, "What really excited me about getting married was not *her* but just being married, doing what I was supposed to do." He wanted to be married to the whole system that defined and supported American manhood.[1]

Marriage defines manhood, but men are supposed to define marriage. That assumption is the keystone of the system that supports marriage, a system that can be called patriarchy or the gender order, a vertical system with men, particularly straight white men, at the top. One of Hollywood's most important functions has been to market conventional patriarchal heterosexuality expressed through marriage as the only means to true happiness.

Because it is impossible to write of masculinity without writing of the groups against which heterosexual men define themselves—women and gay men—I offer here a survey of domestic melodramas that affirm or critique the gender order: works in which a woman's voice seems to dominate but is ultimately silenced, or at least drowned out, by a masculine voice. Gay men play a series of roles in this survey: as the creators of some of the most successful works upholding masculine power and privilege and as the writers of some of the most powerful critiques; as the not-quite-all-male characters who are often allied with the problematic women and as the victims of manipulative women; and, finally, as the tyrants who would wreak violence on both women and straight men.

"WE MEN HAVE TO RUN THIS WORLD, AND IT'S NOT AN EASY JOB."

Opening during the Depression and running through World War II, still the longest-running nonmusical Broadway show, *Life with Father* (1939) continued its life as a successful movie (1947) and a television series (1953–55). Set in a nostalgic New York past quite different from the grim world of the Depression, the play offered a comforting picture of marriage and the family and began a formula we still see in television sitcoms and commercials: the bombastic, domestically inept patriarch outsmarted by his sweet, devoted, clever wife.

When the time comes for him to teach his eldest son about women, Father presents his view of the gender order:

> You see, Clarence, we men have to run this world, and it's not an easy job. It takes work and it takes thinking. A man has to be sure of his facts and figures. He has to reason things out. Now, you take a woman—a woman thinks—no I'm wrong right there—a woman doesn't think at all! She gets stirred up! And she gets stirred up over the damndest things! Now, I love my wife just as much as the next man, but that doesn't mean I should stand for a lot of folderol! By God! I won't stand for it! [2]

It is Father who gets "stirred up," though, to be calmed by his wife, the long-suffering Vinnie: "It's awfully hard on a woman to like a man like Clare so much." [3] Father bullies the maids and rants at his wife for her impracticality, and the stage directions tell us that Vinnie "has a lively mind which darts quickly away from any practical matter." [4] In truth, though, she knows that her duty is to humor her husband while running things her own way. We see that Father's ranting is accepted as normal masculine behavior in his domestic territory. And when the family's seventeen-year-old son, Clarence Jr., is given one of his father's old suits, he finds himself behaving just like the patriarch: "Mother, I can't seem to make these clothes do anything Father wouldn't do!"[5] Young Clarence, like his father, finds himself manipulated by the young woman he tries to master. Such is life in the nuclear family, and the assumption underlying *Life with Father* is that however eccentric, the patriarchal nuclear family is the unquestioned norm. The American commercial theater, like American film, has generally supported the ideology of the nuclear family. As critic Philip Green cogently puts it:

> It's crucial to understand the ideological family not as the "normal" family simply depicted, or even valorized, but rather as the "normal" family (and "normal" sexuality) reconstituted into a special site of moral privilege: not as necessary human unity but as coercive ideological symbol.[6]

This ideological family is structured on the notion of sexual hierarchy as the basis of the gender order. However immature the patriarch may appear, however out of touch he seems in the domestic economy, his preeminent place is unquestioned, and women need to adapt to their secondary position.

In more serious works than this Howard Lindsay–Russel Crouse hit, women are either silenced or learn to accept masculine discourse as authoritative. If they try to find fulfillment outside the domestic sphere, they must learn that the workplace, like the home, is rightfully the man's world. In domestic melodrama one finds, more than anywhere, the gospel of what sociologist R. W. Connell calls "hegemonic masculinity":

> Hegemonic masculinity can be defined as the configuration of gender practice which embodies the currently accepted answer to the problem of the legitimacy of patriarchy, which guarantees (or is taken to guarantee) the dominant position of men and the subordination of women.[7]

One can see the ways in which hegemonic masculinity is affirmed in American drama in two seemingly quite different plays, Arthur Miller's *The Crucible* and David Mamet's *Oleanna*. Both were faithfully translated into film.

"DON'T CALL YOUR WIFE BABY."

Arthur Miller's *The Crucible* (play, 1953; film 1996), required reading in many American schools, is often seen as a parable of one man's fight against the sort of terror and tyranny freethinking Americans faced during the postwar Red Scare. Unlike some of Miller's real-life associates, such as director Elia Kazan, his *Crucible* hero, John Proctor, goes to the gibbet rather than betray his neighbors and his own good name. In creating a drama out of the Salem witch trials, Miller's surrogate for the investigations of the House Un-American Activities Committee, the playwright also created a cogent, uncritical view of the gender politics of the postwar period. At heart, *The Crucible* is a domestic melodrama. The chaos in the play's Salem is caused by adolescent girls (their historical models were younger) led by a forceful, sexually aware orphan, Abigail Williams, who has had sex with the play's protagonist, the freethinking, outspoken farmer John Proctor. With the unleashing of female sexuality, the social order is overturned: The young manipulate and destroy the old, and females have power over men. Abigail's primary goal is the destruction of John's wife, Elizabeth, so that she can have John to herself. John does not have much success in convincing Abigail that their backyard coupling was a one-time thing. "Wipe it out of mind" he tells her, "We never touched."[8] This denial demands of Abigail that she give up not only her feelings for John but also her memory of what was for her a liberating, empowering event. Miller doesn't question the reasonableness of John's demand. Such an incident has no consequences for the man, so the woman—who isn't pregnant, after all—should "wipe it out of mind." Moreover, Miller offers a mitigating circumstance in the person of John's chilly wife. When John enters his home at the beginning of Act 2, he checks the rabbit stew on the fire and adds spice. Like his marriage, it is bland. And though Elizabeth has already fired Abigail as her servant, her suspicions of her husband's infidelity remain to chill their dinner—but John again takes charge: "Let you look to your own improvement before you go to judge your husband anymore."[9] Elizabeth's improvement, it seems, would be to see to it that John's sexual needs might be met at home. At the end of the play, Elizabeth takes responsibility for what has happened to her marriage (and to the town): "I have sins of my own to count. It takes a cold wife to prompt lechery."[10] Her frigidity, though, is mitigated somewhat by her own inferiority complex: "I counted myself so plain, so poorly made, no honest love could come to me! Suspicion kissed you when I did."[11] In writing his screenplay for the film of *The Crucible* (directed by Nicholas Hytner), Miller changed none of these lines. Either he thought the play had attained such classic status since the 1950s that it didn't need rethinking, or his ideas of marriage hadn't changed in forty years. While the performance of Miller's son-in-law, Daniel Day-Lewis, as John Proctor is sexier than the script suggests, displaying a real attraction for Winona Ryder's Abigail, Joan Allen's prim Elizabeth is indeed chilly.

John hangs less for his adultery than to protect his honor: "I have three children—how may I teach them to walk like men in the world and I sold my friends?"[12] Elizabeth, too, will soon die for Abigail's deceit and, it seems, for her own coldness. Elizabeth is allowed to live until her baby is born. After that, she is sentenced to death. Her last words in the play are praise for her husband. She has learned not to judge her husband, but rather to celebrate him—as a good wife should.

The Crucible is revived regularly, somewhat saved from scrutiny by its period setting. Its mores and psychology, however, are those of the 1950s, not the 1690s. How much have things changed? At the end of David Mamet's *Oleanna* (play, 1992; film, 1994; screenplay and direction, David Mamet), when university student Carol, on behalf of her unnamed "group" presents John, a professor, with a list of books they want removed from the curriculum, including a book of his, John says, in clear echo of John Proctor:

> I've got a book with my name on it. And my son will *see* that *book* someday. And I have a respon . . . No, I'm sorry I have a *responsibility . . .* to *myself*, to my *son,* to my *profession*.[13]

Like John Proctor, Mamet's John will resist tyranny and be destroyed in the process, but Mamet's version of the tyrant is a representative of people who do not keep to their assigned place as subordinate to a straight white male. As John and Elizabeth Proctor are brought down unjustly by an adolescent girl, so Mamet's John, a well-meaning professor, is destroyed by a female student who unjustly accuses him of sexual harassment.

Oleanna is comprised of three meetings between John and Carol during which the balance of power shifts totally in her direction. The meetings are punctuated by phone calls between John and his wife and their lawyer over the purchase of a new house, the prize for the higher salary John will earn when he receives tenure. "What about the land?"[14] John asks his wife in the opening line of the play, and the land, John's right to property, his stake in the American dream of home and family, are established at the outset.

Witnessing John's first call is the dull, frightened, Carol, who is curious about a phrase John uses in his phone conversation: "term of art." She asks John what it means, and he replies, "It seems to mean a *term*, which has come, through its use, to mean something *more specific* than the words would, to someone not acquainted with them . . . indicate. That, I believe, is what a 'term of art' would mean."[15] Unwittingly, John is dealing with terms, words, gestures, that have very specific meanings to Carol that are quite different from what John intends, if indeed John intends anything beyond trying to prove that he is a competent, caring teacher. And though John's actions with Carol in their first encounter are ludicrously unprofessional—nowadays a professor would be crazy to allow a student to stay in his office after hours with the door shut—John is simply trying, albeit awkwardly, to establish a positive teaching relationship with a troubled student. And when Carol misreads as a sexual overture John's claim that he likes her, as she misreads his embrace when she cries, we are to see this as a terrible injustice to John's good intentions and proper role as teacher and male.

The rest of *Oleanna* is an expression of masculine panic. Carol's accusations of sexual harassment lose John his tenure. By the final scene, she has accused him of battery because he stopped her from leaving his office. John wants what is his: his house, his family, his tenure, his unquestioned authority as scholar and teacher. Neither he nor his creator sees any justice in Carol's claims that all his "silly weak *guilt*" is "about *privilege;* and you don't know it."[16] And she does not mean merely professional privilege; she means masculine privilege, the privilege to control discourse, to speak and act without having one's authority questioned—by a woman. What provokes John to assault Carol is her order that he not call his wife "baby." For Mamet, this is an issue of freedom of speech, and of justice, though John's words belie deeply seated misogyny:

> You vicious little bitch. You think you can come in here with your political correctness and destroy my life?
> *(He knocks her to the floor.)*
> After how I treated you . . . ? You should be . . . *Rape you* . . . ? Are you kidding me . . . ?
> *(He picks up a chair, raises it above his head, and advances on her.)*
> I wouldn't touch you with a ten foot pole. You little *cunt* . . . [17]

Carol's response to this nastiness is a simple "Yes. That's right."[18] John has shown his true, naked feelings, and Carol can complete her destruction of this representative of privileged white males. What is most shocking about *Oleanna* is that Mamet has stacked his cards against Carol so carefully that audiences cheer John's attack—until they realize that he has just given Carol more ammunition to destroy him.

At stake in *Oleanna* is a man's right to dominate language, to fix its interpretation. Throughout the first scene, John is constantly silencing and correcting Carol, interrupting her words. When she does this to him in the final scene, it is presented as a cruel reversal, an impertinence. "Why do you hate me," Carol asks, "because you think me wrong? No. Because I have, you think, *power* over you."[19] Mamet isn't content with an analysis of the shifting balance of power between Carol and John; he must demonize Carol, make her a tyrant. In the film version of *Oleanna*, directed by Mamet, Carol's costume gets more butch as the narrative progresses, so that it is possible to read her behavior as lesbian revenge.

John's final words to his wife are "I can't talk now, Baby."[20] Carol has managed to silence him in both his professional sphere and his domestic sphere. He has lost his financial security, thus the wherewithal to buy the "good home" so important to him. Carol, his nemesis, "of some doubtful sexuality," has no respect for John's domestic security, or the domestic hierarchy on which it is built.

In discussing two ultraconservative attacks on multiculturalism in the university, Dinesh D'Souza's *Illiberal Education* and Allan Bloom's *The Closing of the American Mind,* two books whose politics bear a kinship to those of *Oleanna,* author Sally Robinson observes: "The real crime [according to these writers] of feminism and multiculturalism is not that they make *truth* relative, but that they make *white masculinity* relative, by placing white men within the field of identity politics, by marking them as the embodiment of a particularity that 'just happens' to coincide with the normative, and putatively, unmarked, self."[21] Even at the end of *Oleanna,* John does not see that he has never questioned his right to the privilege of his position, that there is validity in Carol's demands.

Mamet's play is of a piece with the conservative diatribes of William Bennett, George Will, and Rush Limbaugh, and their call for a return to the rule of straight white men, an end to the strident voices of "feminazis" and other voices of multiculturalism. They want a return to "traditional family values," another term for the preliberation gender order assumed in works like *The Crucible.* Above all, they want to erase the gains made by women in the years between *The Crucible* and *Oleanna.*

What happens when the voice of a gay man is added to the depictions of the silencing of women seeking empowerment? In the next pages, I will be examining some classic films and two plays, George Kelly's *Craig's Wife* and Tennessee Williams's *Orpheus Descending,* both of which have been faithfully adapted to films more than once.

"ESSENTIAL MANHOOD"

George Kelly's play *Craig's Wife,* a Pulitzer Prize winner in 1926 and thrice adapted for the screen, served for decades as the definition of the monstrous middle-class housewife, a female corollary to Sinclair Lewis's harsh carica-ture of bourgeois masculinity, *Babbitt.* Here, presented in a hard, rational play, was the unloving, man-hating wife who made her house, bought with her husband's money, into a fortress. *Craig's Wife,* written by a closeted ho-mosexual who was one of the most successful commercial playwrights of the 1920s and '30s, is a textbook example of a work in which the woman's voice, first dominant, is literally silenced by her husband.

For the first half hour of the play, we hear only women's voices, and they all focus on Mrs. Craig; however, nothing speaks more loudly for or against her than the play's setting, the home she ruthlessly rules and whose appearance she obsessively polices. The stage directions tell us that this living room "reflects the very excellent taste and fanatical orderliness of its mistress."[22] Mrs. Craig's "fanatical orderliness" is not atypical. Mrs. Harrold, the housekeeper, tells one of her subordinates, "Oh, there's plenty like her—I've worked for three of them; you'd think their houses were God Almighty."[23]

For Harriet Craig, marriage is "a bargain" she has made with a man, though it is clear that she despises the gender. Her husband gets a wife and a home; she gets material security and protection. In addition, Mrs. Craig wants "emancipation" (still a politically charged word in the 1920s), which she thinks of as "independence of authority—*over* the man I married."[24] And since "romantic" men don't understand hard, practical women, Mrs. Craig controls and manipulates information to maintain her dominance: "But there are certain things men can't be told, Ethel; they don't understand them; particularly romantic men; and Mr. Craig is inveterately idealistic."[25] She has manipulated things so well that her husband's friends won't come near the Craigs' home. As her husband's aunt, Miss Austen, succinctly puts it: "She's a supremely selfish woman; and with the arrogance of the selfish mind, she wants to exclude the whole world—because she cannot impose her narrow little order upon it."[26] When Clarence Day in *Life with Father* claims, "I didn't buy this house to show hospitality—I bought it for my own comfort,"[27] this can be read as a comic assertion of male privilege that will come to naught because his wife ultimately knows best. The same attitude expressed by Harriet Craig is presented as sinister effrontery.

Throughout the play, Kelly is careful to make sure that the audience reads his protagonist correctly and recognizes Miss Austen as his mouthpiece. Craig is told by his aunt that he must fight "for the life of [his] manhood"[28] or be castrated by this woman who doesn't respect his role as "*man* of the house." A good woman knows a man must rule. For those who know Kelly's biography, there's something appropriate about this fastidious lifelong bachelor choosing a maiden aunt as his surrogate. However negative his portrayal of her, there's also something of Kelly in Harriet Craig. He directed his own plays in order to maintain artistic control and was particularly fastidious about the decor and costumes: "Interior decoration is as important to the playwright as to his characters," he said.[29] His biographer, Foster Hirsch, quoting contemporary magazine articles, points out that "even at the height of his fame in the 1920s, Kelly was reclusive, 'the most inward of men,' with something of the reputation of a hermit. He always had 'very few friends and chose them with the greatest care.'"[30] His cautiousness and reticence about his personal life may well have been a way of concealing his homosexuality. Kelly presented his lover of almost fifty years, William Weagly, as his valet to everyone, including his family (Kelly was one of *the* Philadelphia Kellys, the uncle of Grace Kelly, later Princess Grace of Monaco). This was not only subterfuge. It was also a means of placing his homosexual relationship within a hierarchical order analogous to the relationship of a husband and wife in a traditional patriarchal marriage.

In *Craig's Wife*, the Craigs have been married only two years and they are childless, suggesting that Mrs. Craig has successfully kept her husband out of her bed (she rebuffs his onstage demonstrations of affection and desire). Only when a scandal looms on the horizon does Walter come to understand his wife's "presumption." A friend of Walter's has murdered his wife "because she was dishonest." Since Walter was at the friend's house earlier on the night of the killing, Harriet fears people might think he was in some way involved: "I'm interested only in the impression on the popular mind—and the respect of the community we've got to live in."[31] Walter's epiphany comes when his wife calls him a "romantic fool." In Kelly's version of the gender war, the man is the one with the sentimental, romantic devotion and the wife is the ruthless materialist. When Walter realizes that his wife sees him only as a means to an end, that she is "brazenly presumptuous" enough to "set [herself] about to control the very destiny of a man,"[32] he shatters one of her favorite tchotchkes "as a kind of opening gun,"[33] in the war to put his house in order. One of the unintentional ironies of *Craig's Wife* is that Walter chooses to assert his authority through a series of petulant, childish actions: "I . . . smashed it . . . into a thousand little pieces right here on these bricks here. And then I smoked one cigarette after another, till I had your sanctum sanctorum here absolutely littered with ashes and cigarette butts."[34] (Walter Craig's living-room rampage is father to Lester Burnham's plate hurling in Alan Ball's screenplay for *American Beauty,* which also equates petulance with masculine privilege.) Walter Craig ultimately chooses a more mature response to his loveless marriage: He leaves his wife, declaring, "There's something in a man, Harriet, that I suppose is his essential manhood; and you insulted that last night. And I should be too embarrassed here, under your eye, knowing that you had no respect for that manhood."[35] Kelly feels no need to explain what "essential manhood" is. He assumed his audience knew it is expressed by a man's assumption of his proper role in his domestic space. If he doesn't automatically get that, if his wife does not "honor and obey" him, he must either fight for dominance or move on and find a wife who will play her role in affirming his masculinity.

By the final curtain, Harriet Craig has been silenced. Her husband and servants have left, and she has only her empty house to wander through, "her eyes wide and despairing."[36] She has not only learned the error of her ways, but will pay the price in isolation, for the only fulfilling place for a woman, we have been told, is in a proper, loving relationship with a man.

After a 1928 silent-film version, *Craig's Wife* was remade in 1936 by Dorothy Arzner (screenplay, George Kelly and Mary C. McCall, Jr.), one of the few major female directors of the Hollywood studio era (and a lesbian). In this telling, featuring Rosalind Russell in a grand diva performance, Walter's worst indignity seems to be that he can't smoke in his own house. At the end, Harriet realizes too late the error of her ways and weeps, alone, as the door slams in her face. In 1950, the play was turned into a post–*Mildred Pierce* Joan Crawford weepie, *Harriet Craig* (screen-play, Anne Froelick and James Gunn; direction, Vincent Sherman), nowhere near as visually distinguished as the Arzner version, but instructive in its postwar revisions and a lot more fun (see fig. 2). In this version, more credibly plotted than Kelly's play (the implausible murder is eliminated), Harriet is more a compulsive liar than a shrewd manipulator. The last straw for Walter (Wendell Corey) is his discovery that Harriet has lied about her inability to have children, denying her husband (here, they have been married four years, not, as in the play, two) "something that meant more to me than anything in the world." In the era of the selling of the nuclear family, Harriet's sin is less the reversal of the proper gender order than her resistance of her role in the creation of the suburban family. By the end, Walter looks ready to move next door, where he has been regularly, if innocently, visiting a sweet widow and her son. With our hindsight about *Mommie Dearest,* Crawford's Harriet seems eerily auto-biographical. Her performance, with its terrifying close-ups in Crawford's favorite keylight (which makes her look radioactive) and her over-the-top costumes, is vintage Joan in her Cruella De Vil mode. No wonder drag artist Lypsinka chose to re-create Crawford's Harriet Craig! As Crawford's Harriet Craig wanders desolately through her house, being alone without a man is presented as the errant woman's tragic end. However, in this film, as in Kelly's play, one is left to wonder if Harriet hasn't gotten what she wants after all: her precious house and uncomfortable furniture, without the encumbrance of a man. Why is she crying?

"BILL'S HERE, BABY. AND EVERYTHING'S ALL RIGHT."

One thinks of mid-twentieth-century films such as *Sunset Boulevard* and *All About Eve* as camp classics about grand, aging divas filled with lines that have become part of gay argot. They can as easily be seen as corrective tales about what happens to career women who fall outside a man's authority. *Sunset Boulevard*'s Norma Desmond may murder Joe Gillis, but through some Hollywood miracle his voice remains to tell their story, that of a madwoman who kills her gigolo rather than see him enter into a normal heterosexual relationship. Norma's last line, "All right, Mr. De Mille, I'm ready for my close-up," suggests that even at its best, the power of the diva is limited by the men who control her image. And both Norma and Margo Channing in *All About Eve* are obsessed with their age, an issue that doesn't (according to Hollywood in 1950) affect women in good marriages.

All About Eve (1950; screenplay and direction, Joseph L. Mankiewicz), for all its scenery-chewing moments from Bette Davis and Anne Baxter (the mother of all soap-opera villainesses), is a parable about what happens to women who function outside the heterosexual economy. The film takes place in that mythical land, "the theater," the site of so many Hollywood films from Busby Berkeley musicals to backstage melodramas. In "the theater," women and crypto-gay men seem to have power, but the true dominant forces are the heterosexual male playwrights, directors, and producers. The women are either children, like Margo, who will not grow up until they marry; or monsters, like Eve Harrington, crypto-lesbians who use men only to fulfill their own ambitions. Margo and Eve are stars because they believe that the applause of strangers—"waves of love," Eve calls it—is more important than the love of one man. Margo comes to realize that without a man beside her, she's "not a woman." Eve, on the other hand, ends up sharing her apartment and perhaps her bed with a junior version of herself.

The film is split between two narrators: Karen Richards (Celeste Holm), the wife of a playwright and best friend of Margo, and the venomous critic Addison DeWitt (George Sanders). Karen is a good wife. An artist in her spare time, she lives only for her husband and their friends. Karen occasionally feels "the helplessness of having no talent to offer except loving your husband," but in the end it is wifely love that prevails. She notices Eve, shabbily dressed, waiting night after night outside the stage door, and brings her to meet Margo, which sets in motion the rest of the narrative. Karen's friendship can be dangerous because however good-natured she may be, she makes mistakes that could be destructive. Only straight men are truly steadfast.

If anything shows the danger of theater as a site of women, it is Addison DeWitt, the voice of the theater. Foppishly dressed, sporting a cigarette holder, speaking with a posh accent, Addison seems a brother to the elegant, evil, forties-movies queens like Kasper Gutman and Joel Cairo in *The Maltese Falcon* and Waldo Lydecker in *Laura*. Louche Addison belongs in urban interiors. He is totally identified by his relationships with women who are more his pawns than his lovers. When Eve seems to be willing to surrender to Addison's power, the camera lingers on his face, which demonstrates a look of victory, not desire. Addison wants Eve to belong to him: Love is not part of the equation. He appears at Eve's party with Marilyn Monroe's Miss Casswell, but he sends her off to flirt with a producer who might offer her a job. When it becomes clear that she will not succeed in anything but television, horror of horrors, she disappears from DeWitt's life. However crypto, Addison is another homosexual stereotype. In his discussion of the relationship of the queer aesthete and the diva in the Michael Powell–Emeric Pressburger film *The Red Shoes* (1948), Alexander Doty notes:

> The late-nineteenth-century example of Oscar Wilde would forever after link the gay aesthete with the upper-class dandy. Wilde's status as the most (in) famous homosexual in the Western world would also reinforce the connections between male homosexuality and the arts—for both homosexuals and heterosexuals. If they were not already, such upper-class "feminine" areas as fashion and interior decoration, and such high culture forms as opera, theatre, and ballet became bastions of coded, translated or otherwise indirect homosexual expressiveness in the public sphere. During the first half of the twentieth century, these arenas became more and more widely, and usually pejoratively, understood by the dominant culture as homosexual (or somehow queer) as well as feminine—indeed with gender inversion being the most common understanding of homosexuality, "feminine" *was* "homosexual" where men were concerned.[37]

Woman-identified, effete Addison, whose life is the theater, reads as homosexual. He's not even man enough to be a director or playwright. At the same time, he's great fun, adding another element of camp to the proceedings.

Yet the good women, Margo and Karen, are happy in marriage. At the end, Karen's playwright husband, Lloyd, gives his Sarah Siddons Award, the film's version of the Tony, to his wife, "for services rendered beyond the call of duty." Real awards are shared. At the end, Eve's award is in the hands of her new likely successor, Phoebe, who, wearing Eve's cloak, bows before a multitude of mirrors. All the lone diva has is her own reflection and the companionship of fellow vipers.

The voice of ideal masculinity in *All About Eve* is that of Bill Sampson, the director who marries Margo and saves her from the immaturity, narcissism, and viciousness of the theater. Bill is played by macho Gary Merrill, who became Bette Davis's husband shortly after the film was made, lending an air of authenticity to Bill's relationship with Margo. From the outset, Bill wants to marry Margo, who puts him off: It is she who puts career before marriage. In their first lengthy discussion, Bill gives Eve a sermon about democracy in the arts, asserting that all theater, from circuses to Broadway to film, is good, that one must trust the taste of the audience. Bill may be an artist, but he is a democrat, the opposite of hothouse snobs like Addison DeWitt. He also is clear about where he stands in the gender order. When Eve tries to seduce him, he says, "What I go after, I want to go after. I don't want it to come after me." Stanley Kowalski couldn't have said it better. When Addison DeWitt, at Eve's behest, writes a vicious article about Margo, Bill runs to protect her: "Bill's here, baby. And everything's all right." Even a powerful diva like Margo needs the protection of a real man. After their marriage, Bill continues his career, but Margo gives up Lloyd's new play: "I've finally got a life to live." "Life" is marriage and domesticity. The world of theater is heartless, filled with "killers" of dubious sexuality, nasty lesbians, and vicious queens. At the Sarah Siddons Award ceremony, Margo tells Eve, "You can always put that award where your heart ought to be." Women with hearts get married and grow up. Real men turn down women like Eve. Here is the postwar American husband as director, literally telling women—even divas—where to go.

"I SLEEP WITH A SON OF A BITCH WHO BOUGHT ME AT A FIRE SALE."

The leading-lady roles created by the foremost writer of great postwar diva vehicles, Tennessee Williams, were a far cry from the conventional, if a bit temperamental, married women presented in *All About Eve*. Williams placed his heroines in narratives that demonstrated a far more complex and frightening picture of the gender order, in which marriage may be an economic necessity but is at best a compromise, at worst a trap, and in which the silencing of women is brutal and tragic.

During the late 1950s, Williams, never totally a realist though dependent on realist directors for his commercial success,[38] created a series of richly allusive dramas (*Orpheus Descending* [1958], *Suddenly, Last Summer* [1958], and *Sweet Bird of Youth* [1959]) that illustrated his complex, radical view of the gender order. In the richest of these plays, *Orpheus Descending* (1957, filmed in 1959 and 1990), the woman and the sexual outsider, the sexually transgressive male, are destroyed by men who represent the forces of death in opposition to sex, the life force. Set in a nameless, typical southern town and combining the Greek myth of Orpheus and Eurydice with the Christian myth (the final act of the play, containing the hero's violent crucifixion, takes place the day before Easter), *Orpheus Descending* offers Williams's most codified view of gender relations and the institution of marriage.

In *Sweet Bird of Youth* and *Orpheus Descending* (a rewrite of Williams's 1940 play, *Battle of Angels*),[39] Williams linked his older, battle-scarred female protagonists to another type who was economically subordinate to women and to the straight men who control the economy: the gigolo. As Williams's short stories often glorified the male prostitute as a kind of saintly figure (see "One Arm," for instance), these plays present the supposed heterosexual version of the hustler as a sexual magnet to the women onstage (and to the women and gay men in the audience) and as the most vulnerable person in the economy, dependent on women who are themselves dependent on the men who rule. (We'll see a trashier, homophobic version of this myth in Paul Schrader's *American Gigolo,* discussed in chapter 6.)

Chance Wayne, in *Sweet Bird of Youth,* who seems to have no marketable skills except his sexual prowess, services the fading movie star Alexandra Del Lago, a less murderous Norma Desmond. Val Xavier, the outsider and scapegoat in *Orpheus Descending* who becomes the shopkeeper and stud to Lady Torrance, the play's heroine, is an itinerant balladeer, but seems to be known more for his sexual adventures: He learned at age fifteen that "[he] had something to sell besides snakeskins and other wild things' skins caught on the bayou,"[40] and admits that "all [his] life [he has] been selling something to someone."[41] These gigolos die brutal deaths at the hands of straight men who see them as a sexual menace—in other words, as if they were gay or as if they were Williams's substitute for the gay outsider, the black man. (It is hinted that Val, whose entrances in Act 1 and 3 are heralded by the "Choctaw cry" of the Conjure Man who is part black, part Native American, has had male as well as female "admirers."[42])

The setting of *Orpheus Descending* is a store owned by the mortally ill Jabe Torrance, usually unseen, but identified by the knocking sound of his cane hitting the floor to summon his wife, Lady. A general store is an appropriate setting for a play defining gender relations through material relations. People, like objects, are bought and sold. Living by selling his musical and sexual talents, the beautiful Val stops in this nameless, typical southern town when his car breaks down, where he becomes "fox in a chicken coop."[43] Vee Talbot, the first woman to be drawn to him, allows him to sleep in her husband's jail and brings him to Lady Torrance's store to seek a job. Lady hires him, is drawn to him as all the women (and men) are. Val's exchanges with the men of the town suggest their awareness of his sexual attractiveness. Jabe notes that Val is "mighty good looking" and hopes he will attract women to the store. When Val tells the sheriff that he is not wanted for any crime, the sheriff responds, "A good-looking boy like you is always wanted," and has the men rip his shirt open, ostensibly to check for "scars or marks of identification."[44] The feelings Val evokes in the men—desire, envy, fear—can be expressed only in violence. At the end, they burn him to death with a blowtorch. Such violence is possible because the sexual threat Val represents (to the town's women and men), turns him into something other, a black. Val, whose guitar bears the names of black blues singers, is given a "nigger's" warning by the sheriff. Paraphrasing a sign that says, "Nigger, don't let the sun go down on you in this county," the sheriff tells Val "to just imagine that you seen a sign that said to you: 'Boy, don't let the sun rise on you in this county.'"[45]

Ironically, Val, regarded by everyone as a sexual magnet or a sexual threat, is a relatively passive character. He attracts women, but tries to resist their attempts to take or buy from him what they want. He is trying to leave his past behind, seeking not necessarily celibacy, but a life in which he and his sexuality are not commodities: "There's people bought and sold in this world like carcasses of hogs in butcher shops!"[46] he exclaims. When Lady offers him a room, Val sees her as "a not so young and not so satisfied woman, that hired a man off the highway to do double duty without paying overtime for it . . . I mean a store clerk days and a stud nights."[47] Val takes money from the Torrance's cash register and gambles with it in an attempt to win financial independence—he both takes advantage of his commodity status and seeks his freedom from it.

Like an ancient Greek tragedy, *Orpheus Descending* opens with a chorus of women, who set the scene and narrate Lady Torrance's history. The women have husbands with names like Dawg and Peewee, which suggests that these "heavy, red-faced men in clothes that are too tight for them or too loose,"[48] are at worst less than human, at best less than virile. The women hover around the Torrance general store, the local center of commerce, while the men await the return home from the hospital of their buddy, Jabe Torrance, an image of the worst of southern masculinity. Torrance, "a gaunt, wolfish man, grey and yellow,"[49] dying of cancer, is an image of a decadent breed, an ignorant, hateful, violent man who once

rode with the Mystic Knights, the local version of the Ku Klux Klan. The
men of this play are united by the bond of hatred of difference, particularly racial or sexual difference. Marriage, always an economic necessity
for the women, is never loving and is sometimes worse. Beulah, the primary voice in the chorus of women, talks of loveless marriages born in
money and surviving through money: "People can live together in hate
for a long time, Dolly. Notice their passion for money. I've always noticed
when couples don't love each other they develop a passion for money,"[50]
and even respectable marriages can conceal the secret of sexual profligacy
and venereal disease, "not a soul but them knowin' they have to go wash
their hands after touching something the other one just put down!"[51] Vee
Talbot, a sensitive, visionary artist, married to the bullying sheriff, scolds
the women for giving "drinkin' parties an' get[ting] so drunk they don't
know which is their husband and which is somebody else's."[52]

The play's three major female characters have all been thwarted and
victimized by the men. Vee's husband, the sheriff, the voice of what the
men see as respectability, has nothing but disdain for his gifted wife, who
is going blind, or for her paintings. Carol Cutrere, the daughter of the
town's wealthiest family, has become a rebel and outcast after her attempts
to fight for social justice. Charged with "lewd vagrancy" for her protest
against the execution of a black man convicted of having sex with a white
prostitute, Carol decides to live up to the accusation. As a result, she is
paid to leave the county, as Val Xavier will be told to leave the county or
be killed, after the local men misread his empathetic response to Vee.
Carol is an advocate for the wild, free, nomadic life Val is trying to renounce: "You're in danger here, Snakeskin. You've taken off the jacket
that said 'I'm wild! I'm alone!' and put on the nice blue uniform of the
convict."[53] In this apologia for Williams's own restless life, Carol knows
that one settles down in a hostile society at one's own peril. But Carol is
a remittance relative, well-paid by her brother to keep moving and to stay
away from her former home. I have always seen Carol as a kind of crypto-
gay character. Williams's gay characters are either offstage or, through
what critic Stanley Edgar Hyman called "the Albertine strategy," turned
into women.[54] The political activist turned sexual outlaw and pariah, the
adversary of conventional domesticity, the person who knows about Val's
sexually ambiguous past, can easily be read as gay, and as Williams's surrogate onstage. Carol's outlandish makeup, "the face powdered white and
the eyes outlined and exaggerated with black pencil and the lids tinted
blue,"[55] places her in a kind of drag.

Lady's story encapsulates the dark forces at work in the social history of the South. Before the start of the play's action, her Italian immigrant father, who at first enacted a self-parody, playing the accordion, to the accompaniment of a prancing uniformed monkey, opened a nightspot that became the site of sexual pleasure for the young people of the area, including Lady, who had an affair with David Cutrere, Carol's brother, the scion of the wealthiest and most powerful family in the county. Since marriage is impossible for Lady and David in this class-bound society, Lady is abandoned and aborts the child she and David have conceived, and he marries a woman with the money and breeding to match his own. Lady's father burns to death in a fire set by the Mystic Knights, a mob that includes, unbeknownst to her, the man who will become her husband. Lady's father had committed the unforgivable sin of selling liquor to Negroes. (It is all right in this community to buy bootleg liquor from blacks but not to sell to them.)

Having lost her father, the love of her life, her respectability, and her financial independence, Lady marries Jabe Torrance for economic reasons: "I sleep with a son of a bitch who bought me at a fire sale, and not in fifteen years have I had a single good dream."[56] This makes her marriage a corollary to Val's prostitution. Tied to a dying husband she despises and who despises her, Lady lives for the dreamed-of opening of a confectionery: "It's going to be like the wine garden of my father," she says, a memorial to youthful sex and to her first love. When Lady discovers that she is pregnant, she no longer needs Val: "You've given me life, you can go!"[57] Val has fulfilled his procreative function and there is no biological or economic need for him to stay. Jabe Torrance discovers that Lady is pregnant, shoots her in the stomach, killing child and mother, and shouts that Val committed the crime. Death, and the death-dealing spirit of straight men like Jabe, cannot be overcome.

However dominant the voices of the women and of the sexually transgressive man seem to be in the play, they are silenced by the limited, brutal straight men. But this is, after all, a Tennessee Williams play, and however tragic it seems to be, the ending does not totally restore the order that existed before Val wandered into town. Before the final curtain, Carol has bought Val's snakeskin jacket, the symbol of his connection to a world more natural than that of this stifling town, and is wearing it as we hear Val's cries of pain. "Wild things leave skins behind them," she says, "they leave clean skins and teeth and white bones behind them, and these are tokens passed from one to another, so that the fugitive kind can always follow their kind."[58] There will always be "the fugitive kind" like Val who will live outside the violent law of the men of Two River County. When the sheriff enters and orders, "Don't no one move, don't move!,"[59] Carol laughs and walks right past him. Carol represents the freedom and isolation of the nomad in a play that denies all human connection except brief sexual encounter. As Val declares, "Nobody ever gets to know nobody! We're all of us sentenced to confinement inside our own skins, for life!"[60] Val violated that principle of isolation at his own peril. Carol, who warned Val to leave, acquires Val's jacket as she has shared his fugitive creed, but like everything else in the play, this is a commodity exchange: her ring for the jacket, which she purchases from the play's other wanderer, the Conjure Man.

Orpheus Descending is Williams's most powerful repudiation of the sanctity of heterosexual marriage. While here, as in his other major work, one cannot see the sexually transgressive male as anything but an endangered species,[61] Williams nevertheless offers hope for the woman strong enough to evade patriarchal authority.

Tennessee Williams's plays demand above all that most difficult trait to play, sexiness, which isn't taught in any acting class I know of (and which, in this era of college professors terrified by the possibility of sexual-harassment lawsuits, is barely mentioned). Val Xavier tells Lady that his body temperature is that of a dog's and that he can "burn a woman down." However reticent Val may be, the women of the town can't keep away from him and the men recognize his sexual attractiveness. In the original stage production of *Orpheus Descending,* Val was played by Cliff Robertson, a handsome, stolid actor, but hardly a sexual magnet. As in the casting of Ben Gazzara as Brick in the original production of *Cat on a Hot Tin Roof,* Robertson seems to have been chosen to eliminate any hint of Val being anything but conventionally "masculine." In *The Fugitive Kind* (1959), the screen version of *Orpheus Descending,* directed by Sidney Lumet (screenplay, Williams and Meade Roberts) with his characteristic literalness and heavy-handedness, Marlon Brando plays Val. In director Elia Kazan's 1951 film of *A Streetcar Named Desire* (screen adaptation, Oscar Saul), Brando defined the sexy leading man for his time, striking the perfect balance between Stanley's brutishness and his irresistible sexiness. We all know that Brando set the standard for actors of his generation. By 1959, Brando was a bit overweight, aging less than gracefully, and bringing to Val Xavier a touch of self-parody. The head is cocked and the eyes raised heavenward, as if Brando is seeking divine inspiration for his next line. He leaves long, unwritten pauses in the middle of mumbled sentences. The characters in *Orpheus Descending* are hyperarticulate: Brando's halting speech makes his lines seem artificial. What was most powerful about Brando in *Streetcar,* his palpable sexiness, no longer seems palpable, a problem in an actor playing a character who symbolizes male sexuality. Brando's style already looks dated in 1959. Who else might have played Val in 1959? Paul Newman, perhaps, but there must be an aura of rough trade about this uneducated boy from the backwoods who has been selling himself for fifteen years, a quality Newman does not possess. In the 2000 London revival of *Orpheus Descending,* directed by Nicholas Hytner, a hitherto unknown Irish actor, Stuart Townsend, made a sensation as Val, bringing credibility to a nearly impossible part.[62] Val is sexually irresistible but passive, a difficult combination to play, but drop-dead-gorgeous Townsend made it work. The sexual aggressiveness of a Brando is no longer as appealing as it once was, and it's all right now for men to be more passive. (In *The Fugitive Kind,* Brando's Val does not wait for Anna Magnani's Lady to initiate sex, as Val does in the play—that wouldn't be manly.) Townsend's sloe-eyed, still intensity, reminiscent of the stance of male models in magazine fashion ads, was a perfect image of masculinity for the new millennium.

In *Orpheus Descending,* the work of a gay playwright, the male-dominated gender order is impotent but brutal in asserting its authority. The potent male is beautiful but passive. The conventional nuclear family is a joke, as in *Cat on a Hot Tin Roof,* or a sham, as in *A Streetcar Named Desire.* Could anyone read Williams as sustaining the ideology of domesticity? Contemporary gay screenwriters, as we are about to see, are less radical, offering anti-homophobic narratives that nevertheless sustain the notion of a nuclear family that privileges men and silences women.

"GAYS DO LOVE HOUSES."

The Opposite of Sex (1998; screenplay and direction, Don Roos) is, the box for the video tells us, "a lasting, loving, and committed relationship." The women do most of the talking in *The Opposite of Sex.* The narrator of the film is its sixteen-year-old antiheroine, Dedee (Christina Ricci), but while the masculine narrative voice of 1940s film noir represents the prevailing point of view, much of Dedee's narration must be read ironically. This amoral adolescent, the comic descendant of the ruthless femme fatale—Dedee seduces and runs off with Matt (Ivan Sergei), the not-too-bright-but-gorgeous boyfriend of her half brother, Bill (Martin Donovan, in another of his stoic gay performances[63]), steals not only money but the ashes of Bill's dead lover, blackmails, and kills—must learn to appreciate the romantic love and domestic affiliations she scorns in others, as she learns that her homophobia is unfounded. After all, as she tells us early in the film, gay men "look better than straight people. And smell better." And, one might add, have better taste in interior decoration. Lucia (Lisa Kudrow), a lonely spinster schoolteacher, has renounced sex after the death of her brother, Bill's dead lover, from HIV-related infections: "I'd rather have a good back rub. It lasts longer and doesn't involve fluids." Bitter and misanthropic, Lucia attaches herself to Bill, while harshly judging every decision he makes. (Of course, all she needs is one good roll in the hay to make her pregnant and more positive about other people.)

The only person in the film as nasty as Dedee and Lucia is the only flamboyantly gay man, Jason (Johnny Galecki), a young gay activist. Pierced on pec and penis, Jason claims that Bill molested him, thus losing Bill his job as a high school teacher and exposing him to public scandal. For all the film's seeming enlightenment on issues of gender, only women and effeminate men are shown as nasty and destructive; butch men are ethical. While Jason repents at the end, poor Randy (William Lee Scott), the father of Dedee's child and the film's one-balled repository of patriarchal, homophobic values—he, of course, is southern; Hollywood equates patriarchy and homophobia with the South, as if they don't exist in Southern California or elsewhere in the United States—is killed off. "It's the husband's job to decide what happens with the money," he asserts, but one doesn't boss or slap Dedee and survive. The nuclear family is valorized here, but overt displays of patriarchal authority are strictly taboo.

While Dedee and Jason cause mayhem and Lucia kvetches, Bill suffers nobly one humiliation after another. (Martin Donovan has a great hangdog face that radiates martyrdom.) Bill loses his lover, his job, his savings, and his reputation, but remains quietly stoic. "You think you're being nice," Lucia tells him, "but it's really self-destruction."

In a sense, all of Dedee's crimes are justified: She has been trying to find a father and financial support for her child. Though she kills its biological father, she finds the most worthy father figure in her gay half brother. By the end of the film, everyone but Dedee is happily coupled. Bill and Dedee's parole officer are raising her child in Bill's lovely home.

Lucia is married and has a child. Matt is living happily with a somewhat-reformed Jason. From the outset, *The Opposite of Sex* seems to be a cynical, anti-Establishment comedy, but it ends foursquare in favor of home and hearth. Women lose their bitterness when they become mothers. Young, dumb people like Matt and Jason may think that sex is purely for pleasure, but mature men like Carl, Lucia's husband, know that sex is "supposed to focus your attention on the person you're sleeping with. Like a biological highlighter." Throughout the film, women learn from men, straight and gay. If the "straight-looking and -acting" men, the only sympathetic characters in the film, seem gentle to the point of ineffectuality, and if the women come across as tough, it is the men who turn out to be correct in their steadfastness and loyalty. Even dumb Matt wants the people around him to behave ethically.

The Opposite of Sex is one of the wittiest Hollywood comedies in years, far richer than the puerile junk most straight filmmakers have turned out. However, its popularity is partly a function of its adherence to the traditional Hollywood gender order. Only marriage, gay or straight, redeems.

"YOU'VE BEEN HAPPY AS LONG AS I KEPT MY MOUTH SHUT."

At the beginning of *American Beauty* (1999; screenplay, Alan Ball; direction, Sam Mendes), Jane tells the camera (actually Ricky's camera), "I need a father who's a role model. Not a horny geek." She cold-bloodedly says, "Someone should put him [her father] out of his misery." Since her father, Lester (Kevin Spacey), the film's protagonist and narrator, tells us he is going to die (Lester narrates from the grave, à la Joe Gillis in *Sunset Boulevard*), the only question, as the film goes on, is who is going to kill him: his daughter; Ricky, her boyfriend, who offers to do it for her; or his gun-toting wife. Or none of the above.

American Beauty gives us the coming-of-age of a forty-two-year-old suburban American male. In typical American style, Lester's coming-of-age is really his descent into a second adolescence. Unhappy in his career and in his woman-dominated home, where his marriage has dwindled and his daughter despises him, Lester is precipitated into enlightenment by two events: his lust for his teenage daughter's best friend, and his rediscovery of marijuana and courage through the ministrations of the boy next door, who happens to be an extremely successful drug pusher. Ricky (Wes Bentley), the pusher, is also the moral center of the film. Despite an abusive father, a Marine colonel who has turned his wife into a vegetable, and the fact that he is the scorn of his peers, Ricky is the one person who can see beauty in all things, even windswept plastic bags, and who calmly can tell people the truth (though the film never establishes why exactly). Ball and Mendes want their audience to see him as the *fin de siecle* version of James Dean's painfully sensitive Jim Stark in *Rebel Without a Cause* (1955; screenplay, Stewart Stern; direction, Nicholas Ray). He is also the film's true voice of capitalism. When he offers to kill Lester for Janie, he adds, "It'll cost you." Ricky's status as a drug dealer and potential hired gun hardly qualify him as an alternative to the capitalist system, but the film presents him as a sensitive, artistic option to the impersonal bureaucracy in which Lester had to work before his enlightenment.

Clearly *American Beauty* is on the side of the rebellious males, young Ricky and middle-aged Lester. Ricky's father, the colonel, tells him after he punches him: "You can't just go around doing whatever you feel like. You can't. There are rules in life." The message of the film is that those rules are arbitrary and hurtful to sensitive people who should be able to do whatever they feel like doing. Carolyn polices her house like Craig's Wife—in her loveless home, possessions are her only security—but her wise husband knows, "This isn't life—it's just stuff." At the end, we see Carolyn weeping in her husband's closet, embracing his clothes. Is this grief for the man who has treated her miserably through most of the film, remorse for not appreciating him, or guilt for thinking of killing him?

American Beauty may be simply trying, in classic Hollywood style, to have it both ways, or it may be deeply ambivalent on the subject of the suburban nuclear family, the common image of normality in America. Philip Green observes:

> It is possible . . . to express a divided consciousness without disavowal, so that a normative social institution appears rather as the contradiction it really embodies. From the standpoint of radical critique, this kind of ambivalence may appear as evasion, as disavowal of something that has never really been avowed. However, from the standpoint of dominant visual culture, the interpretive ambiguity it courts allows critique, or the suspicion of critique, to insinuate itself into the consciousness of a viewing public that has been trained to be suspicious, if not scornful, of overt politics.[64]

On the one hand, *American Beauty* presents the nightmare suburban marriage we see in Ricky's parents, a brutal, domineering military man and his brutalized wife, whose only utterances are apologies. Colonel Frank Fitts (Chris Cooper) is a gay man's nightmare vision of the homophobic patriarch, complete with southern accent and gun collection. "What a sad old man you are," Ricky calmly says after his father, erroneously thinking his son is gay, brutally attacks him. Colonel Fitts's mistaken belief that his son is having sex with Lester leads him to make his own awkward overture to the man he thinks is his son's lover. For one moment, the miserable, frustrated homosexual beneath the homophobia is revealed. In killing Lester, the colonel vainly attempts to destroy his own homosexual desire.

Lester's marriage is also miserable: He and Carolyn are both worn down by humiliating jobs and the detritus of consumer culture. Yet, in his last living moment, Lester looks lovingly at a picture of himself with his wife and daughter. Too late, he has come to his senses and realized that he loves his family. The film suggests that it is the conformist environment that's stifling, not the nuclear family. At the end, Lester, like Val in *Orpheus Descending,* is martyred because he is seen as a threat to the conventional sex /gender system. His death is the result of a gross misunderstanding. He is not a disruptive force, as his killer thinks he is, but Lester *is* rebelling against the prevailing socioeconomic structure. Though in *American Beauty,* the real capitalist is the teenage boy, Lester yearns to regain the economic position of a typical adolescent, the right to be a consumer without being a producer.

Perhaps the film's ambivalence can be read as the ambivalence of a gay man toward the American suburban ideal (Alan Ball, the screenwriter, is openly gay), for, ironically, the only couple in *American Beauty* that seems happy in suburbia, committed to its rituals of neighborliness and domestic beautification, is a gay couple. After all, in the promised land of the American middle class, now less hostile to gay people than it once was, why shouldn't a couple like Jim and Jim (Scott Bakula and Sam Robards), probably products of the suburbs, enjoy this symbol of affluence? Carolyn turns to them for gardening advice (they *would* have the best garden), and Lester turns to them for tips on getting his body in shape. On the other hand, there's still homophobia on those tree-lined streets, and the violence in *American Beauty* is born of homophobia. If the nuclear family is really a mess, an ideal seldom attained, why do we want to buy into it? Shouldn't we, like young Ricky and Jane, run off to, or stay in, the freedom of the city?

The real culprit in *American Beauty* is age. Hollywood's version of freedom and happiness is a kind of eternal adolescence. Lester laments that his wife isn't the rebel she was when they were in college together. He really wants his youth back. His final narration echoes Ricky's words—the voice of the teenager triumphs. What would Lester do if he'd lived? He'd have to grow up again. In his adolescent rebellion, Lester also wants to assert his authority as head of the household. *American Beauty* may offer its gay viewers a refreshingly anti-homophobic film, but its gender politics aren't far from those of *Life with Father* or *Craig's Wife*. Lester, like Walter Craig, wants his home to be his castle. At the end, his wife, like Harriet Craig, is alone in her home, weeping. The major difference is that Hollywood now believes more strongly than ever that adolescents, not fathers, know best.

Chapter Three

FATHERS AND COWBOYS

Teaching Manhood

The night after the inauguration of George W. Bush as president in January 2001, Time Warner, the owner of the Turner Broadcasting System, was surprised and delighted to discover that a new made-for-television western shown on the TNT cable network, *Crossfire Trail,* had garnered the highest ratings a cable-television film had scored in ten years. Network officials speculated that *Crossfire Trail's* success had to do with the fact that "there were millions of men who did not get their weekly fill of testosterone-inducing action [there was no televised football game the previous Sunday]—and were, thus, ripe for a good, old-fashioned western." According to a network executive, "There's a lot of pent-up demand for westerns."[1] Have millions of red-blooded American men been frustrated since *Bonanza* went off the air? The executive also noted that it didn't hurt that a Texan was now in the White House. In my youth, westerns were steady fare in movie theaters, on the radio, and on television, and, for the characters on the screen and for the young members of the audience, the western was a genre in which "the heroic male [served] as a model for young boys."[2] Certainly the most important such model was John Wayne. As a holiday gift to those men harboring the "pent-up demand," TNT had offered a marathon of John Wayne westerns as their Christmas Day observance in 2000. In his own time, Wayne was an icon of nostalgia for a lost or threatened ideal of manhood. Now the nostalgia is for Wayne himself, as part of a conservative reaffirmation of a lost ideal of manhood.

In this chapter, I will focus on masculinity and patriarchy in the drama and film of post–World War II America, the heyday of John Wayne and the western. I believe that Wayne's persona and the classic westerns of the period represent the mixed message American boys received in the McCarthy era, the era in which I grew up. Normality meant heterosexuality, of course, but it also meant an idealized pure homosociality. The ideal father figure was both John Wayne, the tough loner of the western, and the sweet family men of *Father Knows Best, The Adventures of Ozzie and Harriet,* and *The Donna Reed Show.* The loner may have performed heroic acts, but he was also sterile, producing no progeny, and could offer only violent action. While the loner was heroic, the mature man, according to literature of the period, was the family man.

"THE BOY I MARRIED"

In her book *The Hearts of Men: American Dreams and the Flight from Commitment,* Barbara Ehrenreich observes that "it is difficult, in the wake of the sixties youth rebellion, to appreciate the weight and authority that once attached to the word 'maturity,'" which, she notes, "required the predictable, sober ingredients of wisdom, responsibility, empathy, (mature) heterosexuality and . . . acceptance of adult sex roles."[3] Maturity for a man meant supporting one's family and being a good father. Maturity was, in a word, "normalcy," and as Michael Kimmel notes of the decade after World War II, "What we like to remember as a simple time, 'happy days,' was also an era of anxiety and fear during which ideas of normalcy were enforced with a desperate passion. . . . No wonder Senator Joseph McCarthy so easily linked homosexuality and communism—both represented gender failure."[4] Real men were not sissies or dupes of a tyrannical foreign power. In the mid-1950s, the Cole Porter musical *Silk Stockings* (book by George S. Kaufman, Leueen McGrath, and Abe Burrows), a hit on stage and screen, presented its Communists as a group of effete middle-aged men (Peter Lorre played one of them in the film) led by a mannish woman who was easily put in her place by an American man: "Without love, what is a woman?" the heroine Ninotchka, sings. But did real men need love?

The American man was supposed to be a responsible breadwinner. Failure at earning meant that one was neither mature nor "normal," and this had clear connotations in an age in which homosexuality, like communism, was demonized as an insidious menace. In essence, this is what separated the men from the "boys": Males would either properly develop into husbands and fathers or remain in arrested development, like the Freudian image of the homosexual. In this context, consider Blanche DuBois's description of her late husband, Allan Grey, in Tennessee Williams's 1948 play, *A Streetcar Named Desire,* as "the boy I married," whom she discovered in bed with "the older man who had been his friend for years."[5] The homosexual husband is a "boy" who is also sensitive and poetic. Blanche didn't marry a real man, like macho Stanley Kowalski, who puts food on the table, satisfies his wife sexually, and sires sons. In the bowdlerized film version, Blanche denounces Allan not for his homosexual liaison but for his immaturity, his inability to keep a job: "You're weak! I've lost respect for you!" Blanche cries.[6] Director Elia Kazan was content with this change in the script because, he said, "I prefer debility and weakness over any suggestion of perversion."[7] However, in 1951, when the *Streetcar* film was released, there was a fine line between immaturity, failing to fulfill one's proper masculine role, and homosexuality. A lot of people, though, would nonetheless read Allan's weakness as homosexuality. Barbara Ehrenreich reminds us:

> In psychiatric theory and in popular culture, the image of the irresponsible male blurred into the shadowy figure of the homosexual. Men who failed as breadwinners and husbands were "immature," while homosexuals were, in psychiatric judgment, "aspirants to perpetual adolescence."[8]

Allan Grey found an older friend who was not fulfilling his proper role as mentor to normal masculinity. In this period it was the job of a father or a father surrogate to educate boys into their proper gender roles. That assumed a maturity on the part of the father figure. Bill Reynolds, the prep school teacher overly devoted to his boys in Robert Anderson's *Tea and Sympathy,* is himself a case of arrested development. Anderson echoes some of the language of *A Streetcar Named Desire:* In both plays, a frightened boy-man looks to his wife to save him from his sexual desire: "This was the weakness you cried out for me to save you from, wasn't it,"[9] Bill's wife, Laura, asks. Too weak to be a man, Bill can only play with the boys.

If real men in post–World War II America were supposed to be good husbands and breadwinners and doting fathers, why was the western so popular? The western hero, after all, was a loner, separate from the nuclear family and larger community. If he had any close bond it was with another man, either a companion, as in the homoerotic relationships one finds in Burt Lancaster westerns like *Vera Cruz* and *Gunfight at the O.K. Corral,* or a surrogate son, as in most John Wayne films. These characters, of course, weren't the best role models in American suburbs, where a real-life male-male relationship as in these films would be highly suspicious; however, the western offered a fantasy of men away from cities and suburbs, wives and children, that many men found attractive.

"YOU'RE SOFT. WON'T ANYTHING MAKE A MAN OF YOU?"

"The typical man of the baby-boom generation," Susan Faludi writes, "has been singularly affected by his boyhood experience before a fearfully distant, authoritarian father."[10] Yet the generation in which I grew up saw on the movie screen a version of that father lionized in the huge form of John Wayne. As Gary Wills puts it, "Wayne is the ideal to which no boy's father, or coach, or teacher, or scoutmaster, or religious minister can quite live up. Yet even the ideal figure is flawed, which offers a partial justification for the actual fathers, a way of understanding *them.*"[11] As a boy, I didn't relate too well to John Wayne. Virginia Wright Wexman correctly observes that "Wayne's persona was not identified with the kind of erotic charge that characterized most Hollywood leading men,"[12] but who says "real men" should be erotically charged? Power, professional competence, and self-discipline are their defining traits, which is why I found Wayne more like my overly authoritarian scoutmaster than like someone I could feel anything for.

Even if John Wayne didn't fit into suburban backyards, he was both a hero and a nostalgic version of the ideal father. In John Wayne films, soft, handsome young men had to be hardened by the dominant image of asexual phallic masculinity, John Wayne, but *unlike* Wayne, the young men would, at the end, assume their proper domestic roles. The young heroes in John Wayne films, played by handsome actors like Montgomery Clift, John Agar, and Jeffrey Hunter provided Hollywood's vision of how the values of the frontier and those of the city and suburbia could be resolved.

With the release of director Howard Hawks's *Red River* (screenplay, Borden Chase and Charles Schnee) in 1948, John Wayne moved from playing a young western hero in B-movies to becoming an icon, partly by playing a character older than himself, a man who, though not a biological father, becomes an idealization of the American patriarch, in deadly conflict with a young protégé. The conflict between the unyielding patriarch and a soft young man would be the formula for most of the classic Wayne films from *Red River* onward, whether they took place in modern wartime or on a mythical version of the American frontier. They always took place in a nostalgic past where manhood could be tested.

"You're soft. Won't anything make a man of you?" John Wayne's Tom Dunson shouts at his surrogate son, Matthew Garth (Mongomery Clift), in *Red River*. After Dunson shoots at Matthew and punches him, Matthew starts punching back. Their knock-down-drag-out fight is stopped by Matthew's girlfriend, Tess (Joanne Dru), holding a gun on them: "Anyone with half a mind could tell you two love each other," she says. She's right, of course, but it's a "manly" love, closer than anything they could contemplate with a woman but unsullied by sex.[13] It takes a woman like the cigarette-smoking, gun-toting, pragmatic Tess to recognize and appreciate what the men cannot say. The film's last image is of Dunson showing his new cattle brand to Matthew. The inclusion of both their initials in the brand is a mark of a homosocial union kept pure and given continuity by the son that will issue from the relationship of Matthew and Tess. How does the film "make a man" out of Matthew? His courageous driving of a herd of cattle proves his professional prowess, his Oedipal battle with Wayne's Dunson proves his maturity, and the fact that he seems to have lost his virginity with Tess the night before his battle with the patriarch (we see Matthew the morning after, with that "I'm a real man now" grin) proves his heterosexuality. A number of critics see a good deal of homoerotic desire in the Dunson–Matthew relationship. I see it as a version of the father-son desire at the heart of Arthur Miller's *Death of a Salesman* and Tennessee Williams's *Cat on a Hot Tin Roof.* The father figure desires the son's youth, looks, perhaps even his sexual ambiguity—the son is the image the father would like to present to the world—but at the same time resents the son's difference. Usually, the father has to leave the scene for the son to be able to realize himself. *Red River* is unique in offering a continuing relationship of the mentor and the protégé.

"I'M GOING TO RIDE YOU TILL YOU CAN'T STAND UP."

Sands of Iwo Jima (1949; screenplay, Harry Brown and James Edward Grant; direction, Allan Dwan), made with the full cooperation of the

United States Marines, was not just a World War II film. As historian Gary Wills notes, "It merged the legend of the Marines with the legend of John Wayne"[14] and became a pivotal work for many men who needed a model for macho behavior. Newt Gingrich called it "the formative movie of my life." Mean-spirited parodies of American masculinity and big-time homophobes Oliver North and Pat Buchanan quoted Wayne's lines in their political campaigns. In his memoir, *Born on the Fourth of July,* Ron Kovic, who became a paraplegic as a result of wounds received in Vietnam, ambivalently credited *Sands of Iwo Jima* with inspiring him to become a Marine: "I gave my dead dick for John Wayne."[15]

By the time *Sands of Iwo Jima* was released, the public had seen Wayne in a number of great westerns, including *Red River* and the John Ford classics *Fort Apache* (1948) and *She Wore a Yellow Ribbon* (1949). Wayne, established as a western icon, would bring the value of the western to this war film. There was a fascinating paradox to John Wayne's persona in his most celebrated films. In the twenty-five years after the end of World War II, John Wayne topped most popularity polls as the man most American men admired. His films were seen as models for manly behavior for boys. *Sands of Iwo Jima* made him an icon of military bravery, yet Wayne had assiduously avoided being inducted into the war effort. His characters never had domestic lives (their wives were usually conveniently killed off by Indians), suggesting that the qualities of heroism Wayne embodied did not transfer to the home. Wayne was the father who could teach his son manhood only without interference from a mother. The power that the John Wayne persona held in our culture, like the fraught depictions of fatherhood in American drama, aptly demonstrates what author Carla J. McDonough calls "the desire to cling to a certain model of masculinity, even as it fails, and at times destroys, its participants."[16]

Critic Mark Simpson is right in asserting that "the war/military film is hardly ever about anything other than what it means to become a man and how to become one,"[17] and who could be a better mentor than John Wayne? Fatherhood is presented in complex ways in *Sands of Iwo Jima,* representing postwar ideas of American domesticity combined with nostalgia for the masculine heroics of World War II. The John Wayne character, Sergeant Stryker, is both an ideal military leader and a failed father, haunted by the fact that he never hears from his ten-year-old son, who is being raised by his ex-wife. (Stryker did not contest his divorce because he knew that his military service came before wife and family.) Yet within the military apparatus and the ethos of war, Stryker is a successful father to his platoon, whose members hate him as he bullies them through basic training, but, in battle, come to respect him. At the same time, as Susan Fauldi puts it, "the character repeatedly played by Wayne personifies less the World War II officer than the *postwar* father figure: remote, unreadable, an enforcer of conformity, a cold-war man."[18] There was, of course, another postwar father type, exemplified by television's Ozzie Nelson and Jim Anderson (Robert Young on *Father Knows Best*), domesticated men who were ideal for the television set in the living rooms of America, but Ozzie and Jim would never save the world from the Japanese or communism or save the West from Indians and outlaws.

As usual in John Wayne films of this period, his hard character in *Sands of Iwo Jima* is in conflict with a soft young man who must learn to combine Wayne's toughness with his own domestic impulses. Peter Conway (John Agar) is the son of a celebrated admiral under whom Stryker served and whom Stryker reveres to the point of having named his son after him, but the younger Conway resents his father: "I embarrass my father. I wasn't tough enough for him." Conway resentfully sees Stryker as the kind of man his father would have wanted for a son, but also as another version of his father: "Every time you open your mouth, my father's doing the talking."

Sands of Iwo Jima contains two parallel narrative lines. One, using a lot of Marine documentary footage, centers on the preparation of the Marines for battle and their victory at Iwo Jima, proving the value of Stryker's training. The other concerns young Conway's whirlwind romance with a young woman he meets on shore leave, which leads to their marriage and the birth of a son (virile American men don't sire daughters). Conway's domesticity is contrasted with Stryker's failure as husband and father. These parallel lines embody the mixed message of the postwar John Wayne film. Within a world of masculine action, Wayne is a hero, an ideal, but he can't cope with family life. His world is the past—World War II and the idealized nineteenth-century West of western films. Young Conway is the real hero, the man who balances military heroism with domesticity and peaceful, civilized society. He tells Stryker that he wants his son to be "intelligent, considerate, cultured, and a gentleman," the opposite of the John Wayne man of action.

In its parallel actions of war and heterosexual marriage, *Sands of Iwo Jima* also compares, on one hand, the homosocial world in which men bond and test their manhood in a world without women, and, on the other, the domestic space where men will ultimately live in what Huck Finn would call "sivilization." Whatever the pleasures of domestic life, the world of war, like the western frontier, is where men can truly be men. The one domestic space we see in *Sands of Iwo Jima,* in which Conway proposes to his future wife, looks decidedly anachronistic. With its old-fashioned furniture, it could be a set from some nineteenth-century play. Heterosexuality and domesticity are presented nostalgically, as the traditional American values for which the Marines are fighting. This is consonant with the many wartime and postwar pictures of American family life set in a mythical past (*Life with Father* and *Meet Me in St. Louis* are classic examples).

Conway comes to appreciate Stryker and his own father at the moment he sires a son. The two Marines bond in a foxhole in the heat of battle as Conway shows Stryker a picture of his son, whom he has also named after his father. Once Conway has become a father and learned the value of Stryker's training, anachronistic Stryker can be killed off.

When Stryker is shot, his men find in his shirt pocket an unfinished letter to his son: "Always do what your heart tells you . . . I want you to be like me in some ways but not like me in others." This is the message of the film. The primary issue for men is fatherhood, but the ideal man of the past is a limited model for young men of the future. Softer personal qualities are as important as heroic action. We see throughout the film signs that Stryker has some of those redeeming qualities. His eyes well up with tears when he has to leave one of his men wounded and crying for help on the battlefield. When he learns that a woman he's picked up has a baby, he leaves money for the baby's support but will not have sex with its mother (a scene echoed in Michael Cimino's 1978 film *The Deer Hunter*). However, like the fathers of the past, Stryker cannot admit his softer feelings. He tells his second in command to give his stash of liquor to his men, but not to tell them he supplied it: "Tell them you got it off a dead Nip." Men of the future must be able to show the feelings men of Stryker's generation were taught to hide. Stryker has to die and be replaced by Conway whose last words quote Stryker's favorite order: "All right men, saddle up," a line which links the action in World War II to the western. In war, the lessons of the father are crucial.

"THAT'LL BE THE DAY!"

The training John Wayne's Stryker offered Peter Conway and the other Marines in *Sands of Iwo Jima* was a merger of the qualities men proved in

World War II with the new emphasis on domesticity as well as a presage of the resurgence of militarism and war movies during the Korean conflict, which began the year after the film was released. However, during the post-war years, millions of men looked to the mythical frontier of the American western for the ideal father figure John Wayne offered. The best film he made, John Ford's *The Searchers* (1956; screenplay, Frank S. Nugent), showed the strengths and weaknesses of a purely masculine education. In *The Searchers,* John Wayne's Ethan Edwards is both renegade brother and surrogate patriarch. Ethan returns to the Texas homestead of his brother, Aaron (Walter Coy), in 1868, three years after the end of the Civil War. Though Aaron has a young son, the house seems dominated by women, Aaron's wife and two daughters. The first line of the film is "Welcome home, Ethan," a greeting from Aaron's wife, Martha (Dorothy Jordan), who clearly loves Ethan (wives in westerns are usually smitten with the lone hero), but Ethan is anything but the domestic type. As usual, Wayne is shot from beneath in low-ceilinged sets that make him look too large to be contained inside. His stay in any domestic space is temporary and uncomfortable.

Shortly after Ethan's return, an Indian raid slaughters Aaron, Martha and two of their children. Martha and the eldest daughter, Lucy, were raped before they were killed. The film traces Ethan's four-year journey to find the younger daughter, Debbie, who was taken away by the tribe. Ethan's monomaniacal vengeance is both racial and sexual. He is avenging the rape and murder of Aaron's wife and older daughter, but he is equally obsessed with the idea that Debbie might have sex with an Indian (he seems unconcerned about the deaths of his brother and his nephew). This vision of a white girl's sullied purity is Ethan's Moby-Dick, the motivation for his long journey to kill the defiled girl.

As brothers Ethan and Aaron Edwards represent a classic masculine split between anarchic spirit connected to the natural world and domesticated, feminized male (we'll see this again in Sam Shepard's *True West*), so craggy Ethan and pretty Martin Pawley (Jeffrey Hunter) are one manifestation of the surrogate father–Oedipal son conflict at the heart of most John Wayne movies (see fig. 3). After Martin's parents were killed in an Indian raid, Martin was rescued by Ethan and brought to Aaron's home to be raised (Wayne's character similarly rescues his surrogate son in *Red River*). Ethan's racism does not allow him to accept that this "half-breed" (Martin is one-eighth Cherokee) sees Aaron's family as his true family and Debbie as his true sister. Martin will gain practical knowledge from Ethan, but he will also battle him to save Debbie's life.

Though Martin is first seen through a doorway, as Ethan is, in domestic scenes throughout the film we often see Martin in conversation with women. He is one of the next generation of men, comfortable in domestic settings but in need of harsh education to face the hostile environment outside the home. Much of *The Searchers* depicts Martin's journey into Ethan's world of practical knowledge. Ethan is a tough, unyielding father, a personification of the landscape. Martin will master this world, but he will be able also to live in the bosom of the nuclear family.

The Searchers alternates episodes of Ethan and Martin's search for Debbie with slapstick comic interludes that represent Ford's idea of normalcy. However imperiled it may be by outside forces, there is a celebratory quality to the life of the community that Ethan cannot share. Home and society require adherence to laws Ethan cannot accept. There's always a representative of social order standing around, typically Reverend Captain Samuel Johnson Clayton (Ward Bond), the head of both church and state in this corner of the West, to eye Ethan with suspicion. Yet strong women are attracted to the wanderers like Ethan and Martin, rather than to good, solid husbands who are presented as ineffectual or ridiculous.

Laurie Jorgenson, the daughter of neighboring farmers, is smitten with Marty and *The Searchers* alternates episodes of Ethan and Martin's search with brief visits to the Jorgensen home. After Marty breaks up Laurie's wedding to a man clearly not worthy of her, he and Laurie become engaged. Martin, the new man, has proved himself in rough landscape and against the Indian menace, but also wants family life. He devotes four years to saving Debbie, who isn't really his relative. Is he less of a man for this domestic impulse than John Wayne's Ethan? It is Martin, after all, who kills Scar, the Comanche chief. Later, after Scar is safely dead, Ethan viciously scalps his nemesis.

American men of the 1950s obtained domestic life without the testing in the wilderness Martin experienced. They often had demanding fathers who offered little in the way of affection, thus providing no education in fatherhood. In John Wayne, they had a hero who was a man independent of women, of domesticity, of authority, but who, like a cold father, offers only the lesson that life is tough and men have to be tougher. At the end of the film, Ethan rides off again into the desert. Ethan endures, but the domesticated, feminized society that is building up on the prairie is no place for him. That will be Martin's world.

The western was a nostalgic genre in which the West was a time as well as a place. Its subtext was that men can be men only in a preindustrial America where they fight for what they want and believe in. Yet the West of the western was also a geography, an arid, beautiful, yet hostile land. In *The Searchers,* as in so many classic westerns, the land itself is a crucial character. Sam Shepard has said:

> There are areas like Wyoming, Texas, Montana, and places like that, where you really feel this ancient thing about the land. Ancient. That it's primordial. It has to do with the relationship between the land and the people—between the human being and the ground. I think that's typically Western and much more attractive than this tight little forest civilization that happened back East. It's much more physical and emotional to me.[19]

The tough loner understands and loves the land. He knows as well that human habitation is frail and impermanent against the land and human predators. The family, above all, seems constantly under siege, in need of protection from outsiders like Ethan Edwards. At the end of *The Searchers,* the camera is placed inside the dark Jorgensen house, and all the characters except Ethan walk into the darkness from outside, leaving Ethan framed in the doorway. As he moves off, the door closes, leaving only darkness, as if director Ford identifies more with the bright, beautiful outdoors. *The Searchers* is full of doorways, symbolizing the division between civilization and anarchic nature.

"I LOVE SHANE. I LOVE HIM ALMOST AS MUCH AS I LOVE DAD."

Nowhere is the conflicted image of masculinity between the lone western hero and the domesticated man better articulated than in *Shane* (1953, screenplay A. B. Guthrie, Jr.; director George Stevens), where, as critic Robert Warshow observes, "the legend of the West is virtually reduced to its essentials and then fixed in the dreamy clarity of a fairy tale."[20] The film sets the lone western hero within and against the nuclear family and heterosexual community under siege from an all-male enemy. In typical western style, Shane (Alan Ladd) rides in from an unknown, violent past and briefly finds a place within family and community, where he tries to live a normal life. It isn't clear where the wanderer has been or where he's bound: "One place or another. Some place I've never been."

When Shane arrives at the Starrett homestead in the idyllic Wyoming countryside, he is immediately welcomed by the entire family. Father Joe

(Van Heflin), an almost ideal, kindly, hard working, courageous settler, needs a man to help build and maintain his farm. Shane also can help Joe defend his homestead from the Ryker brothers and their gang, the all male community of cattlemen who want to drive the homesteaders and their families off the range. Joe's wife Marian (Jean Arthur) is immediately attracted to this mysterious stranger. And their nine-year-old son, Joey (Brandon de Wilde), through whose eyes we see the narrative, quickly moves from curiosity to a childhood crush on Shane, whom he sees as a more heroic figure than his father. "I love Shane," Joey tells his mother. "I love him almost as much as I love Dad." Woody Allen, a devotee of *Shane,* notes of Shane and Joey's first meeting: "From the first, because of the way Stevens shot it, you can tell that there is this intense fascination between the kid and Shane; it's almost love at first sight or something."[21]

Because of the emotions he inspires in the Starretts, his willingness to work hard, and his violent past, Shane's presence in the family he visits is both constructive and disruptive. Shane represents a dangerous love of violence that may be spread to the other men in the community and, more important, to young Joey, already in love with guns. The only time Shane seems truly happy in the film is when he and Joe beat up Ryker's men in a barroom brawl, a conventional western scene of drunken "boys will be boys" bonding through violence. Shane and Joe smile at each other—true bliss—not out of love for each other but out of exhilaration at the violence they have enjoyed. And little Joey looks on excitedly, sucking a phallic peppermint stick (It's very easy to queer *Shane*). Marian becomes upset when Shane teaches Joey how to shoot a gun: "This valley would be better off if there were no more guns left in it, including yours." Shane agrees with her enough to leave, but first he must do what only he can do, destroy Ryker's gang, and Wilson (Jack Palance), the hired gun Ryker has brought in to murder Starrett and his fellow farmers. Only Shane can purge the valley of these evil men. And he makes clear to the community that he is doing it to save families. Though a loner himself, he couldn't be a more ardent champion of the nuclear family. But Shane has to leave because he likes the violence—"A man has to be what he is, Joey. Can't break the mold."—and the community cannot countenance the kind of masculine violence Shane performs so well (the fistfights and gunfights in *Shane* are beyond belief—he can fight a dozen men at once and barely get bruised).

However, Shane must leave at the end, not only because he is a gunfighter who likes violence—that very violence has saved the community he visits—but because he is a disruption to the Starrett household, likely to usurp the patriarch's role with wife and child, both of whom have fallen in love with the stranger. Joe even acknowledges that Shane not only is the better fighter, but would also be the better husband and father: "If anything happens to me, you'd be taken care of," he tells Marian, "better than I could do it myself." Joe is too honorable to act on jealousy, Marian is too honorable to cheat on her husband, and Shane is too honorable to commit adultery—or simply not interested. "Are you doing this for me?" Marian asks when Shane prepares to battle Ryker and his men. "For you, Marian, for Joe, and for little Joe," Shane responds. He loves them all equally.

Alan Ladd's Shane isn't the hard, brutal patriarch John Wayne played. There's a gentleness, an elegance, in Ladd that is unique among western heroes. As Robert Warshow observes, "Ladd is a more 'aesthetic' object [than Gregory Peck or Gary Cooper], with some of the 'universality' of a piece of sculpture; his special quality is his physical smoothness and serenity, unworldly and yet not innocent, but suggesting that no experience can really touch him."[22] He is an amalgam of the older patriarch and the pretty young protégé of the Wayne films. At one point he takes his shirt off and the camera enjoys his lithe body, making him an object of specular pleasure in a way Wayne and Cooper never were. He is both the older outsider and the younger man who can fit into the community. But for all the violence, there's a gentleness, a passivity, a sweetness, about Ladd's Shane, just as there is about Van Heflin's Joe. Shane is torn between wanting to be part of a world of families and wanting to be alone and free. When he rides off, he is wounded; he has left part of himself behind, the wish to be part of normal society. Joe, whom Heflin plays with a touching combination of sweetness and strength, is obviously tempted to be like Shane, but he doesn't have the expertise. Shane has to knock Joe out with the butt of his gun to keep him from trying to take on Ryker and his men. Only Shane knows how to do that. But Shane's violence makes it possible for men like Joe to live without violence.

Unlike in the Wayne films, where the protégé is a young man, in *Shane* the protégé is a boy, preadolescent—an innocent who is so obsessed with Shane that he runs miles to follow him to his climactic gunfight. Joey may be learning manhood by balancing the examples Shane and his father offer, but there's adoration and desire in Joey's focus on Shane. Were Joey past puberty, *Shane* would be a gay love story. Like young gay boys who feel their first crush while watching movie heroes, feeling their difference from normal boys while feeling an attraction for the men on the screen, so Joey watches Shane throughout the film. Shane must leave so that Joey, who loves playing with guns, can grow up to be like his father. All Shane can teach him is how to use a gun. The civilized, feminized, heterosexual community in which he is raised will educate him to live a gentler life. The world of violence is an all-male world. But will Joey outgrow his love for Alan Ladd's Shane? Or will he grow up to be like crypto-gay Plato (Sal Mineo) in *Rebel Without a Cause,* who has a pinup photo of Alan Ladd in his locker?

The West of the western is a nostalgic, mythical place. How could its view of pure masculinity do anything but sow seeds of frustration for men in the 1950s? Yet the western was enormously popular then. More than 10 percent of all fictional works published in the 1950s were westerns, and eight of the top ten television shows—a total of thirty prime-time television shows in all—were "horse operas." Fifty-four western feature films were made in 1958 alone.[23] Clearly, the western spoke to a vicarious need of American men at the time. Its values and its conflicted view of manhood played throughout postwar American film, television, and drama. One sees more complex versions of the hard father–soft son formula of the John Wayne films in Arthur Miller's *Death of a Salesman* (1949, the same year as *Sands of Iwo Jima*) and Tennessee Williams's *Cat on a Hot Tin Roof* (1955, the year before *The Searchers* was released), and in much of the work of Sam Shepard.

"IN NEBRASKA I HERDED CATTLE AND THE DAKOTAS, AND ARIZONA, AND NOW IN TEXAS."

"Where is Dad? Didn't you follow him?" Willy asks his older brother, Ben in *Death of a Salesman* (play, 1949; filmed in 1951; televised in 1985 and 2000). While sixty-year-old Willy Loman, born in the 1880s, is a victim of the values of twentieth-century America, of the success myth preached by Russell H. Conwell in his "Acres of Diamonds" lecture and the myths of personality propagated by Dale Carnegie, his roots and ideals are in the nineteenth-century. Willy's father was a nineteenth-century inventor and entrepreneur. Willy's older brother, Ben, remembers him as

> a very great and a very wild-hearted man. We would start in Boston, and he'd toss the whole family into the wagon, and then he'd drive the

team right across the country; through Ohio, and Indiana, Michigan, Illinois, and all the western states. And we'd stop in the towns and sell the flutes that he'd made on the way. Great inventor, Father. With one gadget he made more in a week than a man like you could make in a lifetime.[24]

Willy's father represents a lost era in which a man is the maker and seller of his own products. It is not surprising that this picture of the nine-teenth-century entrepreneur is connected to music—the music of the flutes he made, sold, and played. That music of a lost era of self-reliance opens the play. When Willy was a child, his father disappeared into the farthest reaches of the American frontier, Alaska, probably in pursuit of gold. Like the western hero, Willy's father had to renounce domesticity and light out to the frontier on his own. Willy's memories of infancy are of the West:

> WILLY: I remember I was sitting under the wagon in—was it Nebraska?
> BEN: It was South Dakota, and I gave you a bunch of wild flowers.
> WILLY: I remember you walking away down some open road.
> BEN, *laughing:* I was going to find Father in Alaska.[25]

Willy has always felt this loss of a father, to him the cause of his own feel-ing of emptiness: "Dad left when I was such a baby and I never had a chance to talk to him and I still feel—kind of temporary about myself."[26] But the lessons his father could have taught him would do him no good in postwar America.

Ben literally walked away from the family, too, leaving Willy without a masculine role model in his own family, but Ben haunts Willy's mem-ories throughout the play. Ben is the success, the man who went to Africa and found, literally, acres of diamonds: "When I was seventeen I walked into the jungle and when I was twenty-one I walked out. And by God I was rich."[27] Ben's jungle is literal and figurative. It is Africa, but it is also the jungle of laissez-faire capitalism, the favorite image of naturalistic writers such as Theodore Dreiser and Upton Sinclair, who saw the world of commerce as a world of survival of the fittest. Ben's rules are those of this jungle: "Never fight fair with a stranger, boy. You'll never get out of the jungle that way."[28]

Ben returned to his brother Willy eighteen years before the play be-gins to offer a job managing Ben's timberland in Alaska:

WILLY: God, timberland! Me and my boys in those grand outdoors!
BEN: You've a new continent at your doorstep, William. Get out of those cities, they're full of talk and time payments and courts of law. Screw on your fists and you can fight for a fortune up there.[29]

This could be John Wayne talking! It is no surprise that Ben's proposition frightens Willy's wife, Linda, for the frontier Ben offers is a man's world—"me and my boys." Fortunes must be fought for, and Linda foolishly believes that the urban, capitalistic world the Lomans inhabit offers safety and security for the nuclear family:

> Enough to be happy right here, right now. Why must everybody conquer the world? You're well liked, and the boys love you, and someday—*to Ben*—why, old man Wagner told him just the other day that if he keeps it up he'll be a member of the firm, didn't he, Willy?[30]

Unfortunately, this devoted wife believes her husband's exaggerated view of his professional situation. Willy recalls this conversation—the moment he turned down Ben's proposition of success on the frontier—right after he has been fired from his job. Willy has opted for safety and domesticity. But Ben is dead, and his world of ruthless, renegade capitalism, tied to the jungle and to the limits of the frontier, is also a thing of the past, though Ben has seven sons, a sign of his virility, to inherit his wealth.

Ben and Willy represent the division of their father's industry. Ben became the entrepreneur, making a fortune out of the natural world. Willy became the salesman, but in the early years of the twentieth century, when Willy began, the salesman represented a noble profession. Michael Kimmel points out:

> Salesmen were heralded as the self-made men of the new century. Sales reinforced "independence and individuality," wrote one salesman. Life insurance was described as a "manly calling." The Equitable Company recruited would-be salesmen to a world in which their possibilities for success were "almost limitless," in which an ambitious young man could "reach the top if he have but the requisite ability and energy." America became "a nation of salesmen."[31]

In order to sell anything, the salesman had to believe, above all, in himself, in the force of his personality: "It's not what you do, Ben. It's who you know and the smile on your face! . . . and that's the wonder, the wonder of this country, that a man can end with diamonds here on the basis of being liked![32] Unfortunately, Willy isn't liked and the year is 1949. Television sets are appearing in people's living rooms, and the traveling salesman is about to become a vestige of an outmoded form of capitalism.

Willy is proud of the work he did on his house: "A man who can't handle tools is not a man."[33] His son Biff says, "There's more of him in that front stoop [he built] than in all the sales he ever made,"[34] but Willy believes that being a white-collar worker means occupying a higher rung on the social ladder than a mere carpenter. Working with one's hands is all right for an avocation, not for a profession. Social historian Robert J. Corber is correct in asserting, "For Miller, what was most disturbing about the increasing division of labor was that it prevented men from freely expressing their masculinity."[35] Masculinity is what is at issue in *Death of a Salesman*. For Arthur Miller, Willy's strength is that he won't accept the diluted version of manhood offered by his more successful neighbors, Charley and son Bernard. The play suggests that Willy is right to dream of something better, more manly. If he can't be that himself, at least his eldest son Biff can. That there is no place for Biff in this white-collar world is not Biff's fault; it's the fault of sissy high school teachers, sticklers for the law, and fathers who cheat on their wives. The play also implies that Willy and his sons would have been better off if they had left Linda and the domesticity she represents and gone with Ben into a real "man's world."

At stake in *Death of a Salesman* is what Willy Loman can give to his sons; the drama's central conflict is between Willy and his elder son, Biff, the golden boy in high school, the handsome, popular athlete whose youthful glory did not translate into mature success or practicality. To short, fat Willy, Biff is "magnificence," and Willy expresses utter lack of interest in anyone else when Biff is present, jealous of anyone (including Biff's mother) who tries to get Biff's attention. Willy's love for Biff, totally connected to Biff's looks and athletic prowess, can only be described as desire. If Willy has failed at living up to his illusions, Biff should succeed. At the end, when he has decided to kill himself so "that magnificence" can have the twenty thousand dollars Willy's life insurance will bring, Willy cries out: "I always knew one way or another we were gonna make it, Biff and I."[36] Willy's final illusion is that somehow his sacrifice will reunite him and his estranged son. Miller's world is filled with heterosexual anxiety (which inevitably includes homophobia), so Willy's love for Biff is love for an embodiment of what America values most, physical perfection and prowess, regardless of whether there's anything inside. Biff remains a man of action who can't fit in the urban world of commerce—a downscale John Wayne.

If Willy's illusions center on Biff, Biff's dream is to live in the West, to be a cowboy, but he cannot overcome his guilt at opting out of the American myth of success:

> In Nebraska when I herded cattle, and the Dakotas, and Arizona, and now in Texas . . . This farm I work on, it's spring there now, see? And they've got about fifteen new colts. There's nothing more inspiring or—beautiful than the sight of a mare and a new colt. And it's cool there now, see? Texas is cool now, and it's spring. And whenever spring comes to where I am, I suddenly get the feeling, my God, I'm not gettin' anywhere![37]

But the rural America Biff tries to inhabit is becoming as much a myth as his father's religion of popularity as the key to success. It's another relic of the past. As Willy would have been happier outdoors working with his hands, so Biff wants a life away from the city and the world of business; but the values of postwar America intervene and Biff sees himself as a case of arrested development: "I'm like a boy. I'm not married, I'm not in business. I just—I'm like a boy."[38] As Barbara Ehrenreich has written, "If adult masculinity was indistinguishable from the breadwinner role, then it followed that the man who failed to achieve this role was either not fully adult or not fully masculine."[39] In the 1950 best-seller *The Mature Mind,* the immature man is "the person who cannot settle down, who remains a vocational drifter, or the person who wants the prestige of a certain kind of work but resents the routines that go with it, [people who] are immature in their sense of function."[40] Can one find a more apt description of Biff and his younger brother, Happy? Yet less than a decade later, followers of the Beats, then the hippies, would see as a hero a man unwilling to conform to the strictures of middle-class America.

As Willy has had no continuing masculine role model, so Biff and Happy have had a father whose illusions made him incapable of training his sons for the "real world" of corporate America. Biff knows that the values his father taught him—the crucial importance of "being well liked" as the foundation of the religion of salesmanship, the pretense of petty thievery as initiative that Willy learned from his rogue brother—do not apply in the modern world. Here success goes only to the nerds: neighbor Charley, whom Willy despises but who generously provides money for Willy, and Charley's bookish son, Bernard, who becomes not only a successful lawyer but the father of two boys, the ultimate sign of manliness in Miller's plays.

Is Biff right in asserting, "I know who I am, kid"?[41] All he knows is that he is a failure at those things valued by the American middle class, a "dime a dozen." Perhaps Biff is heroic in being without illusions and rejecting the world in which he doesn't fit. Perhaps this is the heroism postwar drama offers in Tennessee Williams's Tom Wingfield in *The Glass Menagerie* and Miller's Biff Loman: the self-knowledge that impels one to get out of an empty rat race. But where can a young man go? This isn't the nineteenth century of American myth, where a man could find himself in the natural world, the sea, or the western prairie. Willy's experience shows that the natural world is shriveling. His house in the country has become dwarfed by city buildings. "The woods are burning," Willy repeatedly cries, though there are no woods left to burn.

Both Biff and his brother Happy think that marriage will somehow save them by bringing them into the world of normative heterosexuality, but neither is capable of settling down. Nor do we feel that either brother feels much for his sibling. Their first discussion in their old bedroom is a competitive gripe session. In his teens, Happy was the chubby younger brother trying to be noticed when all attention went to "magnificent" Biff. Now he has followed in his father's footsteps, but Biff is still the golden boy his father will literally die for, the beautiful embodiment of his father's illusions.

When Miller was offered the chance to write an original screenplay, this eastern, urban master of domestic melodrama wrote a contemporary western, *The Misfits* (1961; direction, John Huston). The film was a disaster in more ways than one. Its star, Clark Gable (who played a very heterosexual character named Gay, which was as close as Miller ever got to writing a gay character), died shortly after the close of production. Marilyn Monroe, then Mrs. Arthur Miller, had a nervous breakdown in the midst of filming and filed for divorce shortly after. (Turning her into a mindless earth mother was not listed on the divorce affidavit, but should have been.) A ravaged-looking Montgomery Clift plays the Hamlet-like would-be rodeo performer who is distraught over his mother's remarriage and the loss of his patrimony.

According to Miller's screenplay, cowboys are "the last real men left in the world." Manhood in *The Misfits* is a Hemingway-esque futile battle with nature, symbolized in the film by the roping of mustangs. Real men avoid "wages" and working within the capitalist system, but do not see the irony in brutally roping and killing these beautiful animals to sell for dog meat. Cowboys don't do irony. They do express chivalric love for a woman who represents Nature. Filled with hackneyed aphorisms ("A man who's too afraid to die is too afraid to live") and gender politics that were retrograde even in 1961, *The Misfits* shows us how seriously Miller takes Biff Loman's dream of the West, and how he sees the loss of that dream's purity as the true American tragedy.

"WHAT DOES A FATHER LOOK LIKE?"

Nowhere do we see patriarchy and masculinity with more bleakness than in Sam Shepard's sagas of western families. At the heart of the psychic split and crisis of masculinity that so interest Shepard is the central situation of American domestic melodrama: a powerful but failed father, an ineffectual but sensual mother, and two brothers in conflict. The central issue of these plays is the inheritance sons receive from a failed patriarchy. Tangential to this is the question of whether the sons' relationships with women are important or even feasible. In *Buried Child* (1978), Vince tells his girlfriend, Shelly, "I've gotta carry on the line,"[42] but he is speaking not of producing progeny with a woman but of reconnecting with his dysfunctional family history, particularly a physically and spiritually maimed male lineage. In Shepard's plays, generally, the sons are compelled to connect with ideals of masculinity for which there are no real models and with myths of the American land that are no longer relevant. One important expression of those ideals was the classic American western with which Sam Shepard grew up and on which, to some extent, he built his persona.[43]

Compared with the surrogate fathers and heroic, if quixotic, loners of the classic western, Shepard's fathers, seeking refuge in the desert from the strictures of civilization, are usually absent or destructive, wandering drunks or embittered nihilists (Dodge in *Buried Child* seems to have walked out of Beckett's *Endgame*). While they are nominally progenitors, they are surrounded with images and accusations of impotence. Above all, they seem totally incapable of integrating into civilized society.

These images of failed patriarchy and its relation to a lost West are most vividly seen in *Paris, Texas* (1984), directed by Wim Wenders from a Shepard screenplay (adapted by L. M. Kit Carson). Travis Henderson (Harry Dean Stanton), walking through a white Texas desert as a hawk watches him from a high rock (a parody of the opening of countless westerns), couldn't look more out of place, but we discover in the course of the film that he doesn't fit any better into modern American society (see fig. 4).

The desert in Shepard's work, according to critic Lynda Hart, is "that illusory, eminently male landscape that summons Shepard's heroes with a siren more seductive than Circe."[44] Like the landscape around him, Travis is silent—he seems to have lost, or forgotten, speech. Travis is, for all intents and purposes, a vagrant, but that itself echoes western heroes. In our contemporary society there is no place for a man outside the economic system. He is no longer a hero, but as Jack (Kirk Douglas) describes himself in *Lonely Are the Brave,* a 1962 western Shepard admires, "a cripple."

Travis has a brother who is his opposite, a man who has adapted to his world. Walt (Dean Stockwell) has built a successful life for himself in billboard advertising (is there a greater desecration of the landscape?) and lives in that other favorite Shepard setting, the Los Angeles hills, once rugged nature and now suburbia overlooking not valleys, but freeways. "No one walks," asserts Travis's son, Hunter (a name that evokes the traditional masculine role), now being raised by Walt and his wife. When Travis enters Walt's suburban home, Walt's wife says, "Welcome home," an echo of Martha's opening line addressed to brother-in-law Ethan in *The Searchers.* But this isn't Travis's home, and home is an alien concept to him. Travis gradually, reluctantly, regains language and memories of his parents and of his wife. Gradually, too, Travis builds a bond with his son, teaching him to enjoy walking. At the end, Travis restores Hunter to his biological mother in a Houston hotel room and, like the lone western hero, moves on. Travis is incapable of living with the woman he loves and incapable of being anything to his son but a fellow child. The West is reduced to the Los Angeles hills and a Houston hotel. Even the Mojave desert is decorated with highways, motels, and railroad tracks

In *Paris, Texas,* life is movement, whether walking or driving, but this movement is no longer a westward migration to build an agrarian utopia. Like Travis's walking at the beginning of the film, it seems to be constant movement away from something. Other than Walt's home, the only domestic spaces we see in *Paris, Texas,* are motel and hotel rooms, images of transience in this constantly moving society.

Travis asks Walt's Mexican maid, "What does a father look like?" To the maid, a father is a symbol of affluence, the good provider, so Travis decks himself out in his brother's three-piece white suit with a matching white fedora and goes to walk his son home from school, but they walk home on opposite sides of the street. Fatherhood is a role Travis doesn't know how to play. Domesticated Walt and his wife love Hunter, but they don't seem capable of having children of their own. Travis is fertile but incapable of maintaining the social structure of family. Bringing Hunter back to his mother is an ambiguous act, a re-creation of a family unit in which Travis cannot play a part, but also a destruction of the family Walt has created.

"YOU THINK ME AN' SKIPPER DID, DID, DID!—*SODOMY!*—TOGETHER?"

There are very few gay-created works in which fathers play a major role. Gay characters, like many gay men, have had to find themselves separate from their fathers and from the version of manhood our fathers taught us. In the American version of *Queer as Folk* the few fathers we see are intolerant homophobes. In his most autobiographical play, *The Glass Menagerie,* Tennessee Williams, in a piece of artistic wishful thinking, removes his father from the scene. While fictional versions of his mother and sister play prominent parts, the man who called his son "Miss Nancy" is only a picture on the wall. Yet the Wingfield patriarch represents even in his absence a crucial characterization of American masculinity: the lone wanderer who "[falls] in love with long distance." Like the John Wayne persona so pertinent to postwar America, Mr. Wingfield cannot settle down into masculinity. Nor can his son, Tom, who goes off to sea. When fathers in classic American drama leave, like Mr. Winfield, Willy Loman's father, or the fathers in Sam Shepard's plays, they head out for the frontier, to unknown territory. Fathers are the desert, the frontier, the woods, land, in conflict with sons closed into urban or suburban domestic spaces.

Is there any space for open homosexuality in this myth of manhood? Can the patriarch accept a gay son? Some gay young men of my generation saw in the young reluctant proteges of Wayne's persona, the Montgomery Clifts and Jeffrey Hunters, beautiful, young men we found attractive and with whom we could partially identify. Yet they would move off into a world of normative heterosexuality we already sensed would be closed to us, thus moving us farther from the abstraction of John Wayne or the reality of fathers, perhaps more Willy Loman than

John Wayne, but still incapable of entertaining the possibility of a son who wasn't all man. For its time, Tennessee Williams's *Cat on a Hot Tin Roof* comes closest to offering an understanding patriarch and a potentially gay son.

Cat on a Hot Tin Roof (filmed in 1958; televised in 1976 and 1984), portrays an extreme of the powerful patriarch–beautiful, feminized son conflict that infused the traditional western. The setting is a twenty-eight thousand-acre Mississippi plantation, not a western ranch, but Big Daddy, who, like the western hero, came from nowhere, is both the hard man of the western and the patriarch of his family. He may be cruel to his wife and distant from most of his family, but Big Daddy's abiding love is his land. Big Daddy's favored son, Brick, may be a drunk and professional failure, but this beautiful man (and we are constantly told of his beauty), like the pretty young men in the western, is trying to balance the outdoor, physical world, now represented by the rituals of athletics, with the pressures of heterosexuality and domesticity.

The Pollitt family of Tennessee Williams's *Cat on a Hot Tin Roof* offers a more complex picture of what it means to be a mature man, as one would expect of a writer far less sure of the truth of the gender order than Arthur Miller, Sam Shepard, or the writers of Hollywood westerns. Brick Pollitt, the scion of a grand plantation, a vestige of the agrarian south, is twenty-eight and once again in his parents' home. Like Biff Loman, Brick is an aging golden boy, a handsome former athletic star, the favorite of his parents, now deeply lost. After his glory years as a football star, he and his best friend, Skipper (a name that suggests immaturity), tried to relive their football days on a small professional team they started, partly so Brick and Skipper could continue their friendship, which for Brick is "the one great good true thing" in his life.[45] For Brick, his friendship with Skipper is an ideal male bond, purer than his marriage could ever be, precisely because whatever erotic attraction may have been sublimated, the friendship didn't involve sex. This "pure" (in behavior if not in feelings) friendship, akin to the bonding of buddies in westerns and war films, is accompanied, as it usually is, by rabid homophobia. As Brick's wife, Maggie, aptly describes his friendship with Skipper, "You two had something that had to be kept on ice, yes, incorruptible, yes!"[46] Brick's problem is that he adheres so firmly to an idealized version of gender: Women are for sex and men are for emotional intimacy. However, both Skipper and Maggie demand both of Brick. When Skipper tells Brick his love isn't as "pure" as Brick demands, Brick hangs up on him, leading Skipper to drink himself to death.

Brick blames his wife, Maggie, for convincing Skipper of "the dirty false idea" of sexual love between them and refuses to sleep with Maggie, preferring to try to drink himself to death like his lost friend.

At the end of *Cat on a Hot Tin Roof* it is intimated that Brick will resume his physical relationship with his wife, become a father, and run the family business. However, the setting and narrative behind the family business suggest that homosexuality is not so easily shut out. When Brick is shocked that his father would think he might harbor homosexual feelings for Skipper and vents a stream of homophobic epithets, the patriarch, Big Daddy, silences him with his life story. Big Daddy was, in his youth, a poor Southern redneck, and he admits to having "slept in hobo jungles and railroad Y's and flophouses in all cities."[47] before he hopped off a freight train and walked onto the plantation of lovers Jack Straw and Peter Ochello, in whose bedroom the play takes place.[48] It is intimated that his sexual relationship with the two plantation owners led to his being overseer and, eventually, inheriting the plantation and expanding it to its present size and productivity. Big Daddy isn't shocked at homosexuality and silences his son's homophobic attacks on Straw and Ochello. However, Big Daddy still expects an heir from Brick. Youthful sexual adventures have to be given up, or at least put to the side, in order to continue the dynasty. As Robert J. Corber puts it, Big Daddy "is willing to accept homosexual relations only insofar as they do not impede the reproduction of the hom(m)o-sexual [homosocial] system of exchange on which patriarchal property relations are based."[49] Yet the very legacy of Jack Straw and Peter Ochello questions the prevalent notions of the impossibility of homosexual love, the impossibility of homosexual success in the world of commerce, and the inevitability of heterosexual patriarchal power and inheritance. Brick doesn't have to grow up into a Big Daddy, who despises his wife and loves only the land. He could grow up into a Jack Straw or Peter Ochello. This is inconceivable, however, to Brick, who, despite whatever he deeply feels for Skipper, believes all the 1950s canards about homosexuality, as did most of the audience for *Cat on a Hot Tin Roof*. Nonetheless, his heterosexuality seems more an unhappy compromise with his own fears and social reality than an expression of something natural and satisfying to him.

As Willy Loman is more devoted to handsome, athletic Biff than to Happy, who is much more like his father, so Big Daddy has eyes only for Brick. Brick's older brother Gooper, who has done all the right things—become a lawyer to prepare to manage the plantation, married into society and sired six children—is an object of scorn or ridicule. Big Daddy tells Brick: "You and being a success as a planter is all I ever had any devotion to in my whole life!"[50] As with Biff Loman, physical beauty and prowess are the bases for fatherly devotion and wifely fascination. In Act I, we see partially clad Brick through Maggie's eyes as an object of desire, as Maggie expresses her frustration at no longer having sex with Brick. In Act II we see Brick through Big Daddy's eyes. The homoerotic desire that circulates through the bedroom of Jack Straw and Peter Ochello, which may once have included Big Daddy as an object of desire, now circulates from Big Daddy to Brick. I'm not suggesting incest, but a desire for what Brick represents, youth and masculine beauty, which he seems to be throwing away. In Williams's stories "Hard Candy" and "The Mysteries of the Joy Rio," fat, cancer-ridden old men like Big Daddy seek sex with young men in the dark recesses of movie theaters while westerns are playing on the screen. Cancer-ridden Big Daddy loves his beautiful young son who would be more at home in the outdoor world of the western, where he could be asexual in an all-male society.

Williams could only hint that Brick might not be as "normal" as he would like to be, that a heterosexual resolution is not so easily won. The 1958 film version of *Cat on A Hot Tin Roof* (screenplay, Richard Brooks and James Poe; direction, Richard Brooks) presents another narrative altogether, one consonant with Hollywood's fraught upholding of patriarchy and erasure of homosexuality in the 1950s. Gone are the gay ghosts of Jack Straw and Peter Ochello. In the film, Big Daddy is sole creator of his plantation kingdom: "I made a pasture land out of this plantation when it was nothing but a swamp," Big Daddy says at the beginning of the film, and by the end, he is talking about textile mills to weave the cotton he has grown on his farm. He has lived for his success, but in the process has denied his sons the love they need. Gooper sees his inheritance of the estate as "fair play" for doing what was expected of him, but Brick resents the fact that Big Daddy never demonstrated the love he needed: "I don't want to own anything," Brick cries to Big Daddy, "I wanted a father, not a boss." Then, in a tantrum that would put James Dean to shame, smashing the basement full of artifacts from Big Daddy and Big Mama's European buying spree, Brick shouts, "You own us. You don't really love us." In response, Big Daddy brings out an old, empty wicker suitcase, his father's only legacy to him, and reminiscences about the "old tramp," whose poverty made him ashamed. Big Daddy is reminded that his father "took [him] everywhere and kept [his son] with him," that though his father gave him no material comforts, he gave him love.

Big Daddy's focus on success, on his legacy, has left his younger, favorite son lost: "I don't know what to believe in . . . I'm a failure. I'm a drunk." What Big Daddy has to provide for his thirty-year-old son is the patriarchal gift of strength: "I've got the guts to die. Have you got the guts to live?" With this, father and son, already miraculously off the bottle, help each other up the cellar stairs. Brick is ready to take over the estate and impregnate his wife. At the end, Brick orders his wife upstairs into the bedroom—no Hollywood leading man is going to have to be forced into sex as Brick is in the play. Nor can a Hollywood film end with a wife calling her husband "weak," as Williams's play does. That would mean Brick is not manly, which would mean he is homosexual. Yet in fifties popular psychology, what else did overly doting mothers and emotionally distant fathers like Big Daddy lead to?

One fascinating aspect of the film of *Cat on a Hot Tin Roof* is its attempt at erasure of the signs of homosexuality that are all over Williams's play. In the film, after refusing his wife's sexual overtures, Brick locks himself in the bathroom and feels and smells her nightgown, which is hanging on a hook on the door. He clearly is not refusing to sleep with his wife because he isn't attracted to her—no homosexuality there. He refuses sex with his wife because he thinks she had sex with Skipper before he jumped out of an eleventh floor hotel room—a more active, "manly" death than Skipper's lethal mixture of alcohol and drugs in the play, and one that eliminates the hint that Brick is trying to kill himself the same way Skipper did. Skipper didn't fail at sex with Maggie; she, in a fit of virtue, ran from their embrace. Maggie had wanted to have sex with Skipper, not to prove he was homosexual, but to prove he would betray his best friend by sleeping with his wife. Maggie saw Skipper as Brick's albatross, a failure Brick was devoted to holding up. Skipper's phone call wasn't to admit his love for Brick; it was to admit his weakness, that he was dependent on his best friend and terrified Brick would cut him off. Brick hung up on Skipper because he was too weak to help him: "How does one drowning man help another drowning man?" Why was Brick so devoted to a friend who was dumb, feckless, and a failure at athletics, which was Brick's life? Why is Skipper, "the only thing [Brick could] believe in," if Skipper is, as Maggie says, "no good"? The film's answer is that Skipper was a surrogate father, offering the love Brick never received from Big Daddy. The only problem with this narrative is that even within the conventions of 1950s Hollywood melodrama, it makes no sense without some element of homoeroticism.

Having regained his manly strength through telling the truth and bonding with his father, Brick can become husband and father and new lord of "twenty-eight thousand acres of the richest land this side of the Valley Nile." The film of *Cat on a Hot Tin Roof* is a revision of the father-son mythic relationship of the John Wayne western. Big Daddy, the loner who has never accepted domesticity, is in conflict with his handsome son, who represents non-materialistic values. The son has proved his strength in football, a ritualized form of masculine aggression, but has not lost his sensitivity. According to the film and the prevalent attitudes of its time, it is only through marriage and procreation, however, that Brick will truly become a man. The test of manhood is not in the professional world or on the playing field. It is in the bedroom.

A major difference between the play and the film is in the casting of Brick. In the original production, Brick was played by Ben Gazzara, an actor best at playing gruff, stolid, macho types (Gazzara was replaced by Jack Lord of *Hawaii Five-O* fame), eliminating some of Brick's "sensitivity," which might be confused with homosexuality. In the film, Brick is played by lithe, gorgeous, young Paul Newman. Newman is not built like a football player (a place kicker, maybe). When he takes off his shirt, he is slender but muscular, his chest hairless like a boy's. As in the John Wayne films, the sensitive young man is somewhat androgynous, which in itself hints of homosexual possibilities, as does the fact that these beautiful young men were there to be looked at, admired for their beauty. After all, isn't it Brick's beauty, compared to poor heavy Gooper (played in the film by Jack Carson, the comic sidekick in many films of the fifties), that makes him the favorite son? What else redeems this man?

In the final frames, Brick throws his pillow back on the double bed he and Maggie will share. Heterosexuality has been restored, but only by trying to eliminate any possibility of unthinkable homosexuality or even bisexuality. Brick was going through a phase, and through his heart-to-heart talk with his father, grows up. Seeing the film only reminds one of how crucial homosexuality is to Williams's play. The qualified ending of the play does not place Brick unequivocally in the category of heterosexuality.

"YOU'VE GOT NOTHING TO PROVE TO ME, POP."

Set for the most part in a remote western mountain cabin on Big Bear lake in northern California, *Rites of Passage* (1999; screenplay and direction,

Victor Salva), pits an authoritarian, spiteful father against the surrogate patriarch his gay son has chosen to love. As in the western, the issue here is manhood, and whether the tough father's version of hard masculinity is valid. Del Farraday (Dean Stockwell, who played a young gay man in *Compulsion* in 1959), a successful San Francisco restaurateur, has, like most patriarchs in American drama and film, two sons. The elder son, D.J. (Robert Glen Keith), has become a lawyer. The younger son, Cam (Jason Behr), is a version of "the sad young man," deeply unhappy and bitterly angry at his father's displays of disappointment and fury over Cam's lack of manliness. In a flashback, we see Del trying to teach young Cam how to swim. When Cam, hurt and frustrated cries, his father shouts, "You're not coming out of there unless you come out of there like a man and not some pussy." Relations broke off between Cam and his father two years before the film's story begins, when Del discovered Cam and his best friend and lover, Billy, having sex. Del brutally beat up Billy, who disappeared, and a year later, died. Cam and his father haven't seen each other or spoken since.

In attempting to find his beloved Billy, Cam began a correspondence with a prison inmate, Frank (James Remar), who knew Billy's whereabouts, and writes Frank the story of his love for Billy and his fraught relationship with his father. Frank becomes, through his understanding letters, a surrogate father and potential lover for Cam. Through an unfortunate set of circumstances, Del and D.J. show up at the family cabin as Cam is waiting there to help Frank, newly escaped from jail, to recover his stolen money and cross into Canada. Father and sons raise all their old grievances. D.J. admits that he approved of his father's rejection of Cam "because every time you did it, it was me you pulled closer. You're a hard man to get close to, Pop." And Cam is furious that the father who would never accept his son's homosexual feelings expects his sons to accept his adultery. As in *Death of a Salesman,* the discovery of the father's betrayal of his wife totally undermines the validity of everything he has taught his sons. But Del is too much of an authoritarian to take any criticism from his sons.

As their battle reaches its peak, enter Frank and his young cellmate, Red (Jaimz Woolvett), claiming that their car has broken down nearby. Frank introduces Red as his son and treats him with the same sort of authoritarian brutality Del has shown Cam. Frank is far from the kindly, loving, accepting father figure Cam inferred from Frank's letters. Rather, he is a psychopath whose first impulse is to shoot people who cross him. As soon as Frank enters the cabin and accepts Del's hospitality, he impugns Del's manhood—"You are one solid gold pussy"—and challenges Del to a bout of arm wrestling, to which Del, in order to prove his manliness, agrees. While Frank arm wrestles with Del, he talks of the challenges young Indians had to take on to prove their manhood: "Now what kind of bullshit rituals do we have today to let the pup know he's grown from a boy to a man? His SATs?" After the Indian ritual, Frank continues, father and son would dance naked, "skin on skin," and during this boldly erotic dance "all the pain and regret between a daddy and his boy would pass away."

The legacy passed from father to son has been a legacy of hard manliness. Frank has been emotionally hardened by the hate he has carried toward his father. Del admits that he raised his sons the same hard way his father raised him, but that he is a watered-down version of his father: "He was the hunter in the family. Fishing and watching football—these are my vices now." And D.J. and Cam cannot get past the anger they feel toward their father, who sees everything as a challenge to his masculinity—particularly Cam: "You be a man, Pop. You be a real man and have the guts to ask yourself why who I am terrifies you." But Cam has to face the fact that Frank isn't a loving surrogate father (it turns out that Red wrote the letters for Frank, has truly fallen in love with Cam, and has escaped to meet him), but a man who has manipulated Cam's feelings to get what he wanted. Frank is what Cam will become if he doesn't deal with his hate: "I'm you twenty years from now. When your heart is as hard as a rock."

The night turns more violent, and eventually Cam must neutralize Frank, who has killed Red, wounded Del, and won't be satisfied until Del and D.J. are dead. Cam manages to vanquish Frank without shooting him, but he must nonetheless suffer the consequences of his actions and go to jail for harboring fugitives. The final scene is a prison embrace of father and son, an echo of the Indian dance Frank spoke of. Has Del come to understand that, as D.J. puts it, there's a difference "between something being wrong and something being different"? Has he come to appreciate Cam because Cam stood up to the trials of manhood Frank set for him? Whichever is the case, a manly father and his gay son finally have a relationship. In typical western style, to effect this male bonding the men have to move outside civilization and away from women. They also have to accept their fathers as their fathers have to accept them.

The artistic problems of *Rites of Passage* are endemic to the genre of domestic melodrama. Father and sons are defined only by their relationships to one another. Does D.J. have a personal life? He is supposedly heterosexual, but how does that express itself? His most important traits are his love and acceptance of his brother and his anger at his father. Does twenty-five-year-old Cam have a job? How does he support himself and his shiny SUV? Or does he exist only to grieve over his lost lover, Billy, and rebel against his father? Cam seems quite chaste for an adult male living in San Francisco, still seeking a surrogate father rather than a lover. We're led to believe that Del has berated his son over the years for being a sissy—artistic rather than interested in or adept at "manly pursuits"—but pumped-up Jason Behr looks as if he spends most of his time at the gym. Perhaps that, like his earring, is supposed to assert his gayness.[51]

The surrogate father–son disputes in most John Wayne films are about professional prowess, expertise in combat or tracking or herding cattle. *Rites of Passage* is more like the plays of Miller and Williams: The stakes are feelings. The message of *Rites of Passage* is that the manhood Del and Frank espouse is destructive to them and to the young men whose lives they touch. Frank kills Red, who has been posing as his son, as he would kill Cam. Del, taking out on his sons his insecurities about his own manhood, has raised two unhappy young men. Nonetheless, ironically, it is the skill Del made Cam learn—swimming—that saves Cam's life. This mixed message is consistent with that of the John Wayne films created half a century ago. The father figure can teach skills, but the son has to learn feelings for himself.

Chapter Four

MANHOOD UNRAVELING
Homosexual Panic and Martyrdom

In his seminal, controversial, 1948 essay on homoeroticism and race in American literature, "Come Back to the Raft Ag'in, Huck Honey!," critic Leslie Fiedler noted that the great nineteenth-century American novels by Cooper, Melville and Twain are "boys books" which "proffer a chaste male love as the ultimate emotional experience."[1] This love remains innocent because, according to Fielder, the reader of that more innocent time found homosexual desire inconceivable. The reader, then, performs the same erasure as men who refuse to see the potential for sexual desire in nominally heterosexual male bonding and male rituals, what Fiedler calls the "astonishing naïveté that breed[s] at once endless opportunities for inversion [the old-fashioned term for homosexuality] and the terrible reluctance to admit its existence, to surrender the last believed-in stronghold of love without passion."[2] Thus, in our time, the endurance of the cruel and ridiculous policy of "Don't ask, don't tell," and the equally ludicrous myth that all athletes are 100 percent straight. In American drama, we see this denial most vividly in ex-football player and sportscaster Brick Pollitt's insistence, in Tennessee Williams's *Cat on a Hot Tin Roof* (1955), on the purity of his relationship with his football buddy Skipper (the purity of which was, at best, one-sided) and his crippling belief that the asexual love of two men is far superior to any sexual love a man might have with a woman *or* a man. By the 1970s, it was more difficult to deny the homoerotic potential in the male bonding celebrated in postwar westerns and war films. Yet a number of films celebrated men returning to nature and to endeavors that would test their fortitude. Those returns to nature were also rituals of male bonding for, as Fiedler put it, "Nature undefiled—this is the inevitable setting of the sacred marriage of males."[3] Unfortunately, nature is now seldom undefiled, nor does pure male bonding seem possible.

This chapter concerns depictions of male bonding in "nature undefiled." The men in these works, either fatherless or victims of abusive fathers, are seeking some connection to a lost ideal of masculinity related to a vague romantic sense of a connection with nature. These works express extreme, almost hysterical anxiety about losing one's manhood, mainly through direct or symbolic sexual violation. They also express the white male masochism analyzed by critics such as David Savran, who observes that in many contemporary works, "masculinity is a function not of social or cultural mastery, but of the act of being subjected, abused, even tortured. It implies that masculinity is not an achieved state, but a process, a trial through which one passes."[4] One question these works raise is whether suffering and endurance can empower a man as much as direct, violent action.

In the postwar period, we saw male masochism most vividly in the fates of the heroes of a gay writer, Tennessee Williams: the immolation of Val Xavier, the castration of Chance Wayne in *Sweet Bird of Youth,* the dismemberment and electrocution of boxer-hustler Oliver Winemiller in "One Arm," the mutilation and death by cannibalism of Mr. Burns in "Desire and the Black Masseur" and of Sebastian Venable in *Suddenly, Last Summer.*[5] In Williams's work, such male suffering is connected to sexual transgression, race (Val and Chance suffer the fate of black men), and gender. Williams's martyrs are prototypes for straight white male characters suffering equally horrible fates in some later films. At the heart of the suffering in these films is the specter of homosexuality, which poisons intense male-male relationships. In our classic literature of male bonding, what had to be killed was the weaker, more sensitive partner in any relationship that veered precariously toward homoeroticism. Queequeg dies in *Moby-Dick,* and his coffin saves Ishmael's life. Joe Buck and Ratso Rizzo could not live in eternal friendship in *Midnight Cowboy,* nor could Jeff Bridges's Lightfoot live in director Michael Cimino's screenplay for *Thunderbolt and Lightfoot* (1974), in which Bridges's character, the buddy to Clint Eastwood's Thunderbolt, even wears a dress during the last third of the film.

Recent studies of masculinity have emphasized the masochism inherent in portrayals of men wounded in a postfeminist age in which white straight male authority—what George Kelly's Walter Craig would call "essential manhood"—is no longer taken for granted. In *Marked Men: White Masculinity in Crisis,* Sally Robinson posits that straight white men, demonized in the 1960s by groups they dominated—people of color, women, gays—create narratives of empowerment in which they are the victims:

> Concern over the place of white men in post-sixties America produces images of a physically wounded and emotionally traumatized white masculinity. White masculinity most fully represents itself as victimized by inhabiting a wounded body, and such a move draws not only on the persuasive force of corporeal pain but also on an identity politics of the dominant . . . [6]

Straight white guys can be empowered by using the same sort of victimization narratives as those who see them as the enemy. Lester Burnham's martyrdom in *American Beauty* is one such narrative of the straight male who feels the need to rebel against the women who don't appreciate him and who is ultimately martyred by a repressed homosexual.

In this chapter, I will look at two films that vividly express male martyrdom and hysteria about the male bond and the potential for homoeroticism, which I will contrast with a recent gay-created work, *Defying Gravity,* in which homophobia becomes the source of physical suffering for a gay man.

"TWELVE-AND-A-HALF INCHES LONG AND TEN-AND-A-HALF INCHES AROUND."

For gay men, mention of the Deep South brings to mind the hatred of powerful old coots like Jesse Helms and Strom Thurmond and the old-time religion of the Bible Belt. It also evokes the Tennessee Williams-like saga of Billy Jack Gaither, a sweet working-class country boy, devoted to his family, and gay, who was beaten to death and immolated on a dirt road in Alabama by two men he thought were friends, a story recounted movingly in a PBS *Frontline* documentary. While the threat to gay men is real, John Boorman's 1972 film of James Dickey's novel *Deliverance* gives us a straight man's nightmare of sexual violation in the southern backwoods. A number of major books on gender politics and American film of the 1970s ignore *Deliverance*,[7] a classic of male bonding and masculine anxiety in a beautiful outdoor setting. British director Boorman turned the film into a critique of Dickey's silly macho fantasy. As Sally Robinson notes, "While Dickey's novel is primarily interested in reinventing an old narrative that will enable him to map a new route to men's psychological health, Boorman's film, rather shockingly, offers a darkly pessimistic view of the therapeutic powers of male release and, instead, leaves its protagonists hysterically torn between repression and expression."[8]

Seeing *Deliverance* recently for the first time in decades brought Saint Sebastian to mind. Sebastian has always captured the imaginations of gay artists, from Renaissance painters Caravaggio and Sodoma to playwrights Gabriele d'Annunzio and Tennessee Williams and filmmakers Derek Jarman and John Greyson. Do we all read our own turbulent love story in the relationship of the Roman emperor Diocletian and his erstwhile favorite, Sebastian, who, having been converted to Christianity, tried to convert the emperor's soldiers? Sebastian was sentenced to his time's idea of a firing squad, a line of archers, but miraculously survived the arrows. Later he was beaten to death for publicly defying his friend the emperor. Critic Richard A. Kaye writes:

> A Christian saint invoked against illness throughout medieval times, exquisite, beardless youth of Apollonian beauty in the Renaissance, decadent androgyne throughout the nineteenth century, and self-consciously homosexual emblem in the twentieth, Saint Sebastian today has sustained his role as a distinctly "perverse" martyr . . . the single most successful deployed image of modern gay identity.[9]

The great paintings of Sebastian show an androgynous young man, tied to a tree or stake, with arrows piercing his flesh. One arrow often comes perilously close to Sebastian's groin. Are we also fascinated by this image of the "ecstatically receptive"[10] male pierced by these phallic arrows? Williams's Sebastian Venable in *Suddenly, Last Summer* is the gay narrative that won't go away no matter how violently it is suppressed, incorporating Williams's fascination with eroticism, violence to the male body, and cannibalism. Jarman's *Sebastiane* (1976; co-director, Paul Humfress), looks like early soft-core gay porn with some light S&M thrown in. Amid the sexual play of scantily clad and nude Roman soldiers speaking Latin, Sebastian is tied up a lot. His newfound religion, for which he suffers at the hands of a jealous Roman captain, consists of poetic hymns of praise to and erotic longing for an unspecified "him." We see the final shot of

Sebastian covered with arrows, but are given no intervention of Saint Irene (who rescued and healed him) or his miraculous recovery. Jarman gives us the homoerotic Sebastian without the religion. John Greyson's *Lilies* (1996), one of the most romantic and erotic gay films (Canadian filmmakers are masters at tragic gay romance), sets the doomed love story of two French Canadian boys in 1912 against a Catholic school dramatization of the martyrdom of Sebastian in which they play the leads. Though *Deliverance,* which combines nostalgia for man's connection with the natural world with near-hysterical anxiety about the violation of the male body, is anything but gay-friendly, the film's repeated images of arrows piercing male flesh, empowering and erotic in gay-created representations of Sebastian, here exemplify not the potential bliss of penetration but terror of penetration and the feminization of men. *Deliverance* is filled with phallic imagery that, rather than celebrating masculinity, denotes profound anxiety.

At the instigation of Lewis (Burt Reynolds), four Atlanta businessmen take a canoe trip on the Cahulawassee River before it is dammed up to create a reservoir. The film gives us little information about these men or their prior relationship. Except for Lewis and Ed (Jon Voight), who seem to be good friends, the men don't seem to know or like each other very much. As urban men, they are products of a fragmented society that does not give them any particular identity or connection. Soft Ed, who spends the first half of the film with an unlit pipe in his mouth, seems to worship hard Lewis, the man who claims the greatest connection to the natural world and the most physical prowess. Sporting a black rubber vest to display his perfectly formed torso, Lewis/Reynolds's body is tanned and muscular, a contrast to his pale, soft-looking companions. In 1972, audiences must have thought he had spent most of his time outdoors in strenuous physical activity; nowadays, we would be more likely to assume he's been to the gym and the tanning salon. Some might even assume that he's the gay friend to a bunch of domesticated straights. Lewis is filled with Iron John platitudes. "Sometimes you have to lose yourself before you can find anything," he tells Ed. He believes that in time the entire machinery of modern life will fail: "Survival's the name of the game." Lewis's need to be in control is presented as headstrong and dangerous, a source of amusement and occasional irritation to his companions. It is difficult to understand what the film is showing us about Ed's feelings for Lewis. In the first half of the film, Ed is shown gracing Lewis with long, admiring, perhaps desiring looks. At one point Lewis asks Ed, "Why do you go on these trips with me?" Gentle Ed, looking pensive, doesn't answer. What kind of answer is Lewis looking for? A commitment to the adventure? An emotional commitment to Lewis? Physical desire? The other two men, chubby Bobby (Ned Beatty) and bespectacled insurance man Drew (Ronny Cox), are even more out of place in the wilderness.

Like the men, the film itself takes a negative attitude toward the people who live along the river. At first, the backwoods seem to be populated entirely by grotesque males who are the products of inbreeding, the embodiments of what prejudiced middle-class city men would call "white trash." After all, they spend their time fixing beat-up old cars rather than communing with nature. The carcasses of abandoned cars along the river signal that these men, too, have been corrupted by the machine. Only Drew establishes any harmony with them, as he plays a guitar-banjo duet with an albino boy; when Drew later sees the boy on a bridge and tries to communicate with him, the boy is revealed to be incapable of speech.

On the second day of their trip, Ed and Bobby leave their canoe and encounter two "mountain men," who force them at gunpoint farther into the woods, tie Ed to a tree, unzip his jumpsuit to the crotch, and threaten him with castration: "You ever had your balls cut off, you fuckin' ape?" one of them growls. Then one of the men rapes Bobby while the other, a toothless man, holds a gun. After this violation, the rapist knocks Ed's symbolic pipe from his mouth and is about to force him to fellate his toothless friend when Lewis, arriving in the nick of time, shoots an arrow through him. The danger the men encounter from the river is exhilarating, but the sexual danger posed by the men who live around the river is the danger of being violated, "impaled," of the male body made permeable. Such sexual violation dehumanizes and feminizes, as Ed is called an ape, Bobby a sow. Dying a slow death from the arrow shot through his torso, the man who raped Bobby becomes a caricature of the sexual violations to which Bobby and Ed have been subjected. His body has been pierced by a phallic arrow, which forces him to his knees. His mouth is open as if ready to receive a penis (see fig, 5).

Over Drew's objections, the men hide and bury the body of the man they killed, the first of a number of scenes of hiding, burying, sinking bodies. As Sally Robinson puts it, "Boorman's film is characterized by a futile attempt to escape the male body, a concern emblematized by the men's frantic efforts to hide the male bodies that keep piling up as they progress down the river."[11] Hiding the bodies serves to hide mounting evidence of the violation of Bobby's body. If the men have to confess to the killings, they will have to confess to the rape as the instigating action. "Let's bury him," Bobby says after Lewis has killed his assailant. "I don't want this getting around." "This" is getting fucked, not killing a man.

The bodies of all the survivors and their victims have been penetrated in some way. After the men silently bury the body of their assailant, Drew, who wanted the men to call the police, seems to commit suicide by jumping from the boat in a rapids. His body is later found mangled against a rock. In the melee, Lewis is injured when he is thrown from his boat. His broken thighbone protrudes from his flesh like an erect penis— his tough, hard, masculine skin is no longer impenetrable. From this point on, powerful Lewis lies passively in the bottom of his canoe as Ed and Bobby, the victims of sexual assault, take over. Later, Ed is impaled by his own arrow as he tries to kill the man he thinks is the other assailant in the sexual attack. He does, however, successfully shoot an arrow through this man (not the right man, it turns out). In trying to lower his victim's body from a cliff, Ed falls into the river and gets tangled up in the rope attached to the corpse, a forced embrace with the man he has killed. The worst nature has to offer is not the violent currents of the river, but the feminization men wreak on one another.

The misadventures of these men occur partly because they leave their domestic surroundings and enter an alien, masculine world. When Bobby and Ed find Drew's corpse, Ed eulogizes him for his domestic virtues. But later domestic scenes are tainted by the men's experience. When Ed and Bobby finally get to shore, they find themselves in a country inn sharing a large dinner table—a domestic, heterosexual feast. Having been served by matronly women, Ed breaks down and cries. Safety exists only in a world filled with heterosexual couples, yet Ed and Bobby are strangers to this communal environment. Even there, the discussion is phallic. Bobby comments on the "special" corn, and one of the women boasts of a giant cucumber she grew, "twelve and a half inches long and ten and a half inches around." The women laugh. Sometimes a cucumber isn't just a cucumber. Meanwhile, Lewis is in danger of losing his leg. Anyone who has ever read *Moby-Dick*, the quintessential American saga of masculinity, quest, homosociality, and homoeroticism, knows what *that* symbolizes. In the film's final scene, Ed, home in bed with his wife, dreams of an outstretched arm rising from a lake like a large, erect penis. He will be doomed forever to such phallic nightmares, which will make a full return to normality impossible. His wife tries to comfort him, but Ed lies awake, his eyes wide open. He has lost his innocence.

Being on the river is being one with a powerful masculine force about to be dammed up, as the men try to dam up knowledge of their secrets of sex and violence. One of the film's final images is of coffins being dug up from a graveyard about to be inundated by the man-made flood. Neither bodies nor repressed memories and anxieties of male violation can stay buried.

"AT TIMES I SWEAR I THINK YOU'RE A FUCKING FAGGOT"

Stan (John Cazale) screams at Michael (Robert de Niro) during one of their many arguments in Michael Cimino's *The Deer Hunter* (1978), a three-hour epic about the perils of maintaining one's manhood, in which the male body is subjected to a series of traumas. Michael is Cimino's version of the Hemingway hero: Economical with language, heroically loyal to his buddies, he is the deer hunter of the title, the man who can kill a deer with one shot: "Two is pussy," he says. Working-class Michael is what middle-class Lewis fails to be in *Deliverance:* a traditional version of masculinity. Michael, often described in the film as "weird," seems most at ease in the mountains, away from the other men, tracking a deer. He is the only one of his friends who can master the cruel landscape and sadistic inhabitants of Vietnam. Like the western hero, he is chivalrous toward, but generally disinterested in women. He erupts, like one of Hemingway's heroes, when one of his companions is undisciplined in language or action. His usual adversary is vain, insecure Stan, the least manly—in terms of self-control—of Michael's friends, the one who doesn't go to Vietnam. *The Deer Hunter* is a lyrical celebration of working-class male bonding. Unlike *Anatomy of a Hate Crime, Deliverance,* and *Boys Don't Cry,* it does not pathologize or demonize men outside the middle class. Yet, for all—or because of—the male bonding and manly endeavor, *The Deer Hunter* can easily be read as a love story between Michael and his roommate, favorite hunting partner, and best friend, Nick (Christopher Walken). Film critic Robin Wood notes, "The narrative of *The Deer Hunter* is posited on, largely motivated by, the love of two men for each other, but this, far from being a problem, is assumed to be unequivocally positive and beautiful; therefore the film is compelled to permit the spectator to pretend that its sexual implications do not exist. At the same time, it leaves remarkably clear, if not always coherent or consistent traces, so that those who wish to see may do so."[12]

Unlike the middle-class men in *Deliverance,* the working-class protagonists of *The Deer Hunter* belong to a coherent social community (both films suggest that the middle-class man suffers from the loss of any cohesive community). Early in the film, at John's bar, where Michael, Nick, Stan, and their friend Steve (John Savage) hang out after work, Frankie Valli's recording of "Can't Take My Eyes Off of You" plays on the jukebox while Nick and Michael play pool. Nick sings along and struts gracefully to the music (Christopher Walken danced in Broadway musicals before he went to Hollywood). The other men sing from the bar. Mike is intent on the pool game. "Can't Take My Eyes Off of You" resonates throughout the film, which presents Michael as an observer who acts heroically when he must. The bar is the men's world, where they can be open, comfortable, apart from women. When Steve's mother comes in to drag him away to his wedding, it is a violation of this male sanctuary Steve is loath to leave. He'd rather stay with the guys. The wedding of Steve and his pregnant (by someone else) bride, Angela, is filled with old-world customs, from the Russian Orthodox service to the folk music and dancing at the reception. These people are bound by the traditions their parents brought with them from the Ukraine. However, the bonds between the men are stronger and more clearly defined than their relationships with women.

At the wedding reception in a VFW hall—a transition for Michael, Nick, and Steve from the world of Clairton, their hometown, to Vietnam—we see Michael watch from a doorway as Nick dances a folk dance with his girlfriend Linda (Meryl Streep). The camera lingers on Michael watching, then cuts to Nick dancing, more energetically and better than anyone else, then cuts to Nick's picture on the wall. (Cimino seems to have cast Walken—in his pre-creepy days—for his lithe frame and androgynous good looks, a contrast to the swarthier men around him.) Nick always seems totally occupied with what he is doing—singing, dancing, socializing. Only Linda acknowledges Michael's gaze, but Michael seems to be looking at Nick. While Michael watches, Nick, totally wrapped up in the joy of this social ritual and anxiety about leaving in two days for Vietnam, asks Linda to marry him. We know nothing of the history of Nick and Linda's relationship, but this proposal doesn't seem totally serious: "I don't know what the hell I mean," Nick says. Is Nick proposing to Linda so as to keep some connection to his community while he is away? Cimino's economy with background information allows us to read whatever we want into his characters' actions.

After the wedding, eager to rid himself of the trappings of civilization, Michael runs down the street, stripping off all his clothes. Nick runs behind him, finally catching up to his friend. Michael lies down, exhausted, and Nick throws his tuxedo jacket over Michael's genitals. Nick then sits on the ground with his back to Michael. This moment of heterosexual bonding would be sullied by any sense that Nick is interested in Michael's body, that these men might have any physical connection. But aren't Nick's concern to cover Michael and his inability to look at him, signs of awareness and fear of the erotic potential of the moment? Throughout the film, Michael is the looker and Nick the one looked at. Even at this moment, Nick places himself in front of Michael to speak with him: "If anything happens, don't leave me over there. You've got to promise." Nick exacts this pledge not because of any acknowledged feeling for Michael; rather, he blurts out, "I love this fucking place." If Michael is all control, Nick, as his singing and dancing suggests, is far more emotionally open, but it is his inability to control his feelings, to be "all man," that will destroy him.

From the outset, Nick's beloved Clairton ("clear town") is established as a masculine place. We first see a phallic tank truck rush down a street. Then the camera is inside the local steel mill, where great spurts of flame and streams of molten steel are accompanied by roaring noise. Giant, phallic pieces of machinery abound. In contrast, Vietnam is associated with the sight and sound of hovering helicopters that transport the men into danger more effectively than they rescue them from it (Michael has to save Steve when he falls off a helicopter), and with cruelty to and commodification of men. We see Michael shooting a flamethrower at a Vietnamese soldier who has just killed a group of innocent villagers. In the last Vietnam sequence, Saigon is a hellish vision of flames.

The film moves into bizarre sadomasochistic fantasy when Michael, Nick, and Steve are imprisoned by the Vietcong. As in *Deliverance*, danger comes less from nature than from sadistic men who represent an evil "other." Deer hunting is replaced by Russian roulette, to show how death has become senseless amusement rather than the result of a meaningful ritual of bonding with nature and a male friend. Kept caged in a river, submerged from the waist down, the prisoners are dragged out and forced to play Russian roulette while their captors take bets. Michael, the strongest, exhorts his friends to be courageous. When he shoots the gun over his head, Steve is placed in a cage full of rats. Eventually, infections from the rat bites lead to the loss of his legs. His failure to face death in a manly fashion leads to his unmanning. When Michael and Nick are forced to play Russian roulette together, Michael, who insists on playing with three bullets as part of an escape scheme, becomes Rambo and shoots his captors and rescues his friends. While Michael bravely sees the game as a way to escape, a necessary death-defying ritual, Nick is traumatized—out of horror or because he realizes that he loved the experience?

As the second half of the film begins, the camera lovingly lingers on a shell-shocked Nick as he sits on a wall in a Saigon hospital looking at the body bags lined up on the lawn below. In place of the active figure of the first half of the film, he is now passive and feminized, posed with his shirt open, the object of *our* gaze, weeping uncontrollably when a doctor questions him. Nick's descent is marked by hints of homosexuality. He has become obsessed with the meaningless death he has witnessed. Once he is released from the hospital, Nick wanders through the nighttime streets of Saigon. He goes to a telephone center to call Linda but decides against it. In rejecting Linda, Nick is rejecting Clairton's vision of normality, which includes compulsory heterosexuality. Some profound sense of loss or alienation keeps him in Saigon. Or does he realize that he has been initiated into something alien to Linda, his friends, his community, his country, something represented by the sexualized ritual of Russian roulette, a ritual connected to masochism? (In the prison, the men were slapped brutally if they were reluctant to pull the trigger on the gun held to their head.)

Wandering around Saigon, Nick encounters a wealthy, decadent Frenchman in a sports car watching two men dump a dead body—the loser in a game of Russian roulette. This is one of the queerest scenes in the film. The Frenchman, brandishing a bottle of champagne, attempts to lure Nick into a den where Russian roulette has become a blood sport for gamblers, the sign of the ultimate decadence of Western capitalism in Saigon. His overtures can also be read as a thinly veiled sexual invitation. The French man claims that Nick, like him, is looking for something "quite different." He holds Nick's arm as he insists "But you must come in." "You've got the wrong guy, ace," Nick claims, but he allows the Frenchman to lead him inside. There, Nick puts the gun to his head once, pulls the trigger, and rushes out, but when the Frenchman pulls up next to him, Nick gets in his car and drives off with him, scattering his winnings. Michael, observing Nick in the Russian roulette den (clearly he too has fixated on Russian roulette but can remain in his customary spectator position), runs after Nick but can't catch up to him. It looks as if Nick, turning around as the car drives off, can see Michael running behind the car. Has Nick thrown the money he won at Michael? Becoming the Frenchman's commodity is equated with becoming a sexual commodity: Nick's fall into drug abuse and a life as a professional Russian roulette player is equated with male prostitution. But this association with homosexuality is also an association with depravity and self-destruction. Nick's obsession is with death. It is an addiction to which he has succumbed.

On Michael's return to Clairton, he is shown sitting on the floor of a motel room (he is emotionally unable to go to his and Nick's home, where Linda has organized a surprise party) and staring at a picture of Linda. The idea of Linda and the ideal of heterosexual love she represents is more important than the reality. Neither Michael nor Nick is prepared to be the loving partner she desires. When Linda wants to go to bed with Michael, so they can "comfort each other," Michael sleeps, dressed, while Linda comes to bed naked, prepared for sex. Is this chivalry, loyalty to Nick, or lack of interest? When they finally do have sex, it is in a motel (Michael will not sleep with Linda in his and Nick's house), and Linda initiates it. Whom are they having sex with—each other or Nick?

Returning to Saigon to find Nick and bring him home, Michael discovers his friend, now drugged out, in a roulette den as the city is falling to the Vietcong. Michael tries to reach Nick, who doesn't seem to recognize him, by telling him, "I love you," qualified immediately by "You're my friend." The love Michael can offer is the pure, asexual love of comrades, not physical love, and the love of comrades can be expressed only in rituals of male bonding like the hunt, rituals perverted by the Vietnam War. Nick's response is to spit into Michael's face, perhaps rebuffing what he sees as a sexual overture. During their game of Russian roulette, Nick does show a glimmer of recognition when Michael, putting the gun to his head, proving how much he is willing to sacrifice for his friend, once more says, "I love you." The round is empty and now it is Nick's turn. "One shot," Nick says, a reminder of Michael's hunting days, then fires a fatal bullet into his own head. Cradling Nick's bloody head, Michael cries, "No," as much for his inability to control circumstances as for the final loss of Nick. Michael cannot fulfill his promise to bring Nick home alive. All he can bring home is Nick's corpse.

In the film's last sequence, after Nick's funeral, a group of men and women gather in what had been the all-male enclave of John's bar. Angela is with Steve. Linda is there, too. Instead of the boilermakers the men usually drink, the group has breakfast. Men and women may be together, but we get no sense of romantic coupling. Michael looks as if he is trying to get Linda's attention, to say something important to her, but there is no connection made. The only thing that ties the group together, other than their sense of loss, is the singing of "God Bless America." Vietnam has intensified the group's sense of national identity, but only to underscore the confusion and sense of loss America can evoke.

For Robin Wood, the film posits "the universal bisexuality our culture strives to repress."[13] I see *The Deer Hunter* as both deeply homoerotic and deeply skeptical of all sexual-romantic relationships. The happiest moments are collective rituals connected to music: the dancing at the wedding reception, the men listening to John play Chopin on the piano after the hunt. Sexual relationships are always fraught. However much desire circulates between the men, sex would destroy their bond. It is Stan's sex talk—about Angela's child, Michael's homosexuality, his own misadventures—that brings the greatest disharmony between the men. Virginal Steve has to be dragged off to his wedding by his mother. Real men don't know how to handle sex. This is why Nick's corruption in Saigon is rife with signs of homosexuality as depravity.

Michael is not defined by his job, his military heroism, or his devotion to his friends: He is "the deer hunter," the solitary individual communing with what is left of nature. "I love the trees," his friend Nick says when they talk about hunting, establishing him as the only worthy partner for Michael.

FAG BASHING IN THE WILD WEST

When these straight images of the violated, wounded male body, images infused with terror of homoeroticism, become transferred to products of gay culture, the result is politicized images of martyrdom representing the perilous state in which gay men can find themselves in a homophobic society. The most vivid contemporary image of gay martyrdom has been that of young Matthew Shepard, beaten to a pulp, tied to a fence, and left to die somewhere in the wilds of Wyoming. Amidst a number of brutal murders of gay men, Shepard's had particular resonance, which led to wide media coverage and increased support for hate crimes legislation. His murder and its aftermath were the subject of a superb play, the Tectonic Theater Project's *The Laramie Project,* and an MTV telefilm, *Anatomy of a Hate Crime* (2000), geared to that network's teen audience.

Would the murder have had the same resonance if it had taken place not in Wyoming but in the gay ghetto of an American city where gay bashing, celebrated in the rap lyrics of creeps like Eminem, has long been a sport for screwed-up straight adolescents of all ages? The desolate setting of Shepard's beating, alien to most of us except for what Hollywood has shown us, was central to the media's presentation of the murder. The western landscape was, after all, a site for the straightforward presentation of models of heterosexual masculinity. Young Matthew Shepard seemed so out of place in Wyoming, so alien to the landscape in which he was killed. The many photographs of the fence to which he was tied and left to die in a form of crucifixion attest to a wilderness spoiled by hate, but there's no hero to ride in and make things right. We've seen the prototypes of Shepard's assailants before: the young, angry, walking wounded. They're the novice gunmen itching for a fight who usually die long before the western is over, the runts who demand a respect they haven't earned. Wyoming is cowboy country. Shane rode through those hills and valleys! Like much of the West, Wyoming is idealized by those who have nostalgia for former, better-defined visions of manhood.

The Laramie Project delineated the effect of Shepard's death on members of the community to which, as a transient university student, he didn't really belong. It explores what the glaring eye of the media does to a group of people whose town becomes a setting for and symbol of a highly publicized hate crime. Matthew Shepard is not a character in the play; he is a catalyst for a community crisis. *Anatomy of a Hate Crime,* more concerned with individual motivation than group dynamics or identity (it is, after all, a made-for-television movie), made Shepard a lonely, troubled youth, who had spent his life moving from place to place around the world and returned to Laramie, where he'd spent some time as a boy, to find a place where he could belong. What was most interesting about this telefilm was not its oversentimental treatment of Shepard as the stereotypical sweet, lonely queer (unlike gays of yore, he had a support group and a potential boyfriend) but the detailed account of the friendship of his killers, Aaron McKinney and Russell Henderson, from their meeting until their imprisonment. More sophisticated filmmakers would have built some irony into this structural juxtaposition of the narratives of a straight male couple and a solitary gay victim. While both the killers have girlfriends, fatherless Henderson sees in violent McKinney a powerful masculine figure who can express Henderson's anger and hostility, while McKinney needs a disciple and a defender. Neither of these insecure little guys feels safe alone. It is clear from their girlfriends' complaints that these young men would rather be together than with their heterosexual partners. Was there more? McKinney's vicious treatment of Shepard, his later false testimony that Shepard made sexual overtures to him,[14] and the gay-panic defense all suggest that there was a sexual dimension to McKinney's violence against Shepard. To what extent did McKinney have to destroy Shepard to allay any suspicions about and hatred for his own feelings? The film presents Henderson's participation in Shepard's death as the actions of a frightened follower destroyed by his relationship with his sociopath friend. It may be a sign of how far we've come that fag bashing as a means of establishing the normality of the bond between male friends, a common element in buddy films of the 1960s and '70s, is now presented as pathological.

"ARE YOU, LIKE, IN LOVE WITH HIM, DUDE?"

The resolution of the love triangle at the heart of *Defying Gravity* (1997; screenplay and direction, John Keitel) takes place in a deserted spot high in the Southern California mountains. Todd (Niklaus Lange), anxious and furious that his best friend and fraternity brother, Griff (Daniel Chilson), has stopped confiding in him and seems emotionally out of control, has taken Griff off to spend the night in the mountains, away from all vestiges of civilization, to cool off and to rebond with him. Though Todd has a girlfriend with whom he claims to be in love, Griff is the most important person in his life. This mountain trip is another reaffirmation of a pure male bond in a natural setting. Now, however, this bond must in some way acknowledge homosexual desire. Looking over the beautiful mountain landscape, Griff can finally open up to his friend. "It's amazing," he says of the scenery. "It makes you feel so insignificant. It makes everything so insignificant." Haltingly, elliptically, he tells Todd of the afternoon in which his life changed. Alone in the fraternity house with their friend Pete (Don Handfield), horseplay turned to sex and the safe bonding of fraternity brothers turned to love. "It's as if you're one person," Griff explains. "You're defying gravity together. All at once, everything is different." When Todd asks, "Are you, like, in love with him, dude?" Griff finally, haltingly admits, "I've never been so sure of anything." After this confession, Todd puts his arms around Griff and they sit quietly together, sharing their own intense but nonsexual form of love.

Later, when Griff moves out of the fraternity house to be with Pete, Todd sounds like a grieving ex: "I don't want you to go." Griff, however, has faced the fact that he, like Pete, no longer belongs in the homophobic world of the fraternity, that he must face the fear of entering a new life. He gains the courage to do this only by bonding with the landscape and with his straight friend.

Defying Gravity is no masterpiece, but it manages to capture the relationship between intense male bonding and homosexual love, which all-male organizations like college fraternities (and the military and the Boy Scouts and the Catholic clergy) feel they must deny or chaos will ensue, and it eloquently presents one young man's crisis when his emotions and libido don't match his social training. The resolution can come only with the physical suffering of the most passive, most openly gay member of the trio. While Griff and Todd embrace in the wilderness, a bruised and bandaged Pete is in a coma in a hospital, the victim of a fag bashing wrought by a couple of Griff's fraternity brothers. It is Pete's suffering that forces Griff to face his feelings and his sexuality.

Griff is a typical student at an unnamed, typical university, active in his fraternity, fashionably mediocre in his academic work. He sits in the back of lecture rooms with his fraternity brothers, reading newspapers and talking sports. Griff wants above all to fit in, to be "well liked," as Willy Loman would say. When we first see him, he is frantically jumping out of Pete's bed (Pete moved out of the fraternity house when he realized his sexual feelings placed him in a different milieu) and running back to his fraternity house to brag about his *hetero*sexual exploits of the previous night. The fraternity, the central social unit for Griff and his friends, manifests the paradox of male bonding: It is an all-male environment in which the talk is constantly of heterosexuality and the greatest danger is to be connected in any way with homosexuality. When Griff and Todd pick up Pete on the way to a football game, Pete, with considerable irony, talks about his night of sex with "her" while wearing the hat Griff left on his bedroom floor. Griff's game of playing straight frat boy and having sex with Pete won't work anymore. Pete wants to be more than a furtive fuck and demands the same attention Griff gives "Buffy and Muffy." When Pete arranges for Griff to meet him in a gay coffeehouse to talk about their relationship, Griff becomes frightened and defensive. "This is not about sex, Griff," Pete says, but it is easier for Griff to think about sex with Pete as simply getting his rocks off than to admit that what he feels may be love. "Your whole life is a goddamn lie," Pete cries as he walks away from Griff. Shortly afterward, he is gay-bashed and left in a coma. Guilty and anxious, alternately withdrawn and hostile, Griff can't open up to Todd, nor can he be comfortable with gay men. He goes back to the gay coffeehouse to grieve over what happened to Pete, but he can't accept the friendship and concern of the owners. The coffeehouse could provide an alternative social world for Griff—Pete clearly felt comfortable there—but it's too frightening, and Griff can only worry about being "caught" there. In both coffeehouse scenes, it is made clear that Griff most fears being identified with an effeminate, long-haired gay activist, shown in threatening close-up (which suggests that the film's creator is as frightened of men who aren't "straight-looking and -acting" as Griff is—notably, the coffeehouse owners are classic "butch gays"). Yet though Griff sits silently through a fraternity-house meeting on the subject of Pete's attack, his frat brothers' defensive, homophobic response makes him painfully aware that he doesn't belong there either.

Griff's withdrawal confuses and upsets Todd, who acts like a spurned lover: "You can't shut me out like this, man." Todd's anxiety, almost as hysterical and violent as Griff's, shows the intensity of this male bond threatened by Griff's realization that he must move away from the heterosexual discourse that maintains such bonds. Griff has halfheartedly tried to do what is expected of him and establish a relationship with Gretchen (Nicki Lynn), a clone of Todd's girlfriend, Heather (Lesley Tesh). During a two-man volleyball game, Todd tells Griff how, when he looks in the mirror, "I see how Heather sees me. I see Heather's boyfriend. It's like I'm connected in a way I've never felt before." We next see a lengthy shot of Griff, shirtless, looking in a mirror, clearly trying to figure out whom *he* sees. Later, at the gay coffeehouse, echoing Todd, he tells Pete, "When I look in the mirror, I don't see this. I see me. I don't see you." What Griff cannot see is himself as a gay man, an outsider to the world he knows.

"How do you do this whole thing?" Griff asks his new friend Denetra (Linna Carter), a black lesbian who is as new to her sexual feelings as he is to his. Even as he tries to tell her about Pete, he has to put their relationship in words that don't commit him to homosexuality: "We're close friends. Nobody has a clue about this." As Pete lies comatose, Griff slowly deals with his love for Pete and his guilt and his own cowardice: He won't tell the police what he knows for fear of being considered gay. Slowly, cautiously, he comes out: to Denetra, to Todd, and in a hilariously awkward and unintentional way, to Pete's mother. When Pete regains consciousness, Griff admits his love and his desire for a relationship. At the end, Griff and Pete are double-dating with Todd and Heather. Homosexual love has been integrated into the paradigm of heterosexual coupling. Griff has kept his intense comradely bond with Todd and is beginning a life with Pete. Robotic Heather, largely a silent presence in the film (Heather and Gretchen look and act like future Stepford Wives), seems to understand that Todd won't be happy with just her—he needs his male buddies.

Defying Gravity is as focused on Griff's relationship with Todd as on his burgeoning romance with Pete. Griff and Todd can embrace on that idyllic mountaintop because Griff has found a way to present his love for Pete as a corollary to Todd's love for Heather: "Imagine if Heather is right next to you. All you have to do is reach out your arm to touch her. But you couldn't." By equating homosexual desire with heterosexual desire, Griff can accept his love for Pete, and Todd can accept his friends' homosexuality. Todd can offer his support by maintaining the equation of his romance with Griff's: "I would do anything, anything I had to do, to make sure I didn't lose her," he says, a comment that impels Griff to commit fully to Pete.

At the end of *Deliverance,* the river is gone. The men float past the tops of trees that have been submerged as the new dam creates a lake. With the death of the river, a corollary to the healthy expression of masculinity, men are lost, forever wounded. At the end of *The Deer Hunter,* Michael goes back to the mountains, but his one-shot ritual, his way of expressing a connection to and mastery of nature, is gone. The more optimistic ending of *Defying Gravity* links the hard-won resolution of comradeship and homoerotic desire to the harmony of men and nature. In all these works, the wounded or murdered male body has signified a psyche riven by the inability to integrate desire into the male bond.

1.   *John P. Clum (Audie Murphy) looks disdainfully at an Indian scalp in* Walk the Proud Land *(Museum of Modern Art Film Stills Archive).*

2.   *Harriet Craig (Joan Crawford) picks up the pieces of a beloved vase after her husband (Wendell Corey) asserts his masculinity (Museum of Modern Art Film Stills Archive).*

3. *Tough love: Ethan Edwards (John Wayne) grabs Martin Pawley (Jeffrey Hunter) by
the scruff of the neck in* The Searchers *(Museum of Modern Art Film Stills Library).*

4.   *Travis (Harry Dean Stanton) wanders through the western landscape in Wim Wenders's film of Sam Shepard's* Paris, Texas *(Museum of Modern Art Film Stills Archive)*.

5.   *The* Deliverance *mountain man who has sodomized Bobby (Ned Beatty) is impaled as his friend looks on (Museum of Modern Art Film Stills Archive).*

6. *"Now don't you look fine." Otero (George E. Stone) lovingly admires his boss, Rico (Edward G. Robinson) in* Little Caesar *(Museum of Modern Art Film Stills Archive).*

7.   *The ambiguously gay trio (Elisha Cook, Jr., Peter Lorre, Sydney Greenstreet) has a temporary victory over Sam Spade (Humphrey Bogart) in* The Maltese Falcon *(Museum of Modern Art Film Stills Archive).*

8. "Here's to the three of us": Johnny Farrell (Glenn Ford), Ballin Mundson (George Macready), and the phallic cane/dagger in Gilda (Museum of Modern Art Film Stills Archive).

9.   *Not the happiest of couples: Phillip Morgan (Farley Granger) and Brandon
Shaw (John Dall) in* Rope *(Museum of Modern Art Film Stills Archive).*

10. *Which one is the killer queer? Gary (Tom Berenger) and James (William Atherton) in* Looking for Mr. Goodbar *(Museum of Modern Art Film Stills Library).*

II

LEARNING GAYNESS?

Chapter Five

GAY KILLERS

"I was more ashamed of being a homosexual than a murderer," confesses the killer who has castrated and killed a trick in *The Detective* (1968; screenplay, Abby Mann; direction, Gordon Douglas). It may be difficult to believe that there was a time in which a film like *The Detective* would be seen as affirming to gay men, but I remember, at that confused, married period of my life, feeling validated by a film that at least suggested there were homosexuals in the world (something one could forget at the time in Durham, North Carolina), while concurrently offering me a sermon on the deadly perils of straying from the safe, if sad world of compulsory heterosexuality. The flouncing queens, tortured youth, and gay killers, the only role models we had in film at the time, hardly inspired gay pride. Still, *The Detective* offered some solace by intimating that perhaps the unjust treatment of gay men may have been a cause of their antisocial behavior.

This chapter is devoted to a selective, non-comprehensive sixty-year survey of gay and crypto-gay killers, their relationship to Hollywood stereotypes of gayness and conventional masculinity, and their potential for subverting those stereotypes. I am particularly interested in how the gay murderer plays into various forms of desire, both thwarted sexual desire for an unavailable or recalcitrant male object, and realized desire. More important, I want to focus on how this male-male desire is often linked to signs of affluence.

At the end of *Little Caesar* (1930; screenplay, Francis Edward Faragoh; direction, Mervyn LeRoy), our protagonist, Rico Bandello (Edward G. Robinson), is riddled with bullets shot through a billboard advertising a new movie starring Rico's former sidekick, Joe (Douglas

Fairbanks, Jr.), and his dancing partner and lover, Olga (Glenda Farrell). On the billboard Joe and Olga appear in the sort of elegant dress that would soon be associated with Fred Astaire and Ginger Rogers. The film is titled *Tipsy Topsy Turvy*, which suggests a zany inversion, but is the inversion Rico's downfall and death, the end of his parody of the American success myth, or is it the faux-elegant picture of normative heterosexuality presented on the billboard? Neither Rico's underworld nor Joe and Olga's Hollywood myth exemplifies the way most real Americans lived during the Depression, though crime and show business seemed the only means of achieving a fast buck. Nonetheless, both Rico and Joe covet the signs of affluence. Normative heterosexuality defeats Rico: Joe squeals on his old friend to protect his relationship with the woman he loves, but isn't there something weak, less than "manly," in Joe's virtuous actions? Yet Joe lives to confess because of Rico's love for him. In *Little Caesar*, the gangster's homosexuality is part and parcel of his challenge to American capitalism. We see the same theme worked out in the plays of the greatest of the Depression-era playwrights, Clifford Odets, and in forties film noirs like *The Maltese Falcon* and *Gilda*.

Though few avowedly homosexual figures appear in films of the thirties and forties (homosexuality is at best hinted at), killers Nathan Leopold and Richard Loeb, who defined homosexuality for many Americans, become paradigms of the affluent, murderous homosexual, a connection gay artists like Tom Kalin and John Logan later attempted to recuperate, as writer-director Anthony Minghella tried to turn Patricia Highsmith's murderous Tom Ripley into a sympathetic, quasi-tragic personification of the dangers of the closet.

"THIS IS WHAT I GET FOR LIKING A GUY TOO MUCH."

In *Little Caesar*, the first great American gangster film, homosexuality, perhaps scarcely noted by viewers in 1930 but obvious in our gay-obsessed age, is a logical, if bizarre part of the gangster's all-male parody of the American success myth. In a world in which women are only molls, useful for sex and ornament but just another purchase, men's emotional (and perhaps physical) needs will be directed toward other men.

Little Caesar, despite its primitive sound technology, which restricted movement in dialogue sequences, remains a potent character study, fascinating for its interweaving of homoeroticism with the saga of an Al

Capone–like figure who rises from robbing gas stations to running the Chicago gang and then descends to a flophouse existence and the inevitable violent, ignominious death. The "little" attached to Cesare Enrico "Rico" Bandello's name connects first of all to his physical stature. Rico is shorter than most of the men around him, and like any man worried that folks might think he's little all over, he adorns himself with phallic appendages: cigars, canes, and, of course, guns. In an age in which movie actors were almost invariably cosmetically perfect, Edward G. Robinson's squat, homely antihero is a shock. Above all, Rico's size is attenuated by his constant self-aggrandizing talk. In classic masculine fashion, Rico is constantly measuring himself against other men he sees as softer than himself, "yellow." He challenges men who actually have more power, including his nemesis, the laconic police sergeant Flaherty (Thomas E. Jackson).

At a diner after a gas-station heist, Rico tells Joe, "Money's all right, but it ain't everything. I wanna be somebody. Look hard at a bunch o' guys and know that they'll do anything you tell them. Have your own way or nothin'. Be somebody." For Rico, identity is power—but strictly power over "guys." Women play no part in his equation. When they reach Chicago, Rico and Joe pursue different ideas of being somebody. Rico joins a gang run by a particularly dim-witted boss, and Joe, with his leading-man good looks, joins forces with Olga and pursues a career as a ballroom dancer.[1]

Little Caesar contrasts the parallel careers of Rico and Joe. As soon as Joe reaches Chicago, he finds a job as a dancer (where did he learn that?) and a devoted girlfriend. "I need you," Joe tells Olga at what seems to be their first meeting. When they embrace, Olga discovers the (literal) gun in his pocket and becomes the adversary to his criminal associates. Rico's world is all-male, a criminal fraternity in which, despite his tendency to shoot the wrong people, he rises very quickly. At the end, Joe and Olga have become stars while Rico dies alone and—what he most feared being—a nobody. Critic Joan Mellen writes, "Rico is presented consistently as a male to be admired in contrast to his effeminate buddy, Joe Massara, whose ambition is to go straight and become a dancer! The choice is to become a ruthless man of action or a mincing pansy!"[2] It is true that Rico says, "Dancin' ain't my idea of a man's game"—Rico wants to make other people dance—and accuses Joe of becoming a sissy because he prefers his career and his love for Olga to the life of a gangster. But "mincing pansy" is an odd term for the only man in the film in a heterosexual relationship. Mellen has it all wrong here. Show business, even dancing, was a way out of poverty for a number of poor men, perhaps the only legitimate fast route to success for the uneducated and underprivileged. Why shouldn't a handsome young man avail himself of the opportunity? Does his love for Olga make him a "mincing pansy"? Only in the eyes of Rico's society would Joe be so harshly judged. The hints of homosexuality in *Little Caesar* are not tied to conventional thirties stereotypes like those played by comic actors Franklin Pangborn and Eric Blore—the "mincing pansy" image Mellen projects onto straight Joe. They are linked to the ruthless gangster.

What Rico most disdains is Joe's love for Olga: "Love! Soft stuff!" There's no place for women and love in Rico's manly world. Though he welcomes the molls to a banquet in his honor, he sits at the all-male head table. The successful man in Rico's world is judged only by the standards of men; for the most part, however, the men are little and infantile. The black tie banquet in Rico's honor turns into a food fight. Critic Jonathan Munby points out the "patronizing view of the ethnic underworld" *Little Caesar* presents: "[Rico] adorns himself with the signifiers of social success: smart suits, cigars, diamond rings, marble tables, classic realist paintings, cars. Yet the running joke is that he and his compatriots of Italian extraction, while they can accumulate the outward signs of 'making it,' have no way to actually appreciate the artifacts they have collected."[3] These gangsters aspire to culture but fail. The bookshelves of Arnie Lorch, Rico's first boss, look decidedly fake. Rico, in his formal wear at the palatial home of the underworld kingpin, drops his cigar ashes on the floor. The film's emphasis on these gaffes does seem a bit snobbish, but its disdain seems as much gender-related as class-driven. The film seems to question whether culture can prevail in an all-masculine society. The giant billboard of Joe and Olga demonstrates the superiority of performed as well as real heterosexuality. After all, Joe and Olga represent show business's simulacrum of elegance, no more real than Rico's attempts at aristocratic demeanor. Yet a dancing team like Joe and Olga would become the center of some of the most popular fantasies Hollywood created in the 1930s films, in which normative heterosexuality was defined against a series of homosexual stereotypes.[4]

When Joe insists that his love for Olga is more important than his loyalty to Rico and his gang, Rico offers one of his unintentionally humorous threats: "You go back to that dame and it's suicide. Suicide for both of you." In Rico's view, Joe (and Olga) would bring death upon themselves for Joe's violation of the cardinal principal that one never walks out on a gang. A number of critics have alluded to the potentially homoerotic attraction that Rico, who has no interest in women, has toward Joe. As critic Jack Shadoian puts it: "That Rico loves Joe is beyond doubt. That Rico is ugly and charmless and wants to keep his 'beautiful' friend to himself for private needs and public display is also beyond doubt."[5] Certainly the most emotionally powerful moment in a rather cold, ironic film is the extreme close-up (close-ups are rare in this film) of Rico's tearful face when he realizes he can't bring himself to kill Joe, even though his friend is about to rat him out to the police. This long close-up is also garrulous Rico's longest silence in the film. Joe's challenge and Rico's feelings for Joe unnerve and silence him. In not killing Joe (he has murdered another potential stool pigeon), Rico seals his own fate: "This is what I get for liking a guy too much." To some extent, Rico's fascination with Joe is founded on Joe's indifference to him and to his success. Rico wants a mirror, but Joe has someone else to look at.

Joe's dancing and emotional neediness may not seem as "masculine" as Rico's bravado and killings, but Rico displays even more stereotypical signs of homosexuality. With more costume changes than Auntie Mame, Rico is the consummate fop, tempting fate by parading down Chicago streets in his fancy outfits. He finds his ideal mirror in Otero (George E. Stone), also described as "little," who offers the film's strongest hints of homoeroticism. After Rico has been shot in the arm in a botched assassination attempt, he is shown lounging in bed in a silk dressing gown, sporting a neatly arranged sling. Otero, sitting on what looks like a stool at the foot of the bed, moves to lie next to Rico, and gazes lovingly at his hero. They smile at each other as the scene fades out. In the next shot, Otero is brushing the crotch of Rico's formal trousers as Rico stands on a chair looking at himself in a full-length mirror. Then we see Otero looking adoringly at Rico in the mirror. "You look great, boss," he says. "Now don't you look fine!" (see fig. 6). Otero's batting of his eyelashes and worshipful smile would put Lillian Gish to shame. Otero is Rico's constant companion, his lackey, his mirror, and, it is hinted, his lover. Otero is what Rico has dreamed of—a disciple who will do whatever Rico tells him to do—yet Rico is more fascinated with Joe, the man he can't control, who will calmly walk out of Rico's apartment when ordered to stay.[6] Despite the presence of the adoring Otero, Rico tells Joe, "Who else [but you] have I got to give a hang about." Like the self-hating homosexuals of the past who could love only straight men, Rico will rudely dismiss Otero in favor of being rejected by handsome Joe.

When Rico can't kill Joe, Otero tries to shoot him (as Jack Shadoian notes, "He knows who his rival is"[7]), but Rico deflects his shot. Otero then accuses Rico of being "soft." Within a few minutes, Otero is shot by the police and dies in Rico's arms. In one shot, we see Rico's cheek against that of the dying Otero. With Joe's betrayal and Otero's death, Rico is alone, a hunted man, moving inexorably toward his death behind that advertisement for Hollywood heterosexuality.

"YOU USE ME LIKE A GUN!"

There are distinct echoes of Rico Bandello's materialism and thinly veiled homosexual desire in the gangsters Clifford Odets created in the 1930s—particularly Eddie Fuseli in *Golden Boy* (1937)—products of the playwright's complex response to American materialism and sexual and family values. Odets's gangsters share some of the traits of Rico Bandello and his ilk. They tend to be garrulous, vain, and untrusting of the women they might love, and to harbor an intense, if ambivalent love for the leading men they ally with. For this reason, like Rico, they can be caught in a triangular relationship with the "good guy" and his girlfriend. Also like Rico, they are without families of their own (the only maternal figure Rico communicates with cheats him out of his money), but Odets often presents them in domestic settings in which the presence of the gangster underscores the families' problematic relationships to the values of the world they inhabit. In *Golden Boy,* Eddie Fuseli, the killer, chastises Joe Bonaparte, the boxer hero, for turning his back on his family and is, at the end, in Joe's family's living room. Gangsters in these plays are part of the domestic space, yet they also represent alternatives to family life and escapes from the poverty in which the families are enmeshed.

The gangster's materialism is the temptation away from conventional family life. Sanctioning the criminal and his crime is a means of challenging the audience to see the price of materialism. In a world in which life is printed on dollar bills, as one Odets character memorably phrases it, conventional morality is no longer operative. In an insightful essay on Clifford Odets, Robert Warshaw describes the morality of the Depression-era urban Jews that Odets so skillfully dramatizes: "The best they could find for their life was a worldly compromise: Money is filth, but money is all you'll ever get."[8] No one understands this compromise better than the gangster.

Golden Boy, made into a film in 1939 (screenplay, Lewis Meltzer, Daniel Taradash, Sarah Y. Mason, Victor Heerman; direction, Rouben Mamoulian) and, twenty-five years later, into a Broadway musical for Sammy Davis, Jr. (book, Clifford Odets and William Gibson; music, Charles Strouse; lyrics, Lee Adams), presents a series of interlocking love triangles. Joe Bonaparte, the cockeyed violinist turned boxing champion, is in love with Lorna, the mistress of his manager, Tom Moody. Joe dies while driving in his beloved car with Lorna after he has decided to quit boxing and make a life with her (as in *Little Caesar,* one must leave an all-male world—crime or boxing—in order to have a heterosexual relationship). In leaving boxing, Joe is also leaving Eddie Fuseli, the homosexual gunman who has taken over much of his life and who occupies the third side of the Joe-Lorna-Eddie triangle. In his first appearance in the play, Eddie, "a thin dark man" with hair graying at the temples, enters quietly and, later, "coolly drifts out of the scene on his cat's feet."[9] Eddie's lean look is typical of the description of gangsters of the period: Rico, in the novel *Little Caesar* is based on, has a "pale, thin face."[10] Fight promoter Roxy Gottlieb points out that Eddie Fuseli came back from World War I with a gun: "He's still got the gun and he gives me goose pimples!"[11] Eddie, like the amputee Moe Axelrod in Odets's *Awake and Sing!* and many other characters in classic postwar American literature (Hemingway's heroes are the prime examples), is a casualty of the war spiritually, if not physically.

Homosexuality was rarely mentioned in thirties drama, but Eddie is described as a "queer" and clearly is as in love with Joe as he is capable of loving anyone. Odets might have used Eddie's homosexuality as a stereotypical sign of the character's moral bankruptcy, but Eddie, no more morally bankrupt than many of Odets's heterosexual characters, clearly loves Joe, though he can express that love only as material possession. For years, critics projected their homophobia onto Eddie. Edward Murray judges Eddie on the basis of his theory of sexuality: "There would seem to be no real love in a homosexual relationship. Hence Eddie appears to dote on Joe, but at bottom he ruthlessly exploits the fighter for money."[12] Actually, Eddie does both. Gabriel Miller states that Eddie, "Odets's first truly loathsome character . . . is clearly the villain of the play, and when Joe adopts him as his manager, his fall is complete."[13] I see him not as a villain but as another in Odets's gallery of sympathetic but emotionally maimed characters. Like Odets's other gangsters, Eddie will do what it takes to get what or whom he wants. That could be seen as reprehensible, but in the America of Odets's plays, nice guys finish last. Eddie's disease is materialism, which he shares with the straight characters, not homosexuality.

After Eddie involves himself financially and emotionally in Joe's career, he becomes jealous of Joe's feelings for Lorna and wary of Lorna's destructive potential. When Lorna decides to marry Tom Moody instead of returning Joe's love, Eddie is outraged: "Get outta my sight! You turned down the sweetest boy who ever walked in shoes! You turned down the golden boy, the king among the ju-ven-iles!"[14] Characteristically, Eddie's diatribe is linked to threats of physical violence and death: "If he [loses] . . . the trees are ready for your coffin."[15] But Eddie is merely the most violent character in a violent world in which boxing is a metaphor for the way in which people are bought and sold, a world in which a fortune can be made from beating someone to death, as Joe does. Joe is partly right when he says that "Eddie is the only one who understands me."[16] Both men make a living from violence and both have a religious faith in money and things. As Joe puts it, "I'm out for fame and fortune, not to be different or artistic."[17] Joe forsakes playing the violin, the only thing that makes him feel whole, for boxing because, as he says, "When you leave your room . . . down in the street . . . it's war! Music can't help me there."[18] Eddie is the best soldier in that war.

Joe gives over fully to violence as commerce when, at the end of Act 2, he renounces his family and, temporarily, Lorna, and takes on a new triangle: "Now I'm alone. They're all against me—Moody, the girl . . . you're my family now, Tokio [Joe's trainer]—you and Eddie."[19] Edward Murray, in the characteristic homophobic style of critics in the 1960s notes that "an aura of perverted sexuality hangs over Joe's new menage" of Eddie, Roxy, and Tokio,"[20] who replace family and conventional heterosexuality. Homoeroticism is certainly evident in the words of Eddie, the loving owner, and Tokio, the trainer. In an interesting gender dynamic, Tokio realizes early on that the only way to get Joe to fight properly is to "treat him delicate, gentle—like a girl,"[21] yet it's Joe's "femininity," his reluctance to surrender totally to the violent, masculine culture in which he has placed himself, that redeems him. When Joe weeps at the thought of his father's disapproval, Tokio, massaging him, says "*in a soft, caressing voice:* 'You're a real sweetheart . . . You're getting good, honey,'"[22] while his "*busy hands start up the back of* [Joe's] *legs.*" For motherless Joe, a trainer's endearments replace real love. Ultimately, though, Tokio candidly assesses Joe's problem:

Joe, you're loaded with love. Find something to give it to. Your heart ain't in fighting . . . your *hate* is. But a man with hate and nothing else . . . he's half a man . . . and half a man . . . is no man. Find something to love, or someone.[23]

In the materialistic world of Odets's play, *someone* to love is a secondary alternative to *something* to love. Even Roxy Gottlieb, who owns a piece of Joe, responds sexually when Tokio says that Joe has to be treated "gentle—like a girl":

ROXY: Like a girl? Why didn't you say so before?
MOODY: No, Roxy, not you—you just treat him like a human being.[24]

Eddie Fuseli, who is "embarrassed" at his first sight of Joe, does love him. When Tom calls Joe a "real nutsy-Fagan," Eddie responds, *"repressing a trembling voice"*: "I don't like no one to laugh at that boy."[25] But Eddie, conditioned by his world, has to turn Joe into *something,* a possession. Eddie shows his affection by showering Joe with gifts, binding him with obligations. Joe quickly comes to see his benefactor as "a crowd of Eddies all around me, suffocating me, burying me in good times and silk shirts."[26] And Eddie's obligations can in fact be suffocating: "You're in this up to your neck. You owe me a lot—I don't like you to forget."[27] Eddie, after all, comes to own 70 percent of Joe. It is no surprise that Joe comes to think of himself as another of Eddie's phallic weapons: "You use me like a gun! Your loyalty's to keep me oiled and polished."[28] But what does Eddie love better than his gun?

Odets gave Elia Kazan, who originally played Eddie, a lengthy character sketch:

His main activity is to hunt for possession. . . . His homosexuality may be only partly conscious. . . . He is completely shut off from other people. Doesn't even want to handle the details of the fight. The reason he wants to have a champ is that he would be Eddie's boy to be proud of. He would have dominance over him and possession. His love has a certain element of pride. "He depends on me and needs me."[29]

Eddie's limitation is not his homosexuality, which simply drives him to possess men instead of women. His limitation is that, for him, materialism has become confused with love. Eddie truly believes a person can own another:

JOE: I want some personal life.
EDDIE: I give Bonaparte a good personal life.[30]

Note that Eddie speaks of Joe—to Joe—in the third person. Devotion and detachment are linked in Eddie's feelings for Joe. Yet what is the "personal life" Eddie gives Joe? There is no hint that it is sexual—that would be taboo in American drama of the period. Eddie gives Joe what he knows: what money can buy.

At the end of *Golden Boy,* Eddie is there in the Bonaparte living room to receive the news that Joe is dead. Eddie is both outsider and supporter of Joe's family, but Eddie, the creature of the world as it is, doesn't fully understand the web of love and loyalty that is the ideal, if not the reality, of family in Odets's world. All he knows is facts and possessions:

FRANK: How much does Joe own of himself?
EDDIE: Thirty percent. After tonight I own the rest.[31]

But Joe is already dead, out of the economic jungle in which a man can be bought and sold.

Why is Eddie Fuseli "queer"? In Odets's gendered economic jungle, in which we see social ills through inversions and perversions of the gender order, Eddie is the most successful figure because he is the most masculine—the most aggressive and pragmatic. He is attracted only to men who represent his masculine ideal. Here, as in *Little Caesar,* homosexuality is tied to masculinity, not effeminacy, which one thinks of as the dominant homosexual stereotype in the 1930s. To Odets, homosexuality is just another manifestation of the sickness of American capitalism, no worse than the cruel or cynical heterosexual relationships he portrays.

In the 1939 film of *Golden Boy,* the overt assignment of homosexuality to Fuseli (a properly sinister Joseph Calleia) is excised, thus confusing his motivation. As in the play, Fuseli wants control of Joe (William Holden), buys him shirts, threatens Lorna (Barbara Stanwyck) to stay away, and wants to take Joe to a musical, but here Fuseli's heterosexuality is established with the most obtrusive point-of-view shot in the film—of Lorna's legs. The camera moves up Lorna's body from foot to head as Fuseli admires her physical attributes. Yet from that point on, Fuseli shows no interest in Lorna except as an adversary. Wouldn't this killer, who always gets what he wants, find a way to possess her if he were really interested? For the rest of the film, Fuseli has eyes only for handsome young Joe, and you can't blame him. William Holden captures Joe's ruthless ambition and anger while keeping him sympathetic and sexy. He and Stanwyck, who plays here that combination of toughness and vulnerability that was her trademark, make a terrific couple.

The film of *Golden Boy* ends not with the adoring Fuseli in the Bonaparte household hearing the news of Joe's death but with Joe and Lorna alive and reinstated into his family. Joe has renounced both Eddie and boxing, after killing his opponent in the ring. "Your job is done," he says to Fuseli at their final meeting. "You made a killer out of me." Hollywood could not circulate the tragedy of American materialism Odets created, in which a "queer" killer survives and the hero and heroine die. The film must have its optimistic, heterosexual resolution.

"WHEN YOU'RE SLAPPED, YOU'LL TAKE IT AND LIKE IT"

If in *Little Caesar* and Odets's plays the depiction of gangsters includes a homoerotic dimension in a homosocial, hypermasculine environment, the men who carry signs of homosexuality in film noirs of the 1940s are in complex, ambivalent relationships with *femmes fatales*. In two classics, the 1941 version of *The Maltese Falcon* (screenplay and direction, John Huston) and *Gilda* (1946; screenplay, Marion Parsonnet; direction, Charles Vidor), homosexuals and homosexual desire are crucial to the action of the film, particularly as they relate to the gender order. Richard Dyer, who has systematically catalogued gay stereotypes in films noir,[32] states:

> How gays are represented is always part and parcel of the sexual ideology of a culture and . . . also indicates the complex, ambiguous ways in which heterosexual women and men are thought about in that culture.[33]

In *The Maltese Falcon* and *Gilda,* homosexuality is inextricably connected to women's divergence from their proper, subordinate role and from what one critic refers to as the genre's focus on "challenges to and problems within the ordering of masculine identity and male cultural authority."[34] In these films, the hero's task of controlling women connects to controlling homosexuality.

Huston's relatively faithful screen adaptation of Dashiell Hammett's *The Maltese Falcon* (its third screen incarnation) pits hard-boiled detective Sam Spade (Humphrey Bogart) against untrustworthy women and quasi-comical gay villains who are failures as conventional men. Spade is Huston and Hammett's idea of the successful male. Joan Mellen notes that Spade's "manliness is so manifest that he doesn't even carry a gun, always able as he is to demonstrate his power with his fists."[35] Guns in *The Maltese Falcon* are used by women and crypto-gay men. Mellen fails to note that in the film, Spade's fists are used only on homosexual men half his size. Brigid O'Shaughnessy (Mary Astor), the villainess in this narrative, is capable of performing all the aspects of the conventional female without the requisite subservience and devotion to a man. Spade, who understands women's wiles (the only woman he respects in the film is his devoted secretary, Effie [Lee Patrick], to whom he gives his greatest compliment when he calls her "a good man"), admires Brigid's performance, but he knows it is just that, a performance—like the false grief of Iva Archer (Gladys George), widow of Spade's partner, Miles (Jerome Cowan), who shows up dressed in black to woo Spade back to her bed. Brigid, actually a ruthless murderess who will do anything and ally herself with anyone to get her hands on the jewel encrusted statuette, the Maltese Falcon, is what critic James F. Maxfield calls "the femme noir," "the archetype of the subversive female. In the absence of social, political, or economic means of control she strives to rule men through their emotions."[36] While Spade strings Brigid along, knowing that she probably murdered his partner (in the novel, he's also having sex with her, thus exploiting the exploiter), he saves his brutality for the men who are competing with Brigid for the Falcon.

In the film, Joel Cairo (Peter Lorre) is not introduced as a "queer," as he is in the novel, but he bears all the stereotypical signs of homosexuality, from his gardenia-scented calling card, foppish clothes, and brilliantined hair, to his small stature and high voice. It is difficult to pinpoint exactly when such elegance became a sign of homosexuality in drama and film. Some have suggested that the association is a result of the Oscar Wilde trials, which linked Victorian aestheticism with sodomy and pederasty. One sees it in plays like Mordaunt Shairp's 1933 London and New York hit, *The Green Bay Tree,* which is about—though it is never overtly stated—the corruption of a young man by an elegant old queen. (The worst thing the predatory older man does is turn the young man into a wealthy hedonist.)[37] In most film noirs, one sees the homosexual interested in signs of affluence and luxury in his costume and decor. As Richard Dyer notes:

The ideological pairing of male homosexuality with luxury and decadence (with connotations of impotence and sterility) is of a piece with
the commonplace linking of women with luxury (women as expensive
things to win and keep, women as bearers of their husband's wealth)
and decadence (women as beings without sexuality save for the presence
of men). The feeling that gay men are *like* women yet *not* women pro-
duces the perverse tone of this mode of iconographic representation.[38]

When Joel pulls a gun (a little one, of course, befitting his questionable
masculinity) on Sam, the detective looks amused—until Joel tries to frisk
him, at which point Sam knocks him out. Does Sam punch little Joel unconscious out of self-defense, or because he finds the idea of Joel touching
him so loathsome? Sam's treatment of Joel is really fag bashing, which is
clearly justified in the minds of Hammett and Huston (the scene is played
in the film exactly as it is presented in the novel). When Cairo regains consciousness, he says, always the queen, "Look what you did to my shirt."
Later, Brigid both slaps and pistol-whips Joel and when he tries to hit her,
Spade hits *him*. When Cairo observes, "This is the second time you've put
your hands on me," Spade rejoins, "Yes, and when you're slapped, you'll
take it and like it," and slaps him again.[39] Spade, functioning as an arbiter
of proper masculine and feminine behavior, can treat Cairo viciously because Cairo is a failed man, not because he is one of the bad guys.

   This violent constraint extends as well to short, tough-talking Wilmer
(Elisha Cook, Jr.), who kills for Kasper Gutman (Sydney Greenstreet).
Spade refers to Wilmer as a "gunsel," which means not only a hired gun,
but also "a homosexual young man who is living with and supported by
an older man."[40] Cook doesn't look like the "kid" described in the novel.
He's older and much creepier than Hammett's Wilmer. Were the filmmakers afraid of the whiff of pederasty that would arise from having a
teenage actor play Wilmer? The gunsel is little more than a joke to Spade,
who mocks and humiliates him at every turn and tries to talk Gutman
into making him the fall guy. Later Spade knocks Wilmer out. In the
novel, Cairo tries unsuccessfully to seduce Wilmer;[41] the film, however,
more filled with innuendo, hints at a relationship between Gutman and
the young gunman. Does Spade despise Wilmer because he's a little caricature of a real gangster or because the little thug isn't the real man he pre-
tends, with his street talk, to be ? Though it is only hinted, this "band of
criminals [Joel; Wilmer; and Guttman, the elegant, fat, older queen] is

rather like a gay family,"[42] as James Naremore correctly observes, but a gay family invented by straight men invested in their era's notions of masculinity and homosexuality (see fig. 7).

Spade's frustration is that he can't find a real male adversary. The closest thing he can find to a foe worth his masculine effort is a woman. Yet according to the film's logic, straight men are at risk as long as the dangerous woman and gay men are around. Lesser men might not be able to disarm them as easily as Spade does. What is interesting is that Spade fights so viciously and dirtily against these little men. Clearly he is striking blows for masculinity against men who fight dirty (as women do). In the twists and turns of the narrative of *The Maltese Falcon,* Spade is fighting above all for masculinity and the gender order.

"YOU MUST LEAD A GAY LIFE."

The relationship between homosexuality and masculinity is much more complex in one of the most fascinating postwar film noirs, *Gilda,* for here homoerotic desire is so connected to the central male character and so embedded in the narrative and the acting that it is difficult to accept the film's heterosexual resolution as anything but Hollywood necessity.

After winning a crap game (with loaded dice) in a waterfront dive on his first night in Buenos Aires, Johnny Farrell (Glenn Ford) is saved from armed robbery by the cane (a phallic device with a large dagger in its tip) of Ballin Mundson (George Macready). When Johnny asks Ballin what an elegantly dressed man is doing in a sleazy part of town in the middle of the night, Ballin answers, "I came down to save your life." The audience either accepts Ballin's metaphysical riposte or draws the obvious conclusion. Ballin's formal attire suggests elegance, which suggests homosexuality. His foreign accent suggests decadence; his facial scar suggests danger. It can be inferred that Ballin is out cruising for rough trade. When Johnny remarks, with no apparent irony, "You must lead a gay life," a clear overture to anyone in the know, Ballin offers another cryptic comment: "I lead the life I like to lead." Ballin moves away and Johnny insistently follows him, keeping the conversation going. The scene is played with Ballin and Johnny usually kept in tight two-shot, as if Johnny is encouraging Ballin to pick him up. Instead Ballin gives him a key to his gambling casino.

After Johnny is caught cheating at the casino, two bouncers bring him up to Ballin's office and rough him up, while Ballin watches in the

shadow. In the ensuing scene, Glenn Ford's Johnny couldn't be more os-
tentatiously flirtatious as he tries to talk Ballin into hiring him: "You have
no idea how faithful and obedient I can be—for a nice salary." Ballin asks
Johnny about his past and Johnny coyly responds, "I was born the night
you met me in that alley." Ballin buys Johnny as an employee and, perhaps, more: Johnny is given the key to Ballin's house as well as his office.
Ballin's only condition: "This I must be sure of. That there's no woman
anywhere." Johnny is happy to acquiesce. In the next sequence, during a
celebration of the end of World War II, Johnny comes into Ballin's office
with cocktails. Ballin doesn't want to toast Allied victory,[43] so Johnny suggests a toast "to the three of us" (Johnny, Ballin, and Ballin's phallic
cane/dagger) and intimates that he, like Ballin's cane, would be ready to
kill for Ballin (se fig. 8). Clearly, Johnny has happily settled into his role
as Ballin's property in a world without women.

According to John Kobal, Glenn Ford, and George Macready were indeed aware of "the implications in the relationship between the men in the
early part of the film."[44] I'm not so sure about Macready, but it seems clear
that Glenn Ford is aware of the gay subtext and is playing it to the hilt.
Note, too, Ford's costume changes: the sloppy attire of the first crap-play-
ing sequence, then the ill-fitting suit and ugly tie he wears when he first
goes to Ballin's casino (the men's room attendant, the film's Greek chorus,
calls him a peasant), then the elegant attire he wears once he is "employed"
by Ballin. Glenn Ford never looked better in a film, but as Richard Dyer
notes, Johnny "has no observable talent apart from being pretty."[45]

After a period of absence, Ballin returns married to the tempestuous
Gilda (Rita Hayworth). When Ballin observes, "It's quite a surprise to
hear a woman singing in my house, Johnny," Johnny replies ruefully,
"Yes, quite a surprise." Johnny is both irked at having lost Ballin to Gilda
and jealous that Gilda (his ex-lover, as it turns out) is married to Ballin.
With Gilda's appearance, the film becomes a complex bisexual triangle in
which two men vie for the same woman *and* a man and a woman vie for
the same man. After Johnny gives Ballin back the key to his house and
storms out, he tells us (Johnny narrates the film in classic noir fashion):
"I wanted to go back there and see them together. I wanted to know . . .
I wanted to go back up there to that room and hit her. What scared me
was that I wanted to hit him too."

Despite Johnny's omniscience as narrator the film, he doesn't seem as
aware of his position vis-à-vis Gilda and Ballin as they are. When he accuses
Gilda of marrying Ballin for his money, she responds: "That wouldn't be

the pot calling the little kettle black, now would it?" When Johnny explains his relationship to Ballin, "I was down and out—he put me on my feet," Gilda wryly retorts, "What a coincidence." Ballin flaunts his control of Johnny and Gilda: "I bought her, Johnny, just as I bought you." He seems aware that the dynamic between Johnny and Gilda can bring them together: "Hate can be a very exciting emotion. It's the only thing that warms me." If anything, Ballin seems fascinated with what will happen when he throws his two possessions together. Describing his previous relationship with Gilda, Johnny tells Ballin, "I taught her everything she knows, Ballin. Does that satisfy you?" The implication is: "I got there first. What you like about her is really me. Even what you like about her sexually is really me." This would explain why some of Gilda's lines ("I was born on the night we met.") echo Johnny's.

Johnny, however, tries to be noble, proving his loyalty to Ballin first by trying to keep Gilda away from other men: "I don't care what you do but I do care what it looks like to him." Gilda sees Johnny's supervision of her behavior as desire for her. She is only half-right. She has no idea how faithful and obedient Johnny can be. If he doesn't love Ballin, he loves the fortune his position in Ballin's world has brought him. Throughout, Johnny projects his motives onto Gilda. He joined with Ballin for money, so he assumes she did (actually she married Ballin to get close to Johnny).

When Ballin fakes his death, Johnny marries Gilda, then keeps her captive as punishment for her supposed infidelity to Ballin and prior infidelity to him. Johnny is obsessed with Gilda, displaying what Detective Obregon (Joseph Calleia) calls "the most curious love-hate pattern I've ever witnessed." Obregon also knows "Gilda didn't do any of the things you're losing sleep over. Not any of them. It was all an act." All evidence to the contrary, this femme fatale is a good girl, just trying to make Johnny jealous. Even bad girls were innocent in postwar Hollywood—Hollywood sold *Gilda* on Hayworth's sexuality and naughtiness while maintaining her character's virtue. Gilda may seem like a slut, but there's a good woman beneath the shimmy.

In the final reel, the film reverts rather suddenly to normative heterosexuality, begging the question of why Gilda would want a man who has treated her so terribly. The specter of homosexuality (Ballin) is killed off once and for all—by a men's room attendant! Once Johnny realizes that Gilda is really a "good girl," he can become a proper heterosexual male and they can return to a mythical place called "home," where he will support her. Unfortunately, Johnny has no legal means of support, and does anyone believe Rita Hayworth's Gilda will be happy in American domesticity? Conventional heterosexuality is far less credible for these characters than the homoerotically charged triangle we have witnessed.

As in Odets's plays, in *Gilda* a man can't be "all man" in a culture that makes him a commodity. If a man allows himself to be bought, he becomes like a woman. And what else, in the thinking of the period, is an unmanly man, but a homosexual? It is only when Johnny has to give up the power and possessions he gained form his relationship with Ballin that he can achieve heterosexuality and his true love.

"YOU'RE QUITE A GOOD CHICKEN STRANGLER."

Rope, which Alfred Hitchcock made for Warner Bros. in 1948, centers on homosexual murderers and is filled with stereotypical signs of homosexuality. *Rope* is an adaptation of and an improvement on *Rope's End,* a 1929 hit melodrama by Patrick Hamilton. The playwright was supposedly appalled at the extent to which the homosexuality implied in his play was foregrounded in Hitchcock's film.[46] In his memoir, *Original Story By,* Arthur Laurents, who co-wrote the screenplay for *Rope* with Hume Cronyn and Ben Hecht, and was star Farley Granger's lover at the time, remembers that "At the Warner Bros. studio in Burbank where *Rope* was shot, homosexuality was the unmentionable, known only as 'it.' 'It' wasn't in the picture, no character was 'one.' Fascinating was how Hitchcock nevertheless made clear to me that he wanted 'it' in the picture."[47] Hitchcock's games with the homosexual subject matter show how aware he was that he was playing with a taboo. In the trailer for *Rope,* Hitchcock offers us a romantic springtime scene in a New York park involving a good-looking, well-dressed young couple, David and his fiancée, Janet. In this scene, which is not in the film, David proposes to Janet and she coyly tells him he will have his answer "at Brandon's party." James Stewart then appears on the screen to tell the viewer that this is the last time Janet saw David alive. In the 1940s, Hitchcock's most successful films combined suspense with romance: Cary Grant and Joan Fontaine in *Suspicion,* Grant and Ingrid Bergman in *Notorious,* Gregory Peck and Bergman in *Spellbound.* Here to advertise *Rope* were two attractive, though unknown, young actors on a park bench, promising a heterosexual romance that leads to murder. James Stewart, not then associated with Hitchcock films, becomes the

authoritative voice, standing outside the action and separate from the other
characters. We are then shown unflattering close-up shots of the other characters, all looking decidedly suspicious, and then a two-shot of John Dall
and Farley Granger, who play the two murderers, Brandon and Phillip.
Stewart tells us that Brandon and Phillip are "the two who are responsible
for everything." What we see through Brandon and Phillip's shifting gaze
are two men who look weak and suspicious and who are angry at each
other. So the trailer gives us a heterosexual couple we never see in the film
and, though it is never directly stated, a homosexual couple. The structure
of the trailer and his star billing give James Stewart power over characters
and narrative. Even more clearly than the film does the trailer for *Rope* establish Brandon and Phillip's crime as a brutal disruption of the heterosexual order, which only a strong heterosexual male can restore. One
advertisement for *Rope* falsely claimed that it is "the most excitement-filled
love story ever told," an odd claim for a film in which one of the heterosexual lovers is murdered in the first shot. Or is the "excitement-filled" love
story that between Granger's Phillip and Dall's Brandon?

Rope offers us a depiction of homosexuality through stereotype and
inference that 1948 audiences may well have ignored ("They are just
good friends."). Brandon and Phillip are wealthy, well-educated, artistic,
and well-dressed. They are throwing a dinner party for which they don't
have dates. Phillip may just be visiting Brandon, but they are treated by
their guests as if they are a couple, and, like a couple, they are about to
spend a long visit with Brandon's mother. For the first half of the film,
Brandon and Phillip are almost always in the same frame, as close together as two people can be without embracing. Only the mention of the
bedroom hints that they sleep together. Hitchcock, his gay screenwriter,
and the two gay actors playing Brandon and Phillip are carefully working
within and against a powerful taboo. As Robin Wood deftly puts it, "It's
not simply that *Rope* cannot tell us that the two men sleep together; it also
cannot clearly tell us that they don't, since that would imply that they
might."[48] In his essay, "Anal Rope," critic D. A. Miller, points out: "Until
recently, homosexuality offered not just the most prominent—it offered
the only subject matter whose representation in American mass culture
appertained exclusively to the shadow kingdom of connotation where in-
sinuations could at once be developed and denied."[49]

What can be offered are more sinister clues to their sexuality. Though
Farley Granger is much better looking than John Dall, there is a resem-
blance in build and hair color, emphasized by the similarity in clothing,

suggesting narcissism and young men who are attracted to a mirror image. More important is the masculine-feminine dynamic, reflecting what Richard Dyer notes about the assumptions underlying the treatment of homosexual relationships in film noir, which assume that "such relationships are sick, decadent, etc., but also . . . structured according to the male-female norms of heterosexual relationships."[50] Brandon is controlling and able to master his emotions. Phillip verges on hysteria throughout the film (see fig. 9). At one point Brandon slaps Phillip in the face, the way men in film conventionally slap hysterical women. Brandon's relationship to Phillip seems to be one of control: He manages Phillip's concert career and dominates his life.

What develops during the film is not love between Brandon and Phillip, but growing contempt. Early in the film, Brandon says, "I don't think you really appreciate me, Phillip," to which Phillip responds ironically, "I'm beginning to, Brandon." While Brandon grows increasingly irritated with Phillip's lack of emotional control, Phillip comes to resent Brandon's power over him. When Brandon scolds him for getting drunk, Phillip snaps, "At least if I have a hangover it's all mine." When Phillip gets control of the gun, he says to Brandon, "I'd just as soon kill you as him [Rupert]. Sooner." For Phillip, their killing of David was a private act. For Brandon it needed to be public, an exposure and betrayal of their private bond: "It's what you wanted, isn't it? Somebody else to know."

Homosexuals such as Brandon and Phillip are not only overprivileged, immature, and hyperemotional. They are also dangerous psychopaths, destructively envious of heterosexuals (Brandon and Phillip kill David and serve dinner on the chest in which David's corpse is hidden, as Brandon viciously toys with David's fiancée). In killing David, Brandon and Phillip have disrupted normal heterosexuality.

James Stewart's performance is a classic case of Hollywood miscasting, so as to camouflage the film's prevalent homosexuality. Playing a former headmaster of the killers, Stewart's Rupert strolls through the picture with the air of a suspicious teacher on hall duty. When he apprehends the miscreants and lectures them on the value of all mankind, he's back in *Mr. Smith Goes to Washington*. At the end he is sitting, his back to the camera, a surrogate for the virtuous viewers, holding Brandon and Phillip, both silent, at gunpoint until the police arrive. Like the lone western hero, Stewart has cleaned out the bad guys. This might be a satisfying conclusion to a conventional film, but it goes against the grain of the screenplay. Laurents wrote of Rupert's relationship to Brandon and Phillip:

The three central characters in *Rope* are homosexual. Brandon and Phillip are lovers who carry the Nietzschean philosophy learned from their former prep school teacher, Rupert, to its outer limit; a murder committed to prove superiority. Rupert is a good friend and probably an ex-lover of Brandon's; his is the most interesting role. Caustic with a sardonic sense of humor, overly cynical, he is caught off guard by having to face the appalling result of what he taught and professed to believe.[51]

Hearing James Stewart's deadpan delivery of Rupert's witty, slightly camp banter is bizarre indeed. Instead of being playful and nihilistic, in the style of queens of yore, as the script calls for (Laurents notes that he drew Rupert's characterization from some "silver and china queens" he knew in New York), he is simply out of place. Rupert belongs at the party only if there is a sense of a special intimacy between him and the couple, something beyond a teacher-student relationship. The script makes clear that he is a constant visitor to Brandon's apartment—at his first entrance, he doesn't wait to be admitted. He's clearly on chummy terms with Brandon's housekeeper. What could he share with Brandon and Phillip other than homosexuality? But Stewart is not playing the Rupert of the script. He's playing himself, out of place and disapproving politely of everything he hears. This outsider is in the ideal position to restore order and get the homosexuals arrested. The Rupert Laurents wrote is far more deeply implicated in the action than the one Stewart is acting. In the screenplay, Rupert has taught his protégés that "moral concepts of right and wrong don't hold for the intellectually superior." And who are the intellectually superior, but the homosexuals who hold the heterosexuals in thinly veiled contempt? "Murder is—or should be—an art," Rupert has taught his charges. This is the same sort of evil aestheticism for which Oscar Wilde was punished and which is presented, in works like *The Green Bay Tree,* as the danger of homosexuality. Teach a boy to be an aesthete, and you have taught him to be a homosexual and a sociopath. In this stereotypical pattern, Rupert is the real villain, and realizes his responsibility for what Brandon and Phillip do. Stewart is too morally righteous. Perhaps ten years later, the Stewart of *Vertigo* would have known how to play Rupert, but to some extent the most interesting and frightening aspect of the obsessives Stewart played in Hitchcock's films is that they never fully realize their destructiveness.[52] Because of Stewart, *Rope* becomes a more conventional heterosexist narrative. The homosexuals who dominate the film literally move silently to the background as the supposedly heterosexual (or, like the western heroes, asexual) savior solves the crime and offers society's judgment.

Rope may reinforce the negative homosexual stereotypes of the period, but in foregrounding homosexuality at all and by offering homosexuality in the beautiful form of Farley Granger, one of the few Hollywood actors who did not hide his homosexuality, the film breaks the era's silence on the subject. In discussing the 1944 film noir *Laura,* and gay actor Clifton Webb's role as crypto-gay villain Waldo Lydecker, social historian Robert J. Corber notes, "In an era in which gay men threatened to become invisible, the impact of the film's representation of Lydecker may have been more progressive than regressive, despite the way in which it reinforced homosexual stereotypes."[53] A charming actor, Granger is playing out a set of gay stereotypes—the sensitive young man, the elegant queen, the weak sister, the uncontrollable and effeminate male, the self-hating homosexual—but he's playing them honestly and sympathetically. If only John Dall's Brandon were less obnoxious. He plays the overbearing side of Brandon without showing what Phillip and others might find likable. Perhaps Robert Walker, a more ingratiating actor, might have brought to Brandon the raffish charm he would bring to Bruno Antony, Farley Granger's crypto-gay nemesis in Hitchcock's masterpiece, *Strangers on a Train.*

"AND THEY LEFT NO HUMAN EXPERIENCE UNTRIED."

The clearest signs of homosexuality in *Rope* are its echoes of the 1924 Leopold-Loeb murder case in Chicago. In many ways, the highly publicized case defined the twentieth-century American image of homosexuality as the Oscar Wilde trials defined homosexuality in fin de siècle Britain. Nathan Leopold and Richard "Dickie" Loeb, two brilliant, wealthy, Jewish young men, filled with notions of their intellectual superiority and some Nietzsche, murdered fourteen-year-old Bobby Franks in order to experience murder and to commit the perfect crime. Famed attorney Clarence Darrow, who would soon brilliantly defend the teaching of evolution in the Scopes trial in Tennessee, used all his estimable rhetorical skills to save the two killers from the death penalty. The graphic details of the sexual relationship of Leopold and Loeb (Loeb would allow Leopold to insert his penis between Loeb's legs as payment for being Loeb's partner in crime) became an integral part of Darrow's defense.

Though both young men claimed to have engaged in heterosexual activity (indeed, having sex with two women was their alibi), their occasional homosexual acts, and the relationship of those acts to their criminal acts, were prominent in the scandal surrounding the case. Darrow made a convincing case for mitigating circumstances—if these young men could engage in homosexual acts, they must be insane, even if they knew right from wrong—and Leopold and Loeb got life imprisonment. Loeb was brutally murdered in prison twelve years later by a man who falsely claimed Loeb was propositioning him. Leopold, a model prisoner, was released in 1958, moved to Puerto Rico, and married. In later life, Leopold still thought of Dickie Loeb as both "the man who ruined my life" and "the best friend I ever had."

The Leopold-Loeb case tied together a number of stereotypes that were often applied to homosexuals: immaturity, wealth, intellect (the two were geniuses who finished college in their teens), sadism (not only was the relationship between the murderers sado-masochistic, but they poured acid on their victim's face and penis), atheism, and psychopathology. During the period of the House Un-American Activities Committee and the shenanigans of Senator Joseph McCarthy, Leopold and Loeb again became prototypes for the criminal homosexual stereotype. Gay men weren't just pansies and sissies; they were downright dangerous. As historian John Loughery puts it:

> The attempt to stigmatize homosexuals as a menace to children and as men whose lives were necessarily furtive and violent, a drive that reached its zenith in America in the years 1935 to 1960, was the work of a society that was awakening to the fragility of its own dichotomies: healthy/sick, married/promiscuous, masculine/feminine, active/passive, heterosexual/homosexual.[54]

Rope hinted at a sexual relationship between its murderous central characters. In 1956, Meyer Levin published a fictionalized account of the Leopold-Loeb case, *Compulsion,* which he turned into a play (1957), and which was made into a movie in 1959(screenplay Richard Murphy; director, Richard Fleisher). Nathan Leopold was outraged enough at the film's depiction of a homosexual relationship between Dickie Loeb and himself and its theory that he murdered to kill the feminine side of his own identity that he sued, unsuccessfully, for "invasion of privacy."

The trailer for the film of *Compulsion* hints at the homosexual relationship between the leading characters. "Do you know the strange relationship that existed between them?" we are asked, and then we're told that "they left no human experience untried." If the creators of the trailer couldn't name exactly what human experiences the two young men did try, they could at least suggest that they tried everything, including the unspeakable.

Artie Straus (the Loeb character, played by Bradford Dillman) says at one point to Judd Steiner (the film's Leopold, played by Dean Stockwell) "You said you wanted me to command you," to which Judd responds, "I do, as long as you keep your part of the agreement." End of conversation, though those in the know can read Artie's "part of the agreement" as sexual. Later Artie says, "We agreed to explore all aspects of human experience." Judd responds, "But together, Artie." While Artie may be the more murderous, Judd is the one with the stronger feelings of romantic attachment, though his separation from normal sexuality obviously pains him. Closer to the facts of the Leopold-Loeb case than *Rope*, *Compulsion* depicts a power relationship in which Judd, clearly smitten with brasher, more popular Artie, does what he is told. Dillman's Artie is a rash fraternity boy (the real Loeb was told by one fraternity that he could join if Leopold, whom they thought was homosexual, stayed away), brilliant perhaps, but an exhibitionist. Artie can't help talking to the police, pretending to play detective, to show how clever he is. Dean Stockwell's sad looking Judd alternates between intellectual arrogance and neediness. The film clearly wants the audience to sympathize somewhat with Judd, who is seen through the eyes of Ruth (Diane Varsi), a young woman Judd befriends but attempts to rape in order to prove his masculinity. Guilt prevents the assault, not homosexuality, and he runs away in a fit of anguish. Asked to testify in Judd's defense, Ruth says: "He couldn't go through with it. He was like a child, a sick, frightened child." Ruth's testimony that Judd's inability to rape her was a sign of weakness (and homosexuality?) helps seal the case of "extenuating circumstances" that saves Artie and Judd's lives.

Immaturity is the primary theme of *Compulsion*. Artie and Judd are sad cases of arrested development. They are not fully men, in terms of maturity or sexuality. However heinous their crimes, then, they are not fully culpable. If *Rope* judges its homosexual killers through the eyes of a heterosexual male, *Compulsion* gives us a young woman's judgment. Judd, a potential object of female desire who stands outside the spectrum of normal sexuality, is presented as potentially heterosexual. Had he been able to establish a relationship with Ruth instead of with Artie, he might have been saved, made normal. Ruth leaves the courtroom arm in arm with her fiancé—heterosexuality triumphs.

Until the AIDS-related outings of celebrities like Rock Hudson and Liberace, Nathan Leopold and Richard Loeb were arguably the most famous homosexuals in America. Wealthy and privileged, but social outsiders and misfits, they planned and executed a murder with no show of remorse. They are the worst possible poster boys for gayness, but at the same time they were the first American gay couple to be celebrities. Fascinating to straight artists like Alfred Hitchcock, they became obsessions to some gay artists. John Logan remembers that during the research of his Leopold-Loeb play *Never the Sinner:* "I was seduced. I was completely captivated by Leopold and Loeb. Their flash and glimmer and panache and smug brilliance had taken hold. To my mind, they were the two most magical human beings who had ever lived."[55] If *Rope* and *Compulsion* presented postwar views of the Leopold-Loeb case that reflected their era's view of homosexuality as pathological, Tom Kalin's film, *Swoon,* offers an antihomophobic interpretation of these young men whose gayness has often been seen as synonymous with their brutality.

"I'LL DO WHAT YOU WANT"

Tom Kalin's 1992 film, *Swoon,* removes the normative voices that interpreted and judged Leopold and Loeb in the earlier films and presents their story in their own voices. The film opens with a highly stylized presentation of Dickie Loeb (Daniel Schlachet) and a group of women and drag queens reading from a novel depicting a heterosexual sadomasochistic codependent relationship. Dickie reads: "Oh, my God, I will do whatever you command. Be your slave. A mere object with which you can do what you will. Only don't send me away. I cannot bear it. I cannot live without you."

From the outset, the sort of relationship Leopold and Loeb have is not necessarily homosexual. Nathan Leopold (Craig Chester) walks into the frame and disrupts the reading: "We're late." We see that Dickie's reading has been performed in front of a painted canvas, as part of a filming. His performance places his desire within a heterosexual framework that has been part not only of the previous filmic treatments of the

Leopold-Loeb case, with their coyness about the characters' homosexuality, but of film's overall erasure of homosexual relationships. Kalin's fictionalized account of the Leopold-Loeb case, interweaving history and fantasy, past and present (the film is full of anachronisms such as touchtone telephones and television sets), will present the case within the framework of a gay love story, a challenge as well to the prevalent contemporary antiseptic depictions of the homosexual-as-victim-with-AIDS.

Nathan and Dickie leave the setting of the filming and walk through a bleak urban wasteland. First we see them playfully, if dangerously, throwing glass bottles at each another. They then run into an abandoned building. Light and smoke pour through openings in the ruined edifice while Nathan kisses Dickie. Then Dickie lifts two rings off his tongue and the couple engage in a mock wedding ceremony. As they walk out, arm in arm, we hear their "marriage vows":

"I'll do what you want."
"I'll do what you want."

The murder is part of a marriage pact. Dickie will invent crimes for the boys to commit, after which Nathan will be allowed to have sex with Dickie. Here, Nathan is as powerful in the relationship as Dickie. At one point Nathan tells us, in a voice-over, "I've waited six weeks since our last crime. He's letting me down again." Nathan proudly admits to the police that he is, as the police put it, "the aggressor in this relationship." After the murder of Bobby Franks, Nathan tells us again in voice-over "Killing Bobby Franks together would join Richard and I [sic] for life. I wanted to murder the idea of suffering as my condition." For Nathan, murder is an act of love and empowerment, a way to move away from the notion of homosexuality as inevitably associated with suffering and victimization. Though sex is seen as a payment for complicity in crime, we also see scenes of sincere physical affection and intimacy between Nathan and Dickie.

Leopold and Loeb's crimes (killing Bobby Franks was the capstone of years of petty crimes) are presented against a backdrop of the violence of Chicago in the 1920s, thus implicating to some extent their era's culture. Was the murder they committed publicized more than other murders in Chicago in that period because of its homosexual angle? The trial in *Swoon* becomes a trial more for perversion than for murder. "The basic motive in this case," the prosecutor tells the court, "is the desire to satisfy unnatural lusts." The film emphasizes the ways in which the young killers are made the focus of a homophobic spectacle. While psychiatrists testify as to the defendants' sex acts, we see Nathan and Dickie making out on a bed at the front of the courtroom. The testimony paints their sexual activity as forceful and one-sided, though we see mutual and affectionate physical activity. In his concluding remarks, the prosecutor asserts, "Because these two are perverts, I have a right to claim they have committed an act of perversion."

In prison, Nathan takes a cigarette and burns Dickie's initials into his thigh; Nathan needs to be physically connected to his beloved. After Dickie is murdered, Nathan takes the "wedding" ring off Dickie's finger and puts in into his own mouth. Then Nathan paces his cell and wails with grief, the only passionate emotion he expresses in the film. Nathan is wrapped up like a mummy, an image that also reinforces the sense that he died spiritually with Dickie's death.

The press inaccurately report that Loeb's murder was his killer's reaction to a homosexual overture and Loeb's killer receives a not-guilty verdict, as if Loeb's death were justified. For six months after Loeb's death, Leopold is kept in the same prison area as Loeb's killer: The officials hope the murderer will strike twice and that Leopold and Loeb both receive the death sentence the judge should have decreed.

The Nathan Leopold who leaves prison in this film is a lost man. Without Loeb to direct him, he is aimless. While historically inaccurate, this version of Leopold fits neatly into the film's romantic presentation of the symbiotic relationship of Nathan and Dickie.

Swoon mimics the look of black-and-white "serious" films of the 1950s (like *Compulsion*) that purport to offer a graphic, realistic presentation of historical characters and events. Nonetheless *Swoon* repeatedly confounds realistic devices and techniques, turning the viewers' eyes more on the homophobic hysteria that surrounded the Leopold-Loeb case than on the crime itself. Tom Kalin wants us to understand and suspend judgment on the relationship of Nathan Leopold and Dickie Loeb.

"BETTER TO BE A FAKE SOMEBODY THAN A REAL NOBODY."

Patricia Highsmith, who as Claire Morgan wrote the best-selling lesbian novel *The Price of Salt,* created two of the great crypto-gay villains of postwar crime fiction, Charles Anthony Bruno, who would become the magnificent Bruno Antony in Alfred Hitchcock's film version of Highsmith's

Strangers on a Train, and Tom Ripley, less crypto-gay in Highsmith's 1955 novel, *The Talented Mr. Ripley,* than in a dangerous, self-destructive state of denial. Anthony Minghella's 1999 film version of *The Talented Mr. Ripley* offers a modern twist on the mid-twentieth-century stereotype of the gay man as elegant criminal demonstrating how a villain can be turned into a sympathetic, sentimentalized figure.

"I suppose I always thought—better to be a fake somebody than a real nobody,"[56] is one of the last things Tom Ripley (Matt Damon) says to his lover, Peter Smith-Kingsley (Jack Davenport), before he strangles him. Ripley's statement has two levels of meaning. Tom Ripley, feeling himself a cipher, is looking for someone to *be,* which in his case is confused with finding someone to *love.* Being, for Ripley, is a matter of possessing the right accoutrements: He can be his beloved if he can possess the things that belong to him. He says to the object of his adoration, the charming, rich, and feckless Dickie Greenleaf (Jude Law), "I've gotten to like everything about the way you live. It's one big love affair."[57] When Dickie cruelly rejects Tom, which leads to Tom's killing of Dickie (manslaughter, not premeditated murder as in Highsmith's novel), Tom tries to take on Dickie's identity. By the end of the film, Tom has managed to get what belonged to Dickie, but *being* Dickie seems more of a devil's bargain.

Tom wants the life that wealthy people like Dickie take for granted, and to some extent, *The Talented Mr. Ripley* is, as Minghella maintains, "a story about class."[58] The film, in different ways from the 1955 novel, can also be read as a work about the closet—indeed, the last shot in the film is of a closet door closing on the solitary Ripley, who has just killed his first real chance at a true, reciprocal love with someone who adores him as Tom Ripley. "Tell me some good things about Tom Ripley," he says to Peter as he is about to kill him, but Tom cannot believe statements of love. Rather than accept the love of a man, he will, as Dickie, pretend to love a woman.

In Patricia Highsmith's novel, Ripley is self-conscious about being seen as homosexual, but never fully admits, even to himself, the implications of his feelings for Dickie, a kind of denial far more possible in the 1950s than today. Yet Highsmith constantly presents Tom Ripley's supposedly sexless feelings in sexually charged language. In New York, long before he leaves for Italy, Tom repeatedly announces to friends: "I can't make up my mind whether I like men or women, so I'm thinking of giving *both* up."[59] In *The Talented Mr. Ripley,* though not in the later novels in her Ripley series, Highsmith's Tom has indeed given up sex, but even though he thinks of himself as "innocent and clean minded,"[60] he can't control his feelings for Dickie or his jealous rage toward Dickie's relationship with his girlfriend, Marge. In one of the most chilling passages in the novel, Tom, after seeing Dickie kiss Marge, has a private tantrum in which he fantasizes himself as Dickie enacting violence toward Marge:

> "Marge, you must understand that I don't *love* you," Tom said into the mirror in Dickie's voice, with Dickie's higher pitch on the emphasized words, with the little growl in his throat at the end of the phrase that could be pleasant or unpleasant, intimate or cool, according to Dickie's mood. "Marge, stop it!" Tom turned suddenly and made a grab at the air as if he were seizing Marge's throat. He shook her, twisted her, while she sank lower and lower, until he at last left her limp on the floor. He was panting. He wiped his forehead the way Dickie did . . . Even his parted lips looked like Dickie's when he was out of breath from swimming, drawn down a little from his lower teeth. "You know why I had to do that," he said, still breathlessly, addressing Marge, though he watched himself in the mirror. "You were interfering between Tom and me—No, not that! But there is a bond between us."[61]

Most telling is Tom's "No, not that!"—his denial, even in fantasy, of his desire for Dickie. At the very moment Tom is having this fantasy, Marge is telling Dickie she thinks Tom is "queer." Later, after Dickie has disappeared, Marge is sure that he and Tom have become lovers. (There is a reference to this suspicion of Marge's in the screenplay, but it rightly ended up on the cutting-room floor. Minghella's Marge wouldn't think this.)

When, after five weeks as Dickie's constant companion, trying to win his exclusive if chaste devotion, Tom sees in Dickie's eyes not the love he wanted, but hatred. He "saw nothing more now than if he had looked at the hard, bloodless surface of a mirror."[62] He realizes that their sense of closeness was an illusion, as it always will be for him with anyone, and that he is doomed to be alone: "He was alone. That was the only important thing. He began to feel a tingling fear at the end of his spine, tingling over his buttocks"[63] Note that Highsmith chooses to emphasize the area near Tom's anus, a potential site of sexual pleasure, at this moment of loss. A few days later, on a beach at Cannes, Dickie speaks derogatorily of male couples on the beach. In Highsmith's sexually loaded language, Tom "felt that *sharp thrust* of shame" (italics mine). At that moment, Tom felt that "a crazy emotion of hate, of affection, of impatience and frustration *was swelling in him*" (my italics).⁶⁴ He decides both to kill Dickie and to become him.

When boorish Freddie Miles shows up at Tom's apartment in Rome, where Tom has taken on Dickie's identity, Tom is threatened not only by Freddie's knowing he is not Dickie but also by Freddie's suspicions that Tom and Dickie are having an affair: "Tom knew what Freddie was thinking. *He stiffened,* sensing danger" (italics mine).⁶⁵ After Tom kills Freddie, he thinks about Freddie's silent accusation of sexual deviation: "Tom laughed at the phrase 'sexual deviation.' Where was the sex? Where was the deviation? He looked at Freddie and said low and bitterly: 'Freddie Miles, you're a victim of your own dirty mind.'"⁶⁶ According to Ripley's logic, if you're not actually doing anything about your sexual desire, you can't possibly be homosexual. Later, Tom has a moment of panic at the thought that Freddie found out his address from someone in a bar, someone who must have followed Tom home: "It shamed him and made him shrink inside his overcoat. He imagined a dark, panting young face following him home. Staring up to see which window had lighted up after he had gone in. Tom hunched in his overcoat and walked faster, as if he were fleeing a sick, passionate pursuer."⁶⁷

Highsmith sees two impulses in Tom Ripley. The first is a desire to annihilate the self he hates by taking on another's identity: "He hated going back to himself as he would have hated putting on a shabby suit of clothes, a grease-spotted, unpressed suit of clothes that had not been very good even when it was new."⁶⁸ The second is a love for Dickie expressed as a lonely desire for Dickie's companionship that continues long after the real Dickie's death:

> If only he hadn't been in such a hurry and so greedy, if only he hadn't misjudged the relationship between Dickie and Marge so stupidly, or had simply waited for them to separate of their own volition, then none of this would have happened, and he *could* have lived with Dickie for the rest of his life. If only he hadn't put on Dickie's clothes that day.⁶⁹

Highsmith's Ripley is a man who despises himself but feels superior to others; he is capable of love but thwarted in his ability to express it because his love is "queer" and because he loathes himself: "He thought he had the world's dullest face, a thoroughly forgettable face with a look of docility that he could not understand, and also a look of vague fright that he had never been able to erase."⁷⁰ That "vague fright" seems to be a fear of his own sexuality; of course, the novel was published in 1955, when separating desire, a mental state, from its physical expression was a common option for homosexuals. Readers follow Ripley because they can't help but feel a kinship to something they have felt in their own worst moments taken to a violent, illogical conclusion. Highsmith's description of Ripley shopping could describe the typical postmodern American consumer: "Possessions reminded him that he existed, and made him enjoy his existence. It was as simple as that. And wasn't that worth something? He existed. Not many people in the world knew how to, even if they had the money."[71] Yet, in expressing and judging himself through elegant possessions, Tom Ripley joins the long list of elegant, sinister fictional queens.

Anthony Minghella's 1999 version of *The Talented Mr. Ripley* is actually the second film adapted from Highsmith's novel. In 1960, the French filmmaker René Clément made *Plein Soleil* (known in the United States as *Purple Noon*), starring the young, gorgeous Alain Delon as Tom Ripley. Clément's version manages to erase all traces of homosexuality, which, except for the Technicolor vision of Alain Delon, seems to remove eroticism from the film altogether. With charming Matt Damon in the title role, Anthony Minghella inevitably gives us a far more sympathetic and definitely gay Tom Ripley.[72]

Unlike the empty dilettante of the novel, this Tom is an accomplished, if unknown, classical pianist, though he supports himself as a men's room attendant at a concert hall. It is through music that Tom is able to ingratiate himself with jazz enthusiast Dickie and to charm classical conductor Peter. Peter's role is much more central in the film. As Minghella puts it, "Peter, the most centered character in the film"—actually, he's the only character in the film who has a successful career, and he's the least self-absorbed, as well (is this because he's an Englishman in a film written and directed by an Englishman?)—"also serves as a reminder that Ripley's pathology is not explained by his sexuality."[73] However much Minghella's caution at overt discussion or demonstration of Tom's homosexuality (wasn't Damon willing to kiss another man?) echoes the reticence of earlier filmmakers, he is careful to offer us in Peter a healthy gay man, and Peter's death is presented as Ripley's greatest tragedy. As Minghella puts it, "In killing Peter he murders his own chance of happiness."[74]

What makes happiness with Peter impossible is the appearance of Meredith Logue (Cate Blanchett) on the ship on which Tom and Peter are happily sailing to Athens. Meredith, a Minghella invention not to be found in Highsmith, is the first person Tom meets when he sets foot on European soil at the beginning of the film, and the first person to whom he claims to be Dickie Greenleaf. Facing this young socialite, the first of the American expatriate set he meets, Tom is too ashamed of his status as a nonentity to offer an honest introduction. It is clear, then, that Tom is looking for someone to *be* more than he is looking for someone to *love*. From the balcony of a hotel in Mongibello, the village where Dickie and Marge live, Tom catches his first glimpse of Dickie through binoculars while he practices his Italian:

> *Questo e la mia faccia.* . . . This is my face.
>   *The golden couple emerge from the sea. Dickie shakes off the water, grins.*
>   *Questa . . . e la mia faccia. Questa e la faccia di Dickie.* [That . . . is my face. That is Dickie's face.][75]

In a film filled with mirrors, Tom sees Dickie as the image of himself he wants. When Tom first walks onto the beach to encounter Dickie, he is chalk-white and wearing a hideous, ill-fitting lime-green knit bathing suit, a stark contrast to the stunning, lithe, golden brown Dickie. By the time Tom takes on Dickie's identity, he is blond, no longer pale, and appears totally self-possessed, as if wearing Dickie's clothes does indeed make the man.

The film's a kinder, more three-dimensional Marge (Gwyneth Paltrow), first feels protective of Tom and empathizes with his love for the charismatic Dickie. "The thing with Dickie," she explains, "it's like the sun shines on you and it's glorious, then he forgets you and it's very cold."[76] Marge can empathize with a man who also needs Dickie's attention. She points out that he isn't the first man Dickie has attracted, and (in a passage in the screenplay cut from the film) Peter tells Tom, "We all fell for [Dickie]. So easy to love, so hard to like."[77] Dickie is equally flirtatious with men and women, and for all his control and skill at winning Dickie's and Marge's friendship, the one thing Tom cannot hide is his desire for Dickie. In an extraordinarily erotic scene, Tom is playing chess with Dickie while Dickie sits naked in a bath. Tom cannot help looking a little too long at the beautiful, naked Dickie. Tom asks if he can get in the tub, and Dickie rebuffs him. Tom covers by saying, "I didn't mean with you in it." Dickie gets out of the tub, his naked form reflected in a mirror. "Ripley looks," the screenplay narrates, "then Dickie turns, holding his look momentarily before flicking him with his towel."[78] Clearly,

Dickie can enjoy being the object of desire as long as he doesn't have to reciprocate. On a train, Tom tries to rest his head on sleeping Dickie's chest, then tries to join their reflections in the window when Dickie wakes up and catches him. Tom can't accept that Dickie is indeed straight and cannot return his love: "The funny thing—*I'm* not pretending to be someone else and you are."[79] After he kills Dickie, Tom lies in the boat by Dickie's body for hours, "in the embrace he's always wanted" according to Minghella's screenplay.[80]

Tom wants to assume Dickie's things, but it is Meredith who forces him to take on Dickie's identity as well. Having introduced himself as Dickie, he is stuck when Meredith appears in Rome. In a sequence that verges on farce, Tom must simultaneously play Dickie to Meredith and Tom to Marge and Peter. When Meredith appears on the boat to Athens and clearly wants a relationship with "Dickie," Tom is trapped. Without the freedom of movement he has on land, he has to choose the safest— but not the happiest—course, which is to play out the deception to Meredith and eliminate Peter and, in the process, Tom Ripley. Unaware that Peter is watching, Tom (as Dickie) kisses Meredith. This is Tom's only kiss in the film and is, as Minghella points out in his commentary on the DVD version of the film, "a Judas kiss," promising the relationship with "Dickie" that she wants, but betraying himself in the process.

What makes Tom Ripley a sympathetic, even endearing, character in the film (beyond casting) is his anguished awareness of his own inner ugliness. He tells Peter:

> TOM: Don't you put the past in a room, in the cellar, and lock the door and just never go in there? Because that's what I do.
> PETER: Probably. In my case it's probably a whole building.
> TOM: Then you meet someone special and all you want to do is toss them the key, say *open up, step inside,* but you can't because it's dark and there are demons and if anybody saw how ugly it was . . . I keep wanting to do that—fling open the door—let the light in, clean everything out. If I could get a huge eraser and rub everything out . . . starting with myself.[81]

Here, at least in Minghella's version, is Tom Ripley's tragedy. Offered unqualified love, he can respond only with his fervent wish for self-annihilation. What redeems him is the wish to be able to accept Peter's love. At the same time, ironically, he is totally honest with Peter about how he sees himself. At the end, before killing him, he tells Peter that Meredith thinks he's Dickie, then admits his sense of entrapment: "I'm going to be stuck in the basement, aren't I, that's my, that's my—terrible and alone and dark—and I've lied about who I am and where I am so nobody can ever find me."[82]

Instead of seeing Tom Ripley kill Peter, we watch Tom's face as, alone in his stateroom, he remembers killing Peter. We hear Peter's cry of alarm, but more important, we hear Tom's loud sobs as he kills his one chance at being loved for himself. Half of Tom's face is in shadow, underscoring the sense of self-annihilation. We then see him from inside his closet, trapped in the center of the frame, as the mirrored closet door shuts and darkness envelops the screen. Tom has gotten away with murder, but he has also killed himself.

Maintaining the film's setting in the 1950s, Minghella has nevertheless presented what amounts to a gay love story, as well as a tale of the perils of self-hatred and of the closet. Minghella's Tom does not deny his sexuality to himself, as Highsmith's Tom does: Audiences of today might not accept or understand such a denial. Having chosen to play Dickie, he is trapped into playing Dickie's heterosexuality, which ensures his loneliness. Tom gets away with murder, but he doesn't get away with his sacrifice of his own identity. Though Tom fits some of the traditional stereotypes associated with gay men (artistic, sensitive, hungry for luxury, predatory), the film is set in a leisure-class milieu where conventional definitions of masculinity are irrelevant and sexuality seems potentially fluid. Is Dickie totally heterosexual or, as Tom believes, merely constrained by the taboos of his time? Isn't Freddie, quick to suspect an affair between Tom and Dickie when he is quick about little else, a bit queer himself? Above all, Minghella has revised the stereotype of the gay killer, putting the onus, as Odets to some extent did, on American materialism and heterosexism.

Chapter Six

SEX AND THE CITY

Nuts, Sluts, and Deadly Queers

"MY FAVORITE. MYSTERY MEAT."

In the first of the urban folk tales depicted in *Urbania* (2000; screenplay Daniel Reitz; direction, Jon Shear), Cassandra (Paige Turco), posing as a Wall Street commodities broker, picks up a handsome young business-man (Scott Denny) at a hot dog stand, where he is holding a particularly vile example of "mystery meat." The two begin their tryst in a taxicab and continue in a sleazy hotel. Cassandra ties her prey to the bed and proffers him drugged wine. A while later, he wakes up in a bathtub full of ice to discover that his kidney has been removed. The wage of sin, of sex, is, if not death, involuntary surgery.

Urbania presents the city as the setting for a raft of stories which demonstrate that "shit happens," often "when you thought you had it all under control." The film is a compendium of elements of the urban horror genre, in which the city is the site of chaos and violence. Earlier urban horror films, from pre-feminist, pre-gay liberation examples of the genre such as the Fritz Lang films *The Woman in the Window* and *While the City Sleeps* to more recent movies like *Looking for Mr. Good-bar* and *Fatal Attraction,* offered narratives meant to frighten their au-dience into staying within conventional sexual mores, particularly monogamous heterosexual marriage. In this chapter I want to examine

some of the films of sex, murder, and revenge in the city and the chang-
ing role of gay men in them. These urban melodramas are another site
of what some critics call "male masochism," in which a protagonist suffers for transgressing his domestic masculine role in a place where "natural" masculine authority is no longer pertinent. While women seem to
deserve their suffering for refusing to accept their assigned social role,
men are humiliated and defeated in a world gone awry because the old
white-male-created rules no longer apply. The reverse of these
masochistic narratives are the urban revenge films in which a man finally lashes out against those who would make him and his loved ones
suffer. As we shall see, there are straight and gay versions of these film
formulae.

The place of the gay man in these films is in itself a complex, fascinating narrative. *Urbania*'s protagonist is a gay man attempting to avenge
the brutal murder of his lover at the hands of an ostensibly straight sociopath, but many of the urban monsters Hollywood has given us are
straight-created gay men, symbols of the evils of sexual liberation. The
city is ther natural habitat.

1. Wayward Straights

"I WAS WARNED AGAINST THE SIREN CALL OF ADVENTURE"

The concept of the city as site of sexual license and violence has been
part and parcel of Hollywood mythology from the beginning. Heroes
like Sam Spade in *The Maltese Falcon* and Harry Callahan in the Dirty
Harry films knew how to avoid temptation and destruction at the hands
of loose women or gay men. What happens to the weaker vessels—men
who are not heroic? One common Hollywood morality play is the narrative of the innocent, innocuous man who is tempted into straying
from his conventional sexual path and falls into a nightmare scenario as
a result.

An example of this formula is Fritz Lang's 1944 classic, *The Woman
in the Window* (screenplay, Nunnally Johnson). Richard Wanley (Edward
G. Robinson in his later, genteel mode) is an assistant professor of psychology at a New York City university. His world is that of domestic con-

tentment with his sweet, dowdy wife, his young children, and his routine dinners at his club with his cronies (Robinson is obviously not dependent on his assistant professor's salary for his affluent surroundings). One night, after sending his wife and children off to Maine for a vacation and having one drink more than usual, Wanley expresses his male-menopausal feelings to his friends: "I hate this solidity, this stodginess I'm beginning to feel." Wanley yearns for some adventure, some break from the routine. His best friend, the district attorney, warns him of the serious consequences of middle-aged men heeding "the siren call of adventure." Later that evening, after a chance meeting with a beautiful woman whose portrait he has admired in a gallery window, Wanley follows the "siren call" his friend warned him against. An innocent drink in the woman's apartment turns Wanley into a cold-blooded killer hiding corpses in the woods and buying potentially fatal drugs to eliminate blackmailers.

Here and in Lang's 1945 companion film, *Scarlet Street,* the central figure is decidedly unglamorous. *The Woman in the Window* begins as something of a Walter Mitty fantasy. Even a short, pudgy, unattractive, bookish, middle-aged man might find himself invited home to a magnificently appointed apartment to drink champagne with a beautiful woman of easy virtue. (Actually, Alice Reed [Joan Bennett], the vamp in this film, seems to collect homely, fat, middle-aged men.) Alice has been the mistress of a temperamental tycoon who arrives suddenly on her doorstep and in a fit of jealous rage, tries to kill Wanley, who stabs the tycoon in self-defense and must then get rid of the body to avoid scandal. However hard he tries to cover his tracks, he leaves clues. Wanley's real problem in the film is that he must act to save himself through Alice, who, however well-intentioned, botches every plan the professor carefully, rationally makes. Women are dangerous, as always in film noirs, even when they try to do good. Wanley's friend, the district attorney, says at one point, "She's got something on her conscience, but what woman doesn't?" Women outside of their subordinate domestic role are dangerous, but it is the anonymity and moral relativism of the city that allows them to live unchecked by masculine authority. Professor Wanley's experience teaches one lesson: Follow a lone woman in the city and you enter a nightmare. The man loses his masculine authority, his manly attributes of rationality and physical strength become irrelevant, and he becomes entrapped.

Even moving to the suburbs does not save the man who has succumbed to temptation in the city. In *Fatal Attraction* (1987; screenplay: Basil Dearden and Nicholas Meyer; direction, Adrian Lyne) happily married New York lawyer Dan Gallagher (Michael Douglas) sends his wife and daughter off for a weekend in the country, as Richard Wanley does in *The Woman in the Window,* and finds himself, after a few too many drinks, succumbing to the temptation of a roll in the hay with a seductive blonde with the androgynous name Alex (Glenn Close). "Are you discreet?" Alex asks. *She* sure isn't! At first, Alex seems willing to settle for a quick no strings fling, but by the next afternoon she is slashing her wrists in a hyper-needy, hyper-mad act to make Dan spend another night with her. Soon she is calling, visiting Dan's wife, boiling Dan's daughter's pet bunny, kidnapping said daughter, and, in the film's original noir ending (not the slasher-movie ending in the final version), framing Dan for her death.

Much has been written about the paranoid vision of women the film offers, but little has been said about its hero. A good, happily married man, according to *Fatal Attraction,* cannot resist the temptation of a forthright, sexually available woman. When Alex hints at the possibility of sex, Dan responds, "I definitely think it's going to be up to you," putting all the power into her hands. This reads as the response of a gentleman unwilling to make sexual overtures, but by surrendering his authority and control, he is also asking for trouble. Other than the weekend fling with Alex, Dan's actions and reactions are those of a decent man wanting to get back to his life without hurting anyone. However, according to the film, one can't reason with a needy, emotionally disturbed woman, and Dan, being a man, is incapable of coping with the unscrupulousness of a bad woman. In the final ending of the film, it takes another woman, Dan's wife, to kill Alex once and for all.

One can read the misadventures of Richard Wanley and Dan Gallagher as the wages of sin. They are also tales of male victimization. Wanley suffers mainly at the hands of violent or unscrupulous men—Alice Reed's violent lover and the blackmailer who has the power to destroy him. Dan Gallagher's only foe is a woman, and Dan does not have the physical or mental tools to vanquish a mad, unscrupulous foe like Alex Forrest. In the age of feminism, men are the victims of powerful women (Alex has a good job while Dan's wife seems to be a housewife).

"ALL I WANT TO DO IS GET HOME!"

Martin Scorsese's *After Hours* (1985, screenplay, Joseph Minion) is a well-crafted example of the urban nightmare film, a sort of heterosexual *Alice in Wonderland* set in Lower Manhattan. At its core is the formula of traditional farce. Its protagonist, Paul Hackett (Griffin Dunne), a cute, meek little word processor, just wants to get laid. A young woman in a coffee shop, Marcy (Rosanna Arquette), notices that he's reading Henry Miller's masterpiece of high-class erotica, *Tropic of Cancer,* and begins a conversation. This seems to be Paul's life: working in a Madison Avenue cubicle all day and reading erotica alone in a coffee shop at night. Marcy can quote Henry Miller and pals around with SoHo artists, sure signs of sexual availability. Loneliness and lust lead Paul downtown, far away from his safe, sterile Upper West Side apartment, into an urban nightmarescape filled with the sorts of symbolic repetitions that dreams are made of. The constant in this narrative is the madness and aggression of women who want simultaneously to entrap and destroy men and to be victimized by them. Marcy seems to be in a sadomasochistic relationship with a sculptress, Kiki (Linda Fiorentino), who also shows an interest in Paul, but who is later seen tied up at the mercy of her boyfriend, a German sadist. Marcy tells stories of being raped by her boyfriend and sends out mixed sexual signals. When Paul runs out of her apartment, she kills herself. An overly needy waitress tries to keep Paul in her rat-infested apartment and later puts up flyers claiming Paul is a burglar. A female driver of a Mr. Softee (what better image of sexual anxiety?) ice-cream truck leads a mob of gay vigilantes against Paul. Finally, another sculptress imprisons Paul inside a shell of papier maché, turning him into a human sculpture. The straight men Paul meets along the way are eccentric, but not as menacing as the women or the gay men hunting Paul down. Throughout, homosexuals are either exotic scenery (two leathermen making out at a bar) or terrifying pursuers. "All I want to do is get home," Paul keeps crying, like Dorothy in *The Wizard of Oz,* but SoHo is a maze he can't escape.

After Hours is an amusing picture of straight male anxiety, less nasty and more enjoyable than, say, David Mamet's *Oleanna,* but Scorsese presents this picture of the straight male under siege without irony. Paul looks out a window to watch a married couple copulating. Later, through the same window, he watches the wife put multiple bullets into her husband's torso. The city at night, when one is let out of the gates of one's orderly workplace, is a chaotic welter of disturbed and disturbing people where a guy's libido could lead him into fatal situations. Here again is the city as a site where sexual permissiveness and perversion seem to have won out, even though, in the formula of classic farce, our hero never gets laid. The real problem is that women and gay men rule here. The straight man is prey.

There's a strongly masochistic aspect to *After Hours,* and its slapstick farce becomes serious hurt. Paul's body is constantly threatened: by fire (does Marcy, who has books on burns and burn ointment intend to burn Paul with the candle she brings in to her bedroom during their abortive tryst?), cuts, bodily harm, death by the angry mob, and finally encasement in papier-mâché. The film offers us a vision of what Sally Robinson calls "white masculinity in crisis," positioning the man as a victim rather than as the holder of the unquestioned power of white, heterosexual masculinity. Paul suffers because he finds himself in an environment in which his assumed position in class (he's always in a white business suit), ethnic (two Latinos, played by the seventies countercultural comics Cheech and Chong, operate mysteriously on the streets and ultimately carry the immobilized Paul away) and gender hierarchy is irrelevant. Throughout, Paul cannot understand why people aren't behaving according to his expectations, why his logic isn't shared, why he must suffer. At the end, still covered in white plaster, Paul goes through the giant gates of his office building and back into his advertising agency, filled with straight white men like himself.

2. Loose Women and Murderous Gays

The threat in classic American urban film noirs was the vamp, a woman playing by what she thought were men's rules, but with the added weapons of stereotypical feminine temptation and amorality. In the early years of sexual liberation, the vamp, the sexually transgressive urban woman who refused to play her proper domestic role, became in Hollywood narratives the victim of the urban sexual chaos into which she had placed herself. In films like Richard Brooks's *Looking for Mr. Goodbar* (1977) or Alan J. Pakula's *Klute* (1971) the vamp, no longer deadly, uses men for her own sexual pleasure and empowerment, though this transgression of the gender order must still be punished. As radically as in the domestic melodramas I discussed in the previous chapter, the sexually transgressive language of the woman is silenced.

In *Looking for Mr. Goodbar,* the danger to the sexually liberated woman is not the straight men she encounters but that denizen of urban dark corners, the gay psychopath, who finds the city a perfect hiding place. From the McCarthy era menace to the pretty-boy killer of *Looking for Mr. Goodbar,* his persona didn't change much.

"HE'S EXACTLY LIKE A LITTLE GIRL, ISN'T HE?"

Take, for instance, the twenty-year-old serial killer in Fritz Lang's *While the City Sleeps* (1956, screenplay, Casey Robinson). Clad in a leather jacket and Levi's, Robert Manners (John Drew Barrymore) could be one of Marlon Brando's buddies in *The Wild One,* but we discover that he lives with his doting mother and is going through a gender-identity crisis. When he confronts his mother with the comment she'd lovingly made about him when he was younger, "He's exactly like a little girl, isn't he," she responds, "You are my son—and my daughter." Mom's aspersions on her son's masculinity propel him toward a life of crime that begins with stealing "ladies' things," then escalates to killing young women. In one instance, he wrote on the wall of his victim's apartment, "Ask Mother." In 1950s America, the kind of hyper-emotionalism Barrymore displays—he seems to be doing an eyeball-rolling imitation of Peter Lorre in *M,* Lang's 1931 masterpiece about a child murderer—would have been considered effeminate, if not overtly homosexual. A film of this period could do no more than hint at a villain's sexuality, but Robert is called a "mama's boy," an assault to his deficient masculinity, which in the nineteen fifties was a step on the slippery slope that led to homosexuality. He is the progenitor of the ultimate cinematic mama's boy, *Psycho's* Norman Bates, and the gay killers of films like *Looking for Mr. Goodbar.*

This killer is a creature of the city, knowing how and where to hide above and below ground, but so are the other men in the film, some of whom are at least ambiguously gay: the ineffectual, cuckolded heir to a newspaper empire, played by Vincent Price with his usual hint of mint, and the ambitious, scheming head of the wire service, played by George Sanders, trying unsuccessfully to temper his customary cynical-old-queen act. Only the hero, played by Dana Andrews, veteran of noir classics like *Laura,* is "all man" in the tradition of stolid Hollywood leading men. Only he is capable of figuring out that the killer is a sissy and of hunting him down in and under the city.

"I'M NO GODDAMN NELLIE!"

Looking for Mr. Goodbar was a highly sensational take on the dire fate that can befall a sexually liberated woman. Its heroine might be able to elude the crazy straight men in her life, but she cannot avoid the wild card of urban melodrama, the murderous queer. Richard Brooks's adaptation of Judith Rossner's best-selling novel offers a typical example of how Hollywood treated homosexuals in the 1970s.[1] In the urban post-liberation sexual playground of *Looking for Mr. Goodbar,* the homosexual is no longer recognizable by stereotypical weakness and effeminacy. He's butch, handsome, and, when he takes off his drag, can pass as straight (see fig. 10). Strangely, he poses a far greater danger than straight men, a notion crime statistics aren't likely to support.

Theresa Dunn (Diane Keaton) moves from her strict Catholic, patriarchal home to the center of the city, the tenderloin area where sex shops and singles bars proliferate. She moves into town to escape her domineering Irish Catholic father (Richard Kiley), a living argument against traditional patriarchy, and to be near her sister, Katherine (Tuesday Weld), who is in a swinging marriage complete with porn movies, drugs, and ménages à trois. Having had her first sexual experience with a predatory, caddish professor (is there any other kind in films of this ilk?), Terry decides to enjoy sex, drugs, and rock and roll while remaining free from men's power. The men Terry meets have other ideas, and the film turns into a nightmare scenario as Terry tries to elude straight men who attempt to possess her: the seemingly gentle James (William Atherton), who wants to be her husband and the father of her children and who obsessively stalks her, and the manic, knife-wielding Tony (Richard Gere), who threatens her with violence. Terry copes with the crazy straight men who want to dominate her, but she is done in by the gay psychopath, Gary (Tom Berenger). Gary has been released from prison for some unnamed act of violence and comes to the city for a place to stay and someone to support him. We first see him kissing an older bearded man in the bar Terry frequents. Are he and this man already lovers, or is Gary putting the moves on this man for money and a place to stay? On the night of Terry's death, Gary, dressed in drag for a New Year's Eve parade, is assaulted by gay bashers, which sends him into homosexual panic. "I'm no goddamn nellie!" he screams at his lover, adding, "We're a couple of freaks." He then runs off to Terry's singles bar, where we see him snorting drugs and playing pinball. Terry asks him to talk with her so that she can elude James, but when Gary goes home with Terry and cannot perform sexually, he freaks out, interpreting her every comment as an attack on his masculinity. She asks him to leave, which he refuses to do. Finally, in strobe light, we watch in gruesome detail his murder of Terry.

Looking for Mr. Goodbar gives us a grim panoply of men that would turn Ally McBeal into a lesbian. All of Terry's dysfunctional pursuers—redheaded Atherton, brunet Gere, and blond Berenger—are good-looking. They just happen to be crazy. But that's what you get when you move into the city and give up your proper feminine role. "I don't want marriage or kids," Terry screams at James. "I don't believe in the future." And, like most fallen women in popular cultural constructions, she is denied a future. But the catalog of nasty men *Looking for Mr. Goodbar* offers also suggests that the sexual revolution has eliminated the possibility of finding the sort of man who would be a good husband, if he ever existed at all. He might be somewhere, but he certainly isn't in the city.

"NOT INTENDED AS AN INDICTMENT OF THE HOMOSEXUAL WORLD."

If there is one gay psychopath out there in *While the City Sleeps* and *Looking for Mr. Goodbar, Cruising* (1980, screenplay and direction, William Friedkin) posits that coming out as a gay man in New York places one in a milieu filled with real and potential killers. In this bizarre mess of a film, sexual violence is everywhere, including in the police department. Policemen corrupted by the urban jungle hate women ("They're all scumbags"), force drag queens to provide oral sex in squad cars, and, in a couple of unintentionally hilarious scenes, bring a giant, scantily clad black sadist into an interrogation room to beat up recalcitrant suspects. They also find the time to pursue a serial killer who is murdering gay men in the leather community in downtown New York. All the police know is that the victims had sex with the murderer and that his semen has a zero sperm count—however virile a leather queen may appear, he's clearly not "all man." Steve Burns (Al Pacino, who once played a bisexual bank robber in *Dog Day Afternoon*) has been chosen to infiltrate the leather bars and find the killer, who turns out to be a graduate student writing a thesis on the origins of the American musical theater (!). Unlike in *Klute* and *Looking for Mr. Goodbar,* there are no female victims in *Cruising,* only a protagonist who succumbs to the sexual chaos into which he is placed to restore order.

While looking for this murderous leather-clad show queen, Steve, working undercover as a leatherman, goes through a personality crisis. He has a girlfriend, but he tells her, early in the film, "There's a lot about me you don't know." He stares, wide-eyed, at the sexual free-for-all of the leather bars he visits. He becomes friends with his neighbor Ted (Don Scardino), a gay playwright (*Cruising* suggests that all gay men in New York are in the theater). Ted exists in the script to show that there are nice gay men who aren't into leather or murder, but he has a violent roommate (James Remar). Friedkin's view of gay men and gay relationships hadn't changed much in the ten years since he'd made the film of *The Boys in the Band.* Like Richard Brooks, he's willing to offer a prurient view of homosexuality, but he is a creature of Hollywood who will always follow the party line on homosexuality and sexual morality.

During the early days of his infiltration of the leather bars, Steve's relationship with his girlfriend becomes fraught and he asks his superiors to take him off the case: "Something's happening to me," he says, "There's stuff going down. I don't think I can handle it." We're never told exactly what he can't handle, but he seems attracted to the sexuality and ritualized violence of the leather culture and S&M bars and clubs. At the end of the film Steve finds and stabs the killer show queen and is promoted to detective. At his promotion, he says to his superior, "I appreciate the chance you gave me." Was it the chance to enter this violent, alternative world he appreciates? He's still got his leather gear at the end, and it is intimated that he, too, has become a killer.

The opening title tells us that *Cruising* is "not intended as an indictment of the homosexual world." I love that term—"homosexual world," as if gay people literally live in a world apart from the "heterosexual world." We are also told later that the leathermen are "not in the mainstream of gay life." The film is part of the continuum of cautionary tales of urban sexual freedom. If the gay leather community is presented as an extreme (Scorsese presented leathermen as part of the bizarre urban landscape in *After Hours*), it is both potentially deadly and alluring. These men, after all, look masculine and Steve Burns seems drawn to that hypermasculinity. The "homosexual world" may be macho, but it's also lethal. As Vito Russo put it, "The audience is left with the message that homosexuality is not only contagious, but inescapably brutal."[2] In urban melodramas non-marital sex of any sort often is brutal and leads to violence. In *Cruising,* as elsewhere, homosexuality is presented as the nadir of the city's depravities.

3. Whores

If the city is a sexual marketplace, the prostitute is the most vivid sign of the commodification of urban sex and the dangers of becoming a commodity. And yet, sexual availability with no consequences has always been alluring. It is not surprising, then, that the person paid for sex has been an object of fascination in popular culture from Dumas's *The Lady of the Camellias* (best known to film audiences as the Garbo film *Camille*), to Elizabeth Taylor's call girl in *Butterfield 8,* to Jodie Foster's young prostitute in *Taxi Driver,* to Jane Fonda's Bree Daniel in *Klute* and her male counterpart, Richard Gere's Julian Kaye in *American Gigolo.* Gay filmmakers, too, have looked with fascination at hustlers. Yet most recent films that center on prostitutes focus on their illusion of power over the customers who pay them, and on their vulnerable lives and the danger of their position. Which is to say that these, too, are moral fables that end ,in their heterosexual versions, in their protagonists forsaking their careers for loving, monogamous relationships.

"FOR AN HOUR, I'M THE BEST ACTRESS IN THE WORLD AND THE BEST FUCK IN THE WORLD."

Alan Pakula's 1971 film, *Klute* (screenplay, Andy and Dave Lewis) is a corrective parable for the sexually liberated seventies. In the course of a missing-person investigation, John Klute (Donald Sutherland), a dour, straight-laced private detective from a small town in Pennsylvania, travels to New York City and meets and becomes obsessed with a call girl, Bree Daniel. Klute is the 1970s version of the stolid hero once played by actors like Gary Cooper—though the chivalric heroes of pre-sexual liberation films seldom went to bed with the women they rescued. The camera lingers on close-ups of Klute's sad face as he watches, with pain, the sordid scenes the city offers him and listens to Bree's X-rated phone calls. Though the investigator would, in traditional film noirs, be the central consciousness and narrator, grim, silent Klute (what must he be like in bed?) comes out of the world of westerns, not Dashiell Hammett.

Though Klute is the title character, we hear much more from Bree, as we are privy to her two voices: the telephone voice of the call girl enticing a john and the troubled voice of Bree confiding in her therapist. Bree's professional voice is that of the sexual swinger. In her tape-recorded voice, heard under the titles, we hear her mantra, which sounds like the epitome of seventies sexual philosophy:

> You should never be ashamed of things like that [wanting kinky sex]. There's nothing wrong. Nothing is wrong. I think that the only way any of us can ever be happy is to let it all hang out. Do it all and fuck it.

Bree's hedonism is rooted in a deep cynicism: "Don't feel bad about losing your virtue," she says to Klute after they have had sex, "I always knew that you would. Everybody always does." According to *Klute* and its ilk, this is the law of the city. No one is good. The villain is a solid family man whose heretofore repressed impulse toward sexual violence is allowed to flourish when he leaves his small town for this fallen urban world.

Bree is a call girl in part because she hasn't succeeded as an actress or model, but more because, as she says, "It made me feel like I had some control over myself, some control over my life." In the first scene after the titles, we see the world over which Bree and other women *don't* have control. A group of women sit in chairs against a giant Abstract Expressionist mural as a male casting agent and his female assistant audibly and deprecatorily assess the physical attributes of each woman. We can see how a person such as Bree could think that if a woman is going to be treated as a piece of meat, she might as well profit from it. Yet her defensiveness with her therapist suggests that Bree is not as confident as she seems—that she might yet be "saved" from her life of sin.

As Bree finds herself falling in love with quiet, decent, emotionally constipated John Klute, she feels the need to sabotage that love by going back to her old, allegedly self-controlled life as a prostitute. Clearly, though, Bree's sense of control over men, even over her own professional life, is both illusory and dangerous. Her fellow call girls become drug addicts, turning tricks for the addicts they love, or are murdered. Bree is pursued by a murderer from whom Klute must rescue her in the nick of time. For all its daring presentation of a world of sexual freedom where anything goes, even S&M, *Klute* comes down squarely on the side of a woman's traditional place in the home, under the solemn eye of a decent man. At the end of the film, Bree, oddly silent, prepares to move to Klute's small-town world. There will be no need for her telephonic skills in the world to which she is moving—or will there be? While there is some question whether she will be able to stand her conventional life there (the story of Bree in a small Pennsylvania town would have to be written by Sinclair Lewis or Grace Metalious), the film suggests that she *should* be content with her new conventional domestic arrangement. She *should* give up her desire for control and follow her man. Above all, she *should* escape from New York City, dirty and deadly, which in *Klute* is a metaphor for sexual liberation.

The portrait of Bree and the narrative of her relationship with Klute is set within a fairly routine and not totally credible murder mystery played at a glacial pace. What made *Klute* a success is that it gave us a seventies version of the whore with the heart of gold in a film as conservative in its own way as *Camille;* and, like *Camille,* it offered the prurient thrills of sexual depravity with a corrective fable. *Klute* ends with the open question of whether sexual autonomy is possible for a liberated woman in the city. Perhaps today Bree Daniel would be a comfortable addition to the women on *Sex and the City.* Where would John Klute be?

"FOR AN HOUR, I'LL BE ANYTHING YOU WANT ME TO BE."

Ben Taylor's *In the Flesh* (1997), an independent film made in Atlanta, gives us a gay version of *Klute.* Twenty-one-year-old Oliver Beck (Dane Ritter) comes from a highly dysfunctional middle-class family in which, it is hinted, he was sexually abused. Like many southern gay boys, he has escaped to Atlanta for the sexual freedom it offers, but Oliver is conflicted about the life he wants to lead. By day, he is a closeted college student majoring in business and psychology and working at a record store. (The biggest gap in credibility in the film is why Oliver is closeted in *très* gay Atlanta, where thousands of gay southern boys go to be out.) At midnight, he is a hustler working out of the Blue Boy, a seedy bar where boys rent themselves to older men by the hour. Oliver seems out of place among the poor, shabby, tough runaways who rightfully think he's arrogant. He's there because he needs a source of drugs for his heroin-addicted sister, but also because he finds in hustling a power and order he finds nowhere else. Hustling is being "in charge." It also allows Oliver the chance to share another's fantasy, which is easier to deal with than his own reality: "For an hour, I'll be anything you want me to be. You just have to use your imagination."

Enter Philip Kirsch (Ed Corbin, instructed, according to writer-director Ben Taylor's comments on the DVD, to play Philip like John Klute), a sad-looking, deeply closeted policeman assigned to investigate drug trafficking at the Blue Boy. A former poster boy of conventional masculinity, a college football star who married a cheerleader—"Did the whole trip. Hated every minute of it"—Philip, who "hasn't been with anybody in so long I don't remember what it feels like," can't take his eyes off Oliver and makes the professional mistake of hiring him for an hour, which only increases his obsession. As in *Klute,* the romance of Oliver and Philip proceeds within a conventional and not totally credible murder mystery, but Oliver is an interestingly drawn character, wanting the love and friendship Philip can offer, but finding it terrifying. At one point, when Oliver offers Philip sex, Philip responds that what he really wants is a moment of holding Oliver. "Holding me!" Oliver responds. "Oh, man! Couldn't we just fuck instead?" Oliver, whose sense of self-worth is nil, ("I'm nothing but a slice of ass, and you're the only one too stupid not to know it"), cannot accept love and runs back to the world of the Blue Boy: "Everything's a lot easier when you know it's not real. But this shit! I don't know how to deal with it." The film offers a tentative reconciliation between Philip and Oliver, then cuts to a final image of the inside of the Blue Boy, as if to suggest that this world of young hustlers will go on without Oliver and still exert its attraction, in contrast to the relationship of Oliver and Philip, which has mainly been depicted in Atlanta's Piedmont Park. Oliver and Philip do guy things—play soccer and fix cars—and Philip wants a buddy as much as a lover. It's the guy stuff that will ultimately save Oliver.

If *In the Flesh* echoes *Klute,* it does so without the moralizing. Whatever relationship will be established between Oliver and Philip (wisely, the film does not suggest that Oliver has been miraculously cured of his hang-ups), it will not be the conventional small-town marriage *Klute* ends with—these guys are gay, after all, and not about to leave Hotlanta—but more of a friendship.[3] *In the Flesh* is no masterpiece, but it does offer an interesting gay rethinking of the classic Hollywood whore story.

Filmmakers like Ben Taylor are interested in hustlers for the same reason some straight filmmakers are fascinated with teenage prostitutes. It's the idea of innocence corrupted, of sexually available youngsters, of sexual allure combined with corrective fable. Scott Silver's *Johns* (1996), grittier, less romantic than *In the Flesh,* is supposedly a fictional collage spun from the real experiences of Los Angeles street hustlers (Silver made documentaries before *Johns*). At the center of the film is the friendship between John (David Arquette) and Donner (Lukas Haas), as it plays out over one Christmas Eve, which is also the eve of John's twenty-first birthday. John is a veritable torrent of talk, a con man whose cons never work, a dreamer who believes that he's "going to be a big fucking star one of these days" but will settle for one night at a fancy hotel. He would love to be independent and invulnerable, but instead is a walking disaster area. In the course of one day he is robbed, stabbed, beaten up, and has his clothes ruined. When the adoring Donner claims friendship, John goes ballistic and starts hitting him: "I'm not your fucking friend. I don't have friends." John soon apologizes and promises to leave town with Donner, who dreams of a trip to Branson, Missouri, the capital of family entertainment. While John does tricks for money, he can't deal with real hetero- or homosexual emotions or desire. The film begins with John being robbed of money and shoes while he sleeps in a park; it ends with his brutal murder in a motel room at the hands of a sick trick. The life of the basically sweet, ill-kempt kids in *Johns* is anything but glamorous, but they didn't choose to be there. Donner comes from a wealthy family but was disowned by his father for being gay. These kids are on the street because there is nowhere else for them. The film is named for the hustlers' clients, who could care less for the well-being of these kids, who are simply commodities in an urban sexual marketplace. Any attempt on John's part to explain his predicament to his johns—his lack of shoes, his hunger, his frustration—falls on deaf ears.

"I DON'T DO FAGS."

Julian Kaye (Richard Gere), in Paul Schrader's *American Gigolo* (1980), is on the classy high end of male prostitution in Los Angeles. He may have come out of the same milieu as the young men in *Johns,* but he would never admit it. Far from the gritty realism of *Johns* or the gay romantic fantasy of *In the Flesh,* even farther from the sympathetic treatment of homosexual desire those films offer, *American Gigolo* is another morality play, a corrective tale of what happens to a man who doesn't know his place in the gender order. If an intelligent, articulate woman like Bree Daniel needs to be silenced and rescued by a man, and removed from the city that allows her freedom to role-play and live out her desire for a modicum of power over men, what happens to a man who places himself in the position of being the object of a woman's sexual gaze and who lives to service women? Any masculine power Julian asserts is pure illusion; he becomes dependent on women and—worse, by the film's values—a black gay man. Like classic gangster movies such as *Little Caesar, American Gigolo* is the depiction of the fall of a man from an illusory position of power and material security. As in *Little Caesar,* the hero's rise and fall are shown through the changes in his clothing and material possessions. Like a Warner Bros. gangster, Julian sees himself as above the law, of which he is disdainful. "Men make laws," he asserts. "Sometimes they're wrong. Stupid. Or jealous." At the end, Julian is saved by the devotion of a woman. While a heterosexual viewer might see Julian as redeemed by his maturity into heterosexual love, a gay viewer can share the skepticism some of the film's characters express about Julian's heterosexuality and see Julian's downfall as the result of his own homophobia.

As Paul Burston points out, Julian "exists in what was in 1980 an identifiably gay world. It is a world of sun-kissed bodies and swimming pools, of pastel interiors and micro-blinds. It is the world revealed in the paintings of gay artist David Hockney."[4] However, the film identifies Julian's chic West Hollywood apartment, his tasteful collection of ceramics and paintings, his perfect haircut and beautiful clothes, to say nothing of his attention to his body—conventional gay traits—as heterosexual attributes. Gay people are identified by tacky decor. In the film's iconography, Julian's high-class pimp, Anne (Nina Van Pallandt), an elegant blonde who looks very much like the heroine, Michelle (Lauren Hutton), lives in a lovely beachfront home, while Leon (Bill Duke), the pimp who wants Julian to do "fag tricks," is a very dark-skinned African American who can be found in gay bars or his gaudy apartment. When Julian finds himself at Leon's mercy, he descends from his gorgeous Mercedes to a plain rental car, from his Italian clothes to what look like work clothes. Exactly when he looks most straight to a gay viewer, we are to see him in the clutches of a gay villain and willing to go back to "fag tricks" to survive. Toward the end, after Julian has accidentally killed Leon, we see him sitting despondently on Leon's garish, glow-in-the-dark sofa. In a film in which even prisons are carefully color-coordinated (there's a scene in which Hutton's outfit perfectly matches the walls of the prison interview room), the bad taste displayed in gay milieus defines their otherness. Or does Leon have bad taste because he is black or a pimp?

Throughout the film, Julian is insistent that he won't "do fags," but we know this wasn't always the case. When he goes to negotiate with Anne, who, like Leon, is angered by Julian's diva behavior, he tells her that if she doesn't like his terms, she "can keep dealing with those retarded faggots who've got no class." "Look who's talking," she responds. Since he certainly acts like he has class and doesn't seem retarded, she must be referring to his sexual orientation. His relationship with Leon suggests that he was not always above "doing fags." Leon says, ironically, "I forgot. You've got scruples now."

For Julian, the ultimate arriviste, moving beyond fags is moving up the ladder of class. Julian is above all a snob, a dangerous thing for a prostitute to be. In one of the first transactions we see, Julian must act as the chauffeur for a rich widow. It is only after he is properly servile that she becomes sexually interested in him. He may be able to escort rich women to galleries and to make learned pronouncements on antiques, but he shouldn't forget that he is his clients' dirty little secret. Julian's allure is built on mystery, on making sure no one knows anything about him. "Anything worth knowing about me, you can learn by making love to me," he tells Michelle, the senator's wife who falls in love with him. But Michelle knows the truth: "When you make love," she laments, "you go to work." Sex, for Julian, is a performance, not an act of intimacy. His pride is in his prowess to bring women to orgasm. He never suggests that sex is enjoyable for him, but insists that he is doing an important service: "Who else would have taken the time or cared enough to do it right?" He wants to be a free agent because he thinks he is the best at what he does and because he has developed the appearance of class so well that he is allowed in all the most fashionable places. However, Julian constantly oversteps his position—with his pimps, with the police, eventually with at least one of his wealthy clients. His ambiguous role in the gender order foils him at every turn.

Am I saying that Julian is gay? I agree with Paul Burston that *American Gigolo* is "noteworthy (if not exactly unique) for the extent to which it actively courts that which it seeks to deny,"[5] the homosexuality of its central character. While surrounding Julian with attributes of gayness, Schrader works hard to make us believe he is straight. The most telling moment is the one in which Julian escorts a wealthy client to an auction. Julian is perfectly dressed and impressively knowledgeable about the materials on auction, but anyone who knows anything about the handsome young paid escorts of wealthy women—and who could take Julian as anything but a paid escort?—knows that they are likely to be gay, and expertise in antiques is almost a gay stereotype. When the woman is afraid of being "caught" by an acquaintance, Julian acts the role of a flaming German queen. The homosexual he plays is loud, tasteless, and totally clumsy around delicate antiques. In order to make Julian convincingly not gay, Schrader has Gere pretend to be a gay man who is decidedly not like Julian. Straights may buy this exoneration through stereotype, but it is Julian who seems like an obnoxious, piss-elegant queen.

Julian doesn't have to be gay to be in a fragile position in the gender order. He is, after all, an ornament, a boy toy. At the film's most famous moment, he appears totally nude, posed like the subject of a classic photograph or painting. As an object of display—as a sex object—Julian is not presented in a typical masculine way. Moreover, as Peter Lehman points out, "Julian is a prostitute, practicing a profession identified almost exclusively with women. He places extraordinary emphasis on fashion; his closet is full of beautiful clothes. Perhaps most significantly, he is a victim who has to be saved at the end of the film—by a woman."[6] In other words, Julian transgresses the gender order by not behaving according to the codes of masculinity. Bree in *Klute,* rebelling against conventional feminine roles, had to be saved by a man—conventional heterosexuality—from her life as a prostitute and from possible death. Julian has to be saved from prison and potential death by a woman, Michelle, willing to give him a false alibi. When she comes to prison to talk about her "sacrifice" (she no longer matches the decor, by the way), Julian says, "My God, Michelle. It has taken me so long to come to you," and organ music swells in the background as Julian bows his head against the glass partition separating the two. This moment of Julian's conversion to his proper role in a domestic couple is presented as his salvation. Never mind that this film is much more about money and class than it is about religion, or that Michelle has lost her marriage and her meal ticket and seems far too vapid to be able to support herself, or that Julian has seemingly forsaken the one job he is good at. How will these two live? Suddenly, in a film devoted to materialism, we're to buy a spiritual renewal. The bleak, conditional ending of *Klute* is far more credible. What does Julian see in Michelle, who is obsessed enough with him to stalk him? She is written as a cipher. Are we to believe he loves her because she is the one woman who has demeaned herself for him, thus proving herself worthy of him? Schrader seems to be saying that Julian has managed to "rise above" homosexuality, through suffering and humiliation and through the selfless devotion of a good woman.

4. Macho Revenge

If the urban villain is gay or gay-acting, the urban hero is, like John Klute, a virtuous outsider, not part of the city; or a hardened loner, like Humphrey Bogart's Sam Spade in *The Maltese Falcon;* or the classic conservative icon of masculinity in the city, Harry Callahan, as seen in director Don Siegel's *Dirty Harry* (1971; screenplay, Harry Julian Fink, Rita M. Fink, Dean Riesner, and [uncredited] John Milius). Policeman Harry Callahan (Clint Eastwood) strides down San Francisco's Market Street, his mouth filled with symbolic hot dog, and shoots down black bank robbers. As he tries to find a serial killer who rapes and kills young women, Harry sees sexual activity in just about every window (as in old-fashioned porn, there are lots of naked women here and no naked men). Scorpio (Andrew Robinson), the vicious serial killer Harry must track down, is a blond, androgynous-looking, hyper-emotional crypto-gay character. On an empty football field at night, the battle of positive and negative masculine images is played out: stolid, impassive Harry, the real man, against emotional, effeminate Scorpio. Once the battle moves out of the city, where effeminate serial killers and sex offenders can hide, and into an abandoned quarry, the real man rules and Scorpio is vanquished. Harry is, like the western hero, a loner, outside of heterosexual relationships (in a later sequel, he has an Asian American girlfriend who is gunned down), but a protector of women. In the next Dirty Harry film, *Magnum Force* (1973; screenplay, John Milius and Michael Cimino; direction, Ted Post), Harry has to save the San Francisco police force from a cell of fascist homosexual officers, so the series moves from a homosexual-acting killer menacing women and schoolchildren to straight-acting homosexual murderers infiltrating the police. The homos have gotten deadlier since Sam Spade slapped them around in *The Maltese Falcon,* and the heroes depend more on their guns than their wits. Harry Callahan, like Sam Spade, is a sadist, but he's got a bigger gun.

Critic Pauline Kael noted the danger of the vigilantism celebrated in Harry Callahan's off-duty pursuit of the killer in *Dirty Harry,* but Hollywood has always celebrated the lone hero who operates outside the mores and institutions of organized society. At least Harry's role as a policeman gave him some sanction for his heroic acts. The hero of later urban night-mares is the civilian operating outside the law to avenge personal wrongs. This is the only heroic action open to ordinary men in a bureaucratic so-ciety in which the police are either corrupt or ineffectual. How can one emulate John Wayne in the city?

"IF WE'RE NOT PIONEERS, WHAT ARE WE?"

In *Death Wish* (1974; screenplay, Wendell Mayes; direction, Michael Winner), an urban saga so successful that it spawned four increasingly tacky sequels, Paul Kersey (Charles Bronson) is a middle-aged New York City real estate developer with good 1970s liberal sentiments—a former conscientious objector, he is all for gun control—until his wife is killed and his daughter traumatized by a brutal rape in the Kerseys' apartment. Sensitized by his family tragedy, Paul now sees that the city is a playground for criminals, on which the police are powerless (too bad Dirty Harry Callahan is out in San Francisco). On a business trip to Tucson, Arizona, Paul has an epiphany in a theme-park simulacrum of a Wild West town: Bad guys should be shot down in New York City the way they were in the mythical West. His Tucson host takes him to a gun club and, as a parting gift, gives Paul a pistol. "This is gun coun-try," he tells Paul. "Unlike your city, we can walk our streets and our parks [sic]." When Paul returns to New York City, he becomes a one-man police force, gunning down anyone he sees committing a crime. "If the police don't defend us," he tells his wimpy son-in-law, "we have to defend ourselves." If Paul just disarmed the assailants he encounters, the film's unquestioning acceptance of his one-man campaign against crime might be acceptable, but, in Wild West - style, Paul shoots each malefactor until he is dead. The publicity surrounding Paul's vigilan-tism inspires other New Yorkers to defend themselves. The police want Paul to stop his activities, but they don't want to arrest him. He has, after all, lowered the crime rate (that is, unless you consider his mur-ders crimes).

Once Paul Kersey's nice, middle-class, heterosexual family is de-stroyed, the film celebrates his acts of vengeance. Paul is merely doing what any brave man with a gun should do. The film offers the message that justice is going to be meted out by the gun-toting individual, not the ineffectual police, hamstrung by laws that favor the criminal.

"I HAD A CHANCE TO SAVE PAUL."

Can this sort of macho revenge fantasy be queered? Gay filmmakers have tried, with varied results. In writer-director P. J. Castellaneta's confused dramedy of the sex lives of twenty-somethings in Los Angeles, *Relax . . . It's Just Sex* (1998), Vincey (Mitchell Anderson) rapes a gay basher in front of his friends, in broad daylight. While his friends are rightfully appalled, Vincey later becomes the voice of correct gay politics.

In the independent gay film *Raising Heroes* (1996; screenplay, Douglas Langway, Edmond Sorel, and Henry White; direction, Douglas Langway), a gay man can't even get a quart of milk in Manhattan without witnessing a Mafia hit. Cute, sensitive Josh (Troy Sostillio) and his older bear lover, Paul (Henry White) are in the midst of a custody battle for little Nickie, the son of Paul's oldest friend, Susan, who has just died of leukemia and who wanted the couple to raise her boy. Susan's mother is fighting to keep the boy away from the gay couple. Josh and Paul are model assimilationist gays with a lovely riverside apartment, good jobs, an SUV, and a beautifully decorated nursery waiting for Nickie. When Josh goes to the neighborhood grocery to buy milk for Nickie, he witnesses a gangland murder. From this point, the film becomes a stir fry of film noir (voice-over narration by Josh), Quentin Tarantino (killers who engage in offbeat banter in parked cars), Sam Peckinpah (the peaceful couple forced into extreme violence to protect themselves), and Martin Scorsese (bumbling junior Mafiosi and echoes of "Are you looking at me?"), with politically correct gay politics thrown in. In two climactic shootouts, with more bullets going into bouncing bodies than at the end of *Bonnie and Clyde,* Paul and Josh manage to kill the entire gang. I'm sure the creators of *Raising Heroes* didn't mean for this to happen, but Paul and Josh, filling their adversaries with bullets, seem more violent than their enemies. There are no legal repercussions to their slaughter. Charles Bronson would be proud. At the end, we discover that Paul and Josh get custody of Nickie and move to the suburbs. They have proven not only that they are the equal of straight couples but, through violence, that they're Real Men, not sissies. Yet they haven't lost their sensitivity— Josh's eyes are filled with tears as he empties two automatic pistols into an adversary. Josh tells us in his final narration that he has overcome his fear of confrontation. Has he ever! All the good guys in *Raising Heroes* are gay. The one policeman we see (Josh never thinks to call the police when he is threatened and a neighbor is murdered) is a gay undercover detective whose lover has been shot by the bad guys. He, too, wants vengeance, not arrests. In trying to give us gay urban heroes, *Raising Heroes* buys uncritically into the violence and vigilante mentality of straight tales of urban revenge.

"WE'VE GOT NOTHING TO LOSE."

Two fine films—writer-director Gregg Araki's *The Living End* (1992) and Jon Shear's *Urbania*—offer gay visions of the urban nightmare-revenge scenario. Gregg Araki's self- proclaimed "irresponsible film" begins in an eerie, blue, fluorescent, nighttime Los Angeles where Jon (Craig Gilmore), a young would-be film critic, meets Luke (Mike Dytri) just after Jon discovers he's HIV-positive. Luke is the unavoidable, irresistible representative of the dark side of human experience. Clothed in torn jeans and a motorcycle jacket, he looks like the iconic 1950s rebellious youth, now gay and placed in a more perilous time. Luke can sit impassively, unlit cigarette in his mouth as a gun is directed at him, because he doesn't care if he lives or dies. The relationship between Jon and Luke is passionate and sexually explicit. Luke may be terrifying, but he's sexually attractive as well. In the film's early scenes, Jon's reaction to his diagnosis is juxtaposed with Luke's witnessing a murder, having his life threatened by two murderous lesbians, and shooting a group of bat-wielding fag bashers. When Luke runs in front of Jon's car, a relationship begins that both terrifies and thrills Jon. Most of the film is devoted to the couple's experiences on the road between Los Angeles and San Francisco, after Jon helps Luke run away after shooting a policeman.

Luke's anarchy is less a response to the prevalent violence than to his own HIV status: "We've got nothing to lose . . . We're totally free. . . . We can do whatever the fuck we want to do." Above all, Luke is at war with the homophobic society Araki portrays in a film dedicated to those dying of AIDS because of "a White House filled with Big Republican Fuckheads." Wandering through a series of bleak landscapes, Jon is alternately attracted and terrified by Luke's violent, sometimes suicidal behavior. "I have a vision of you as a vampire," Jon says, "sucking the life force out of me." It is HIV, however, that is doing the worst violence. "I love you more than life," Luke declares, which in his case isn't saying much. Images of death fill the film, from the first bumper sticker we see—"Choose Death"—to the skeleton hanging on Jon's closet door, to the constant discussions of death, to Jon's ominous illness at the end.

Luke offers Jon the kind of powerful passion–cum–death wish that was the stuff of nineteenth-century romance and that is an element of 1990s gay cinema.[7] The two have unprotected anal sex—safe sex seems unnecessary when they're both HIV-positive. In one scene, Luke wants to be strangled when he reaches orgasm. In the film's final sequence, Jon, now clearly sick, wants to get away from Luke and go home. Luke knocks him unconscious with the butt of his gun, licks the blood from Jon's face, and ties his hands. When Jon regains consciousness, Luke rapes him while holding the barrel of his gun in his own mouth. "What the fuck are you waiting for? Just do it," Jon screams, but the gun is out of bullets. The final shot is an extreme long shot of the two lovers embracing on a desolate beach, away from the city, but equally far from any sane vision of experience.

Araki does not criticize or condemn Luke's point of view, which seems as valid as any toward the world the film offers, and better than Jon's unreflective caution. Violent rage is better than victimization, crazy passion better than solitude.

"IT'S NICE TO KNOW YOU'VE EMBRACED THE HEALING PROCESS, CHARLIE."

Urbania is the culmination of the urban horror film, presented from the point of view of a gay man who, during one night, moves from grief and victimization to regaining control over his life by accepting that much of experience is out of one's control. In *Urbania,* the New York nightscape is not a comic caricature of the more bizarre aspects of the city; rather, it is a reflection of the protagonist's mind. Director Jon Shear presents the kind of labyrinthine narrative filled with false clues that was common in film noir; however, in *Urbania,* the audience is in the role of noir detective, looking for a pattern in the seemingly random and potentially violent wandering of the central character.

Charlie (Dan Futterman), the protagonist, is a writer clearly at the end of his tether. He has lost his relationship with his lover, Chris (Matt Keeslar), his anchor to stability. We don't know at the beginning of the film what happened to Chris, but we know that Charlie is a wreck, unable to work or sleep, and is constantly trying to call Chris from pay phones around the city.

All the other relationships we see in the film are heterosexual and dysfunctional. Charlie's obnoxious neighbor enjoys noisy sex with his overly possessive, insecure girlfriend. A crazy woman microwaves her dog. A wealthy woman offers a bartender hundreds of dollars to see his penis. Most of the men are far more benign: the homeless man Charlie befriends (Lothair Bluteau), the kindly bartender (Josh Hamilton), Brett (Alan Cumming), the friend dying of HIV-related infections, who clearly is in love with Charlie. On the night on which most of the film's action transpires, Charlie seems intent on provoking men with any symptoms of homophobia. "I'm an absolute shit," he boasts in a fantasy conversation with Chris. "People fuck with me, I fuck with them." He becomes hostile and violent toward Ron (Gabriel Olds), the vain, ostensibly bisexual soap opera actor he goes home with. Later, Charlie runs into his upstairs neighbor and his girlfriend in a bar and tells them how he masturbates while listening to them have sex, throwing the neighbor into a fury. Throughout the first half of the film, director Shear and actor Futterman are daring enough to make Charlie pathological and unsympathetic. It is only when the puzzle is put together that the audience can understand and sympathize with his often bizarre behavior.

Charlie's goal is to find Dean (Samuel Ball), "the man with the tattoo," who has caught Charlie's eye during his travels around Greenwich Village. At first it seems that Charlie is hunting for Dean to have sex with him. He tells Brett, "I think I found him. The guy who's going to make everything right." Charlie finally finds Dean in a bar and wanders around the city with him, sharing liquor and drugs. Through flashbacks it is revealed that Dean is Chris's murderer and that Charlie is seeking vengeance. The brilliance of the film is its rich, compassionate presentation of this homophobic murderer and the complexity of Charlie's responses to him: a combination of hate, fascination, and sympathy. As Charlie and Dean wander through the city, Dean reveals himself as a violent loser—spiritual kin to the homophobic killers in *Boys Don't Cry* and *Anatomy of a Hate Crime*—abused as a child, "drunk since he was thirteen," whose frail sense of his manhood is threatened by homosexuals and whose only exercise of power is violence against them (though Charlie stops Dean from gay-bashing as they wander through cruising areas). After Dean passes out, Charlie drives him to a desolate swamp in New Jersey, where he plans to take his revenge.

As Charlie's earlier wanderings were intercut with his memories of happy moments with Chris, so his revenge against Dean alternates with imaginary conversations with Chris, whose death Charlie has not fully accepted. He imagines telling Chris of his violent, vengeful encounter with

Dean as a way to atone for not being able to save his lover, but Charlie is no Charles Bronson. Instead of revenge he receives enlightenment: "There was no point in what he did to us. There was no point in what I was going to do to him." Narratives give events structure and meaning, and Charlie wanted to live a revenge narrative that would justify all that happened, but he learns that human experience is not the same as narrative. Finally, he is able to grieve for Chris and go to sleep.

We accept Charlie's madness (powerfully depicted by the quasi-expressionistic direction and Dan Futterman's brilliant, haunted performance) because it is placed in the context of a mad urban society. In *Urbania,* as in *Death Wish,* the real horror of the city is that it destroyed a stable, loving relationship. The love of Charlie and Chris, idealized and eroticized in the film, is the only truly beautiful thing the bleak, ugly city offers.

In one of his fantasy conversations with Chris, Charlie says, "You're the only home I know," to which Chris responds, "This isn't home." Is home gone, or is it the half-empty double bed to which Charlie returns at the end of the film? What is at stake in all these urban films is the idea of home endangered or destroyed by malevolent forces within the city. The films are full of scenes of women and men who try to expel unwanted intruders from their domestic space and of people finding it difficult to find their way back home. The concept of home is as fragile in films of the city as it was in classic westerns, where frail cabins were dwarfed by their natural surroundings. What is still authorized in urban films is the idea of the loving, loyal, committed couple, straight or gay. In *Urbania,* the image of domestic bliss is a homespun quilt, a metaphor for the historical continuity of the couple, and an assertion that gay couples are as entitled to participate in that ideal as straights.

III

LEARNING LOVE

Chapter Seven

IN THE SHADOW OF CARY GRANT

Gay Romance

Bereft of a supply of films about growing up gay, my younger self had to make do with reading myself into the romantic comedies I saw on film and on television. Once in a while, there was a queer moment, like the end of *Some Like It Hot* (1959; screenplay, I. A. L. Diamond and Billy Wilder; direction, Billy Wilder), which was released my senior year in high school, when Osgood (Joe E. Brown) doesn't care that his beloved Daphne (Jack Lemmon) is a man in drag: "Nobody's perfect," he allows. That same year, I learned Rock Hudson's precise definition of a homosexual (without the use of the "h" word, of course) in *Pillow Talk:* "Well, there are some men who just are very devoted to their mothers. You now, the type who likes to share cooking recipes, to exchange vicious bits of gossip." At least Hudson managed to say those lines without affecting a limp wrist. For the most part, though, I had to do the queering.

Later, as I tried and failed and tried again, for better or for worse, to establish and maintain relationships, I learned that there is validity in the central assumptions of the great romantic comedies, which provide an alternative to the ambivalence of contemporary gay and straight romance. I offer in this chapter a survey of gay romantic comedies seen in the context of the classics of the Golden Age of Hollywood romance and more recent images of heterosexual love.

"I JUST HAD SEX LIKE A MAN."

So says the empowered-feeling heroine on HBO's series, *Sex and the City* after having her orgasm via oral sex without reciprocating: "Sorry. Got to go!" In this comic version of New York City, everyone is interested primarily in sex. In the 1950s, a hit film comedy like *How to Marry a Millionaire* (1953; screenplay, Zoe Atkins, Dale Eunson, Katherine Albert, and Nunally Johnson; direction, Jean Negulesco) would offer sirens Marilyn Monroe, Betty Grable, and Lauren Bacall using sexual allure as their primary weapon to capture rich husbands who would support them in the style they dreamed of. The four women who are the central characters in *Sex and the City* have careers of their own. Marriage, if it comes, is not an economic necessity, and in the show's vision of New York City, marriage seems unlikely and "meaningful relationship" seems an oxymoron. If you want to have sex like a man, you don't settle down. There's always someone better. The only fear is of age, which takes one out of the marketplace. Of course, as always in a consumer society in which desire is the primary emotion, the women are constantly unsatisfied.

In this series, the men are objects, as well as the folks who have set the rules by which the women play. To deal with men on their own terms— to "have sex like a man"—is to treat men the way they treat women. This means that the women must be as attractive, callous, selfish, and promiscuous as the men they want to be with. The men who want more or something other than sex look sad and baffled: the cute but not gorgeous young man (the men on this show tend to be gorgeous and great in bed) who is looking for love from the wrong women in the wrong place and is treated like dirt,[1] and the rich, handsome young man who has bought an apartment and is intent on finding a wife to share it. When Carrie (Sarah Jessica Parker), our heroine, flees from him and his magnificent six-bedroom Upper West Side co-op, he can't fathom why women in the city don't want to marry and have children. (By the end of the third season Carrie is engaged after vomiting at the first sight of the engagement ring and one character is pregnant by a man she has no intention of marrying.)

Sex and the City is produced by a man (Darren Star, who also gave us *Melrose Place*), and many episodes are written by men, so we get, as usual, a man's view of women's sexual desire and mores. Like *Ally McBeal*, another male-created show about sex in the city among thirty-somethings, *Sex and the City* is immensely popular with women and gay men. How different, after all, is the singles world of *Sex and the City* from the uncoupled urban gay world? An early episode of *Sex and the City* pointed out, rightly, that singles and coupled people live on different planets in both straight and gay society.

The city offers freedom and an unlimited supply of sexual partners. This is a sitcom, so there's no danger, no violence, no disease, only fun and a healthy dose of cynicism. If the characters seem to act more like college kids than like folks in their thirties, that's because maturity is to be avoided. One character seems intent on rising in her law firm, but work doesn't seem particularly important to these characters except as a means of providing the wherewithal to play.

Brian (the dreary, miscast Gale Harold) in Showtime's series *Queer as Folk,*[2] a gay version of *Sex and the City,* focusing totally on the world of gay singles, lives to "have sex like a man"—with men. His milieus are the gay bars and clubs where he finds an unending supply of buff sexual partners—in Pittsburgh! According to the writers of this series, all of whom undoubtedly live in West Hollywood, urban gay life centers on sex without the encumbrance of relationships, which Brian thinks are the bane of straight people. "I don't do relationships," he says, because he thinks that the natural state for men is promiscuity. His only morality is a loathing for any form of hypocrisy—in others. Though he is anything but a good friend, he is loved, even admired, by the other characters in the series, who would all like to be Brian but lack the courage or the total insensitivity to emulate him successfully. Brian and his friends live in the city because it is a sexual marketplace. They spend their nights at a club called Babylon, a site for the anticipation or realization of physical pleasure without responsibility.

The protagonists of these hip television series aspire to marriage but fear it even more. The adult romantic comedies of Hollywood's Golden Age either began with a married couple or ended in marriage. Marriage, the ideal combination of sex and friendship, of love over time, was a given. The heyday of American romantic comedy on film was, oddly enough, the Depression, when Hollywood had some of its best writers and wasn't terrified of dialogue-heavy films—listen to the barrage of language in the first ten minutes or so of *His Girl Friday* (1940; screenplay, Charles Lederer, based on the play *The Front Page,* by Ben Hecht and Charles MacArthur; direction, Howard Hawks), which is comprised entirely of two people talking at a desk, unthinkable now but sheer magic in the hands of Rosalind Russell and Cary Grant. *His Girl Friday,* like most comedies of the period, wasn't about sex. It was about what Mark in *Trick* calls "the hard part": friendship, commonality, communication. Hildy Johnson (Russell) and Walter Burns (Grant) belong together because they're devoted to their profession—they are newspaper reporters—as well as to each other. Hildy and Walter have already had sex: Hollywood's way around the physical relationship of their sparring couples was to make them divorced. These two know they're sexually attracted; it's the other stuff they still need to work out after Walter gets rid of Hildy's sappy fiancé.

In the original play and in two other film versions of *The Front Page*, editor Walter sabotages a male Hildy's engagement so that he won't lose his best reporter. It didn't take much revision to make Hildy an ex-wife, and Rosalind Russell's sublime, butch Hildy makes one long for the next remake, with a male Hildy and Walter rekindling their romance. Look at critic James Harvey's description of Russell's Hildy: "She is both regal and ungainly, with a clear element of parody in the down-looking style. That parody is partly self-protective—part of her geniality, too."[3] It isn't difficult for gay men to relate to Hildy and Walter's zany reconciliation. One ex and I used to think of *His Girl Friday* as "our film."

The Philadelphia Story (1940; screenplay, Donald Ogden Stewart, based on the play by Philip Barry; direction, George Cukor) begins with the end of the marriage of Tracy Lord (Katharine Hepburn) and C. K. Dexter Haven (Cary Grant). As Dexter moves his belongings out of the house, Tracy breaks one of his golf clubs over her knee. In retaliation, Dexter knocks her down. We discover that the marriage broke up because Dexter had a drinking problem, which Tracy exacerbated through her superior attitude and, it is hinted, chilliness in bed. *The Philadelphia Story* is a version of *The Taming of the Shrew*. Tracy can do everything—at least everything an aristocratic girl has to do: She rides, dives, and swims, speaks fluent French, reads serious literature. She can also be charming, brilliantly ironic, and, sometimes, magnificently camp. There's always something androgynous about Katharine Hepburn that made it easy for gay men of my generation to identify with. However, Tracy is also arrogant and judgmental to the men in her life: her philandering father and her dipsomaniac ex-husband. Tracy must learn to be worthy of Dexter's love. He, after all, has done his part by giving up liquor. One can cringe at the sexism in the film, particularly when Tracy's father blames his dalliances with chorus girls on his daughter's lack of unquestioning devotion, but in this carefully tailored comeback vehicle,[4] Hepburn is too radiant and the film too much fun to quibble over. The characters may complain about her, but they also extol her virtues.

Tracy is fought over by three men. The issue is marriage and lifelong commitment, not a night in bed, so the qualities that are displayed and tested are the qualities in the individuals and in the chemistry of the couples that make a happy marriage possible. By the end, Tracy and Dexter have been tested and are now mature enough to remarry with a proper ceremony—they eloped the first time. The battle for Tracy is also a class battle between aristocratic Dexter, a reformed playboy; middle-class would-be writer Macaulay Connor (James Stewart), who is something of a reverse snob as well as a romantic; and stuffy fiancé George (John Howard), a self-made man who worked his way up from the mines to a position as Tracy's father's general manager. That aristocratic Tracy ends up with one of her own class seems fitting, particularly when that aristocrat is Cary Grant. The class politics of *The Philadelphia Story* are a far cry from the "bring the rich girl down to earth" populism of Frank Capra's *It Happened One Night* (1934).

While George is a cipher, too self-absorbed and priggish to appreciate Tracy, the real rivals for her affection are Dexter and Connor, and what a superb contrast Grant and Stewart provide. Tall, gangly Stewart seems like an adolescent who has not yet gotten used to his body. His adolescence extends to his adoration for Tracy; he waxes poetic as only a would-be author can: "You're lit from within, Tracy! You've got fires banked down in you, hearth fires and holocausts!" But the last thing Tracy needs is a worshiper. Romantic Connor is better off with his devoted, down-to-earth sidekick, Liz (Ruth Hussey). To Dexter, Tracy is "Red," a decidedly physical being whom he understands, warts and all. Who wouldn't choose Cary Grant over coltish James Stewart? This isn't Grant in his zany mode, the Grant of *Bringing Up Baby* (1938) or *His Girl Friday* (1940). This is more like the intense Grant of Hitchcock's *Notorious* (1946), the romantic lead rather than the comic star. What one notices most is Grant's stillness, the intensity with which he watches and listens to the other characters. Grant is not only handsome in this film; he is downright sexy. He can also steal a scene by playing the straight man, as he does in Connor's late-night drunken visit to Dexter's house. There is no doubt, from his first entrance to the finale, that Grant's Dexter is in control of the proceedings.

Cary Grant is what is absent from today's romantic comedies—a sexy, handsome, mature leading man with a strong sense of irony, an actor who can do just about anything. In his days as a music-hall acrobatic comedian, he learned slapstick; in his days in Broadway musical comedy, he learned to be dashing. In Hollywood, he seemed able to pick up the style of the directors he worked with: Compare his performances in three of the films he made in 1940 and 1941; Hawks's *His Girl Friday,* Cukor's *The Philadelphia Story,* and Hitchcock's *Suspicion.* In an odd way, Grant dominates these films by seeming both outside the world of the other characters and yet in control of their actions. Even when, in a film such as *North by Northwest,* he is put in amusingly outlandish situations (being chased by a crop-dusting airplane, hanging by his fingertips from Mount Rushmore), there is little doubt he will prevail. Yet he never seems quite to belong. Part of it is his power onscreen and part of it his strange British accent (cleaned-up cockney, actually, which to many Americans passes as sophisticated), but there's something else, a sense of guardedness. Film historian Stanley Cavell describes this quality as "the air [Grant] can convey of mental preoccupation, of a continuous thoughtfulness that makes him spiritually inaccessible to those around him."[5] One may speculate that Grant's remove may have been a function of his alleged role as sexual outsider, the homosexual who learned to play the part of heterosexual on-screen and, to protect his career, off-screen. I don't know whether I would go as far as writer David Ehrenstein, who claims that "the charm, the grace, the sophistication, the *je-ne-sais-quoi*-ness of Cary Grant is plainly and simply *his gayness,*"[6] but it is hard for us to ignore what we now know about Grant. It is impossible now not to read his romantic reticence—in Grant's best films, his characters seem more interested in their love interests as pals than as lovers—as that of a gay man as we read his virtues, those qualities Ehrenstein catalogs, as gay.

Hollywood has lost the knack for making romantic comedies in part because they were not primarily about sex. They were about the qualities that make a lasting relationship. Tracy ultimately chooses a man she has known since childhood.[7] The men in *The Philadelphia Story* are sexually attracted to Tracy, but they wouldn't think of taking advantage of her. Chivalry isn't dead. They also love her wit, which is her unique attribute. We also don't have a Cary Grant. We do have a Hugh Grant (no relation), a self-confessed lightweight, limited actor with a small repertoire of verbal and facial tics, and since the few good romantic comedies that have been made in the last decade have been made in England, Grant has been busy. Why England? In part because their class system offers a structure for romantic comedy, as does their cultural character. The basic formula for British-made romantic comedy is Grant playing a stereotypical Englishman—bumbling, disorganized, inarticulate abut his feelings, incapable of being sexually aggressive (this stereotype, by the way, does not fit any Englishmen, straight or gay, that I know)—falling in love with a vapid but sexually experienced American woman (Andie MacDowell, Julia Roberts), whom every man wants. In the best of the Hugh Grant vehicles, *Four Weddings and a Funeral,* only the gay couple seem to know why they are married.

"IF WE CAN'T BE LIKE GARETH AND MATTHEW, MAYBE WE SHOULD JUST LET IT GO."

At the end of *The Philadelphia Story,* C. K. Dexter Haven and Tracy Lord finally get the proper wedding—and marriage—they should have had years ago. At the end of *Four Weddings and a Funeral* (1994; screenplay, Richard Curtis; direction, Mike Newell), Charles (Hugh Grant) announces to his wedding guests that he really doesn't love his bride but loves someone else, the mysterious American, Carrie (Andie MacDowell). "Do you think not being married to me is something you might consider doing for the rest of your life?" he asks her, to which she replies, "I do." These two characters, who are terminally ambivalent about marriage, can make a commitment only by denying commitment. While class is never discussed in the film, Charles's friends all seem to be university-educated folks near the top of society. One of Charles's friends lives in a mansion with 137 bedrooms; the others have spacious London flats and don't seem to worry much about work. The film's four weddings take place in relatively posh settings. Tracy Lord would not be out of place in this world, but what would Charles, who is smitten with the terminally bland Mac-Dowell, do with a radiant creature like Hepburn's Lord? Charles seems to be incapable of controlling a situation. At his wedding, his deaf brother has to sign to him what to say to get out of the marriage.

The norm for a happy marriage in the film is the relationship of Gareth (Simon Callow) and Matthew (John Hannah). "If we can't be like Gareth and Matthew," Charles says at one point, "maybe we should just let it go." While Matthew is a quiet Scot, older Gareth is always the life of the party, sporting wild vests and drinking and dancing up a storm. It is Gareth who is the reason for the one funeral in the film. He has a fatal heart attack at a wedding reception. Matthew's eulogy, the most eloquent testament to the power of love in the entire film, provides the norm for what marriage should be. Before his own wedding, Charles asks Matthew what he thinks of marriage. "I think it's really good if you love the person with all your heart." Charles's aborted marriage to "Duckface" is nothing more than a compromise.

At the end of the film, we see snapshots of all the characters coupled, except Fiona (Kristin Scott Thomas), who has carried a torch for Charles. Even Matthew has a new boyfriend. The film is a celebration of coupledom. What it lacks is what great romantic comedies have: a sense of what it takes, beyond a vague conception of love, to be married. Except for Gareth and Matthew, there is no sense of the abiding friendship, common interests, or understanding that one sees developed in the great comedies of the 1930s and '40s. All Charles and Carrie have going for them is physical attraction. The film does capture one aspect of current ambivalence about marriage: the impulse to marry without a sense of what marriage entails or why one should bother. Carrie's sexual history, which she proudly catalogs for Charles, and which seems to be all she has to offer, hardly suggests that monogamy is important to her.

Given the close friendship of the men in the film, their inability to communicate with women other than physically, and the privileging of the relationship of Matthew and Gareth, the subtext of *Four Weddings and a Funeral* seems to be that real marriage can exist only between men. Yet gay men have a history of ambivalence about relationships and romance that is as fraught as that of heterosexuals. It is inevitable that that ambivalence is so marked in even gay romantic films.

"DADDY, ARE YOU A FAGGOT?"

As Matthew and Gareth are the life (and death) of the parties in *Four Weddings and a Funeral,* so Rupert Everett's George, the chic, charming gay friend of Jules (Julia Roberts) is the best thing about *My Best Friend's Wedding* (1997; screenplay, Ronald Bass; direction, P. J. Hogan), a farce about a woman determined to steal her straight male friend from his bride. What was most revolutionary about this casting was that an openly gay man played an openly gay man. For once we were spared the nauseating, offensive assertions of heterosexuality and implied homophobia we still get, for instance, from some of the cast members of Showtime's *Queer as Folk.* Everett's George was handsome, beautifully dressed, witty, professionally successful, and charming—the gay stereotype for the turn of the twenty-first century. Susan Bordo is absolutely right when she observes that Everett's George is essential "not only to challenge stereotypes of homosexuality but also to reveal the inadequacies of *straight* masculinity."[8] Who remembers the cipher Julia Roberts's Jules was fighting for? Bordo also correctly notes that Everett's George is an homage to the roles Cary Grant once played, but Grant's urbane comic hero, like the actor himself, seemed forced into a romantic heterosexual formula. Everett's George can charm everyone at Jules's wedding reception and dance up a storm, but he remains outside the paradigm of the wedding. Nonetheless, compared to the bland straight groom and the zany female rivals, he emerges as the hero of the film.

The disaster entitled *The Next Best Thing* (2000; screenplay, Thomas Ropelewski; direction John Schlesinger), created as a vehicle for Everett and his buddy Madonna, shows what happens when Hollywood filmmakers try to move a gay man from the periphery to the center of the marriage paradigm. Chaos ensues, which empowers the gay characters at the expense of the woman. In *The Next Best Thing*, Everett plays Robert, a gay Los Angeles landscape gardener (not a convincing profession for the louche actor) whose best friend, Abbie (Madonna), is a yoga instructor. Never for a moment demonstrating any aptitude for acting, Madonna is most hilariously at sea trying to look as if she can teach yoga. Robert's function in Abbie's life—like Everett's George for Julia Roberts's Jules in *My Best Friend's Wedding*—is to help her recover from her disastrous romances with gorgeous but feckless straight men who are not ready to commit. But Robert's love life is also a disaster. His ex-boyfriend is in jail on a drug offense. His best gay friend, David (Neil Patrick Harris, in the film's most winning performance), has just lost his partner to AIDS (as in *Four Weddings and a Funeral*, the loving couple gets the funeral) and his home to his partner's nasty parents, and is himself on the HIV cocktail. Robert's parents are the stereotypical parents of a gay man: the Auntie Mame mother (Lynn Redgrave) and the emotionally constipated father (Josef Sommer) Hollywood thinks gay men have.

One drunken night, Abbie and Robert have sex; shortly thereafter, Abbie announces she is pregnant. Robert decides to move in with Abbie and be the father of their child. "I'm bored with it all," Robert tells David. "Bored with the parties. Bored with the drugs. Bored with the body obsession." (Everett, of all people, manages to keep a straight face saying this!) Robert becomes the ideal father, totally devoted for six years to his and Abbie's son. In true gay form, rather than teach their son, Sam (Marcolm Stumpf), to read properly, Robert turns the book upside down and makes up his own very camp stories. Robert has a romance with a gorgeous cardiologist (a hunk *and* a doctor!) who loves him, but Robert can't be a proper lover because "Sam is everything to me." For mainstream audiences, Robert is sympathetic to the extent that he repudiates any expression of his sexuality except the mere claim that he is gay. Robert's devotion to his son verges on the pathological, but the creators of this weepie want us to see him as the good father who will give up everything for his son. Robert is a reconstituted version of the fallen woman with children Lana Turner played in the 1950s. Perhaps they can remake *Madame X* or *Imitation of Life* for Rupert Everett.

Meanwhile, Abbie, worried at the questions her son is asking about her relationship with Robert—"Daddy, why don't you and Mommy sleep together"[9]—starts dating Ben (Benjamin Bratt), a representative of that new breed, the Straight Gay Man, who has all the qualities of a gay man (good looks, good taste, sensitivity, honesty, ability to sustain a relationship, and just a bit of camp) but is also heterosexual—and rich. Ben is also good with Sam, bonding with him in boy stuff on the beach, not the camp flights of fancy Robert shares with him. At this point, Abbie turns into the Wicked Witch of the West, spiriting Sam off to Ben's house. When Robert tries to sue for joint custody of Sam, Abbie springs the news that he isn't really Sam's biological father. The last third of *The Next Best Thing,* so convoluted and unbelievable that we must read the resolution in the final titles, makes *The Young and the Restless* look like well-crafted, coherent drama. Both Abbie and Robert become hysterical, unsympathetic characters, Robert in his total dependence on his relationship with his son, Abbie in her sudden, inexplicable destruction of that relationship. Only straight Ben remains a good guy. Robert gets his tearful court scene, Abbie plays dirty, and Ben looks noble. At the end, Abbie realizes that she has been unfair, hugs Robert, says "I miss us," and allows joint custody. Abbie is in the wrong, and the guys are noble and long-suffering.

This reactionary Hollywood film was directed by John Schlesinger, the man who thirty years before made the classic gay male–straight woman–bisexual male saga, *Sunday Bloody Sunday* (1971; screenplay, Penelope Gilliatt), in which the gay man and the woman are intelligent, loving people. Now Schlesinger and his collaborators offer their gay characters no real relationships that don't end in prison or death. In order to be a Noble Hero, a gay man must give up the life heterosexual characters are entitled to have. Nor does the film offer much sympathy to the woman in its triangle. Abbie is dishonest and disloyal and allows her best friend to be cruelly humiliated. The men here achieve the moral victory, and the woman is silenced.

While mainstream Hollywood is still skittish about presenting gay characters who are anything but eunuchs, there is a plethora of independent gay films that successfully place gay characters within the category of romantic comedy, a genre Hollywood has, for the most part, forgotten how to make.

I have organized my consideration of these films as a kind of life history of gay relationships: from teenage coming out and romance, through the love lives of twenty-somethings, to depictions of the sad infatuations of older men.[10] There has been virtually no interest in film depictions of the relationships of men over thirty, a clear reflection of the age of the independent filmmakers interested in gay subject matter and the ageism in the gay community.

Teenagers in Love

What gay men have in common is the coming-out process, with its varying degrees of angst and anger. That process has three stages: a realization that one's primary sexual impulse is directed toward members of one's own sex and a decision to act on those impulses, an affiliation with other gay people, and some acknowledgment, at least to the straight people closest to one, particularly family, that one is gay.[11] *Defying Gravity*, discussed in chapter 4, is in many ways a classic coming-out film; however, Griff, its young protagonist, chooses to maintain his relationship with Pete in the social context of his supportive straight friends rather than live exclusively in a world of gay social institutions that would provide an alternative to his homophobic fraternity.[12] For Eric Hunter, the troubled teen in *Edge of Seventeen* (1998; screenplay, Todd Stephens; direction, David Moreton), coming out means accepting his place in a gay bar and, thus, a gay society.

The quasi-autobiographical *Edge of Seventeen* takes place in 1984 in Sandusky, Ohio, which is anything but a gay mecca. The life of the protagonist Eric (Christopher Stafford), seems at first relatively untroubled. He has doting parents, two younger brothers with whom he has a good relationship, and a sweet female friend, Maggie (Tina Holmes), to whom he is much closer than he is with any of his male friends (uh-oh!). Maggie accepts Eric's definition of them as "best friends" but lives in hope that they will someday be more. Like Eric, she seems to be uncomfortable with her peers, hoping to prove herself through a relationship, but her role in Eric's life as couturiere and makeup artist as he looks more and more like someone out of an eighties glam-rock group should have lit a few warning lights. When she pauses to put on her mascara before she and Eric go to a party, he asks her to put mascara on him as well. Maggie is treated with far more sympathy than the gay man's female sidekick is in most gay-made movies. When Eric talks Maggie into joining him at the local gay bar and a drunk yells out, "Hey, Eric, I didn't know you had a fag hag!" the viewer shares her pain and embarrassment.

During this summer before their senior year in high school, Eric and Maggie work in the cafeteria of a nearby amusement park under the management of Angie, an amiable butch lesbian (Lea DeLaria). There, Eric meets and ultimately ends up in bed with an openly gay Ohio State student aptly named Rod (Anderson Gabrych). The first half of the film, chronicling Eric's summer at "Crystal Shores," alternates between Eric's tentative relationship with Maggie and his flirtation with Rod. While everyone, including Maggie, assumes that Eric and Maggie are a couple, Eric can't bring himself to be romantic with her. He tries to kiss her, but it is only an affectionate peck. The only time he is passionate with her is at a drunken party at Angie's, but while above the waist Eric is kissing Maggie, below the waist Rod is fondling Eric. This is how Eric would like his life organized: affection with Maggie but secret passion with Rod. On the last night of their summer jobs, Eric and Rod finally have sex, which leads to Eric falling in love with Rod, who goes back to his Ohio State boyfriend. "How did you know you were in love?" Eric asks his mother. "When I thought so much about him it hurt," she says. Love is what Eric wants—the kind of love he and Maggie could have if only Eric were straight. When he works up the courage to go to the local gay bar, he gets picked up and has sex in the front seat of a car with a trick. "Afterwards he wouldn't even look at me," he complains. "I want to fall in love," Eric tells Maggie, but that isn't what the men he meets want: "I can't have what I want with a guy," he says. But after finally going to bed with Maggie, he realizes that a heterosexual relationship isn't what he wants either. In the film's final sequence, he returns to the gay bar and to a potential boyfriend, Jonathan (Jeff Fryer), who loves music as much as Eric does.

"I guess I thought if I came out everything would get easier," Eric tells Angie in a moment of anguish. The beauty of *Edge of Seventeen* is that it shows adolescent coming out to be a difficult process, not only for the person coming out but for everyone around him. In his ambivalence, Eric is unintentionally hurtful to all the women in his life: his doting mother, Maggie, and Angie, whom he alternately befriends and snubs.[13] Eric is truly happy only in the candid scenes with Rod—a delightfully erotic scene with pie and Reddi-wip and a tender scene of defloration—and in his newfound relationship with Jonathan, who will be the gay friend Eric needs, as well as a lover. The film is also candid in depicting the way gay men can exploit each other: The most painful lesson in coming out is that one cannot mistake sex for love.

Twenty-somethings

"THERE YOU GO AGAIN, PUSHING THIS ROMANTIC THING."

The first American gay-created coming-out film was *A Very Natural Thing* (1974; screenplay Joseph Coencas and Christopher Larkin; direction, Christopher Larkin), the mother of all gay film romances. I remember going to see it with my boyfriend at the time at a movie theater in Greenwich Village. The theater was quite empty. No one film on the subject of gay mores and relationships was going to please everybody, so *A Very Natural Thing* was bound to disappoint. Made on a shoestring budget, it is badly edited, and the acting is amateurish. (Very few actors were willing to play gay roles in the early 1970s.) But now I find it refreshing to see so many natural-looking bodies rather than the pumped-up ones that are currently de rigueur—though where did they find all those avocado-colored percolators? Like many firsts on a big subject, the film tried to be both story and sermon. I don't remember thinking at the time that the film was a classic, but some of us, particularly those with a romantic streak, settled for small favors in those days. How else could one explain the success back then of the silly, romantic novels of Gordon Merrick, the gay versions of Harlequin romances?

Seeing the video of *A Very Natural Thing* recently brought home to me how little gay romantic films have changed. The film tells the story of the liberation of David (Robert Joel), who leaves the all-male, ostensibly celibate world of a Catholic monastery for Greenwich Village in the heyday of gay liberation. We don't see David's decision to come out or his entry into New York gay life. The film simply cuts to David working as a school-teacher by day and by night cruising through New York's gay haunts (which were pretty tacky compared to the fancy bars, restaurants, and nightclubs urban gay men now frequent). David's goal is to follow in the footsteps of his parents, to find a partner and settle down for life in a loving, monogamous relationship. In a bar, he meets Mark (Curt Gareth), a junior executive in an insurance firm. Their one-night stand turns into a romance, illustrated through clichéd slow-motion running in the park, rolling around, candlelight kisses, and Sundays at home with the *Times,* scored to Samuel Barber's "Adagio for Strings," which is a bit morose for such goings-on. But amid these affectionate moments, David blocks out Mark's skeptical comments about romance and relationships. (Relationship junkies are seldom good at hearing warnings or seeing red flags—believe me, I know!) Mark, who is as fond of David as he is capable of being, invites David to move in with him. No sooner has he done this than he is sorry, feels trapped, and starts checking out the countless other items on the menu. When David reacts with soulful, guilt-provoking looks and comments (he was, after all, training to be a priest), Mark yells, "You're just going to have to stop imposing your screwed-up romantic ideas on my life. I'm liberated." To hold on to Mark, David tries to live Mark's way: orgies on Fire Island, tricks, all the accoutrements of an open relationship. He freaks out at the most inopportune moments, Mark gets fed up, and the relationship ends. The film wants to be sympathetic to Mark's feelings of claustrophobia and his desire for sexual freedom—the real question, then, is why he asked David to move in—but Mark does seem something of a cad. Gay film, like straight film, always comes down on the side of the romantic against the free spirit.

After splitting up with Mark, David finally realizes, "Liberating myself is the most important thing for me right now." As in so many cultural productions of the 1970s, "liberation" is offered as a vague, quasi-religious concept, but what seems to be suggested is that David will free himself from conventional relationship patterns and enjoy sexual freedom and variety. On Gay Pride Day, he meets Jason (Bo White), a divorced photographer who is a friend to his ex-wife and devoted to their child, but as tied to the idea of marriage as David was with Mark. When Jason asks David to move in with him, David declines, because he has learned that when two people live together, "'want to' turns into 'have to.'" Jason reluctantly accepts David's liberated, qualified relationship, and for a finale there's five minutes of the couple running nude on the beach, dicks flapping, and romping in the water to quasi-religious music, a visual-aural metaphor for the new liberated relationship pattern they will create.

Seeing the film again, I was struck by how well it reflected what a lot of intelligent, sensitive gay men went through in the early 1970s. As all the documentary testimonials intercut into the narrative of *A Very Natural Thing* suggest, coming out was a kind of religious experience for many of us, particularly those who had been religious. So was liberation, which meant throwing off all restraints and exploring one's sexuality, acting on one's urges. Relationships of all kinds collapsed. Men who had been married, some with children, realized that they couldn't live purely heterosexual lives, and given the either/or our society enforces, they, like Jason in the film, came out. My bridge foursome of a colleague and I and our wives changed around 1970 to the same colleague and I and our boyfriends. Gay couples who had been together for years in devoted relationships broke up because one of the two needed to "explore." What's a boy to do when everyone is sexually available? Often the couples would try to stay together in some kind of open relationship that got stretched beyond its tensile strength. I saw this all around me, even in staid North Carolina. I lived through it in one typical early-1970s relationship in which the guiding principle was supposed to be "Have all the sex with other people you want but stay emotionally faithful to me." One of us was able to have lots of sex without any sense that it might compromise the relationship; the other, incapable of separating sex from emotions, had guilt-inducing affairs and ultimately settled for a monogamous relationship with someone else. Who more betrayed the relationship? Monogamy and commitment seemed alien when every guy seemed to be sexually available; nor were they ideals gay society supported.

Like a classic overture, *A Very Natural Thing* contains the major theme repeated in most of the gay-made films that have followed: the conflict between desire for the stability of a committed relationship and the urge for sexual freedom. In her book *Creating the Couple: Love, Marriage, and Hollywood Performance,* Virginia Wright Wexman asserts as her central thesis, "As a form of modern popular ritual, movies define and demonstrate socially sanctioned ways of falling in love"[14] by "modeling appropriate courtship behavior."[15] Gay film romances serve much the same function. Films like *Beautiful Thing* (1996; screenplay, Jonathan Harvey; direction, Hettie MacDonald) and *Trick* (1999; screenplay, Jason Schafer; director, Jim Fall), aimed at a mainstream audience, both model appropriate gay romantic behavior and serve to raise political issues.

American gay romances pursue the central debate in middle-class American gay life—the extent to which one should assimilate to the same norms as heterosexuals—but they also serve to validate gay mores and relationships for a straight audience. What is clear in gay romances is that romantic love is good, promiscuity bad or unthinkable. As in heterosexual romance, the sexually active man who doesn't want to settle down needs to grow up. Bisexuality is never presented as a positive possibility. As *A Very Natural Thing* depicts Mark as something of a cad for betraying his relationship with David, so too does the first Hollywood film to look at gay relationships, the overly solemn *Making Love* (1982; screenplay, Barry Sandler; direction, Arthur Hiller), make the newly out gay man's first lover a narcissistic novelist incapable of commitment, albeit sensitive enough to regret it. Yet the issue of marriage is a complex one for gay men. On the one hand, in America we have a panic reaction from the religious right and their friends in government. Gay marriage, we are told, "devalues" heterosexual marriage. What stronger evidence does one need that heterosexual institutions are defined in opposition to homosexuality? On the other hand, it may be that a long-term committed relationship simply isn't something many young men—gay or straight—want or are capable of sustaining. What in our culture teaches us to hold on to something—or someone—forever? Many Americans throw out their televisions or appliances and buy new ones rather than get the old ones fixed—why should we feel any differently about partners? The only institutions that fervently support "till death do us part" are those most negative toward lesbians and gay men and our partnerships.

"I KNOW WHAT YOU'RE THINKING. 'WHAT AN ASSHOLE,' RIGHT?"

While Mark's deviations from monogamy are presented unsympathetically in *A Very Natural Thing*, Christopher Bedford's betrayal of his lover in *All the Rage* (1998; screenplay and direction, Roland Tec) is depicted as downright pathological. Christopher (John-Michael Lander) is the stereotypical urban gay man who places sexual conquest above everything. His Boston Back Bay condo, complete with roof garden, his expensive clothing, and his fancy office reflect his status as a successful urban gay professional. *All the Rage* alternates between black-and-white extreme close-ups of Christopher talking to the camera and color flashbacks of the events that lead up his dark night of the soul. Christopher's monologues alternate self-defense, angry accusation, and guilt, punctuated by silence.

Christopher is a successful young lawyer by day and a connoisseur of male flesh by night. "One hundred percent grade-A beef," he calls one trick, demonstrating how he judges his sexual partners. "What I hate most are clingy men," he tells us in his first appearance. His definition of a clingy man is anyone who calls expecting a second date or an emotional response. If anyone does catch him, he never tells the truth. "I don't play games" is his motto, but he doesn't take into account the notion that any of his sexual partners may have feelings. He is organized: He keeps a card file of his tricks next to his bed—not that he would ever want to see any of them again, but as a record of his conquests. He compares notes with Larry (Jay Corcoran), a fellow lawyer, unaware that Larry is smitten with him. Besides his sex life, Christopher has time for a small circle of friends. Susan (Merle Perkins), less dysfunctional than most women in gay-made films, is going through a series of blind dates from hell, and Christopher plays Rupert Everett to her Julia Roberts, though on occasion the roles are reversed. He is also friendly with a gay couple, Dave and Tom (Paul Outlaw and Peter Bubriski), who are going through the seven-year itch, desiring some of the adventure of their past but wanting to keep what they have. When Christopher tells Dave he's sick of the singles scene and wants a boyfriend, which is what he thinks his committed friend wants to hear, Dave and Tom fix him up with their neighbor, Stewart (David Vincent), a book editor. Christopher and Stewart meet at a couples dinner party that makes partnered gays seem every bit as crass as single ones. The discussion among these piss-elegant queens is all money and possessions. "I was thinking of going into publishing," one says to Stewart, "but then I decided to make money." Stewart is smart and nice-looking, but he isn't a 10. He's also extremely shy, though Christopher reads his reticence as playing hard to get, which tantalizes a man who has always insisted on having the power in any relationship. For a few months, Christopher is infatuated with Stewart, or at least with the idea of being in a relationship. As soon as he and Stewart exchange keys, Christopher gets claustrophobic and begins to lust after Stewart's well-endowed gym-bunny roommate, Kenny (Alan Natale), whom Christopher and Larry refer to as "donkey dick." Christopher and Kenny are caught in the act; Stewart, betrayed once too often, dumps Christopher, and Christopher's other friends become decidedly chilly toward him. As in a morality play, *All the Rage* has Christopher endure a dark night of the soul. Cut off from his friends and from Stewart, he goes out to

cruise his old haunts. He first goes to an elegant bar filled with loving couples, then moves on to a dark, smoky place that looks like a boiler room, in
which men lurk around phallic vertical pipes. In the iconography of this
film, moving out of the world of committed couples to that of cruising singles is moving downward. Christopher picks up John (Jeff Miller), a man
he'd slept with and subsequently avoided two years before. After sex, John
reminds Christopher that they had slept together and tries to force Christopher to admit his game of screwing men, then ignoring them. Christopher
breaks down, furiously attacks him, and lets out all the rage that underlies
his behavior: "Why the fuck should I care about a mediocre piece of shit
like you? I fucked you. You're fucked. I'm a fucking winner." As John quietly leaves, the film switches back to black-and-white and Christopher is
left sitting alone in the chair where he has been during all the black-and-
white scenes. Are we to believe he will reform after reflecting on this series
of disasters? Since most of his comments are rationalizations for his behavior, it is unlikely.

Tec goes overboard demonizing Christopher instead of seeing him as
a representative of one aspect of gay culture. Christopher is what Restora-
tion playwrights would call a rake, a man who lives for sexual conquest.
The problem is that gay culture makes such conquests too easy, thus less
dramatically interesting. Perhaps that's why characters like Christopher
keep going out every night, hoping to find a challenge. There might be a
delightful comedy in promiscuous Christopher falling for a man who in-
advertently plays hard to get but then reverting to his old ways amid these
other comic versions of recognizable urban affluent types. Instead, Tec
gives us melodrama, and John-Michael Lander overdoes the villainy and
insincerity—all he needs is a mustache to twirl. At the end, all of Christopher's friends reject him for behaving as he has always behaved. Though
its satire is often on target, *All the Rage* is intolerant toward its central
character's choices. Men who don't or can't choose coupledom aren't villains, and Christopher's ambivalence about relationships is very common
among gay and straight men his age. Even the most romantic recent gay
films have qualified endings.

"I FEEL STUPID SPENDING THE ENTIRE EVENING LOOKING FOR A PLACE TO GET OFF."

Eric in *Edge of Seventeen* is an aspiring songwriter who can't wait to get to
New York. The heroes of two other late-nineties gay romances, *Trick* and

Broadway Damage, are also aspiring songwriters. "I really feel lame telling people that," Gabe (Christian Campbell), the protagonist of *Trick,* tells a young man he meets in a gay bar, "because it makes me sound like such a queen. Which I'm not." But what is a gay young man who writes old-fashioned show tunes, but a queen? Gabe shares a tiny Greenwich Village walk-up with a cretinous womanizer and his parade of bimbos and seems to have only one friend, Katherine (Tori Spelling), an aspiring actress in the advanced stages of neurosis and insensitive self-absorption. Here, at the outset of the film, are the two obstacles to willing suspension of disbelief: that cute Gabe would have no gay friends or romantic life, and that he, or anyone, would find Katherine anything but repellent.

In the gay bar, where Gabe is telling the young man he is not a queen, Mark (John Paul Pitoc), a cute go-go boy, is gyrating on a stage in a red G-string. Later, on a subway, Mark sits across from Gabe and falls asleep, legs suggestively spread. The rest of the film is a comic variation of the urban-nightmare genre, a queer, more benign version of Martin Scorsese's *After Hours,* as Gabe unsuccessfully tries to find a place to have sex with Mark. Mark, on the other hand, hopes that Gabe sees him as something more than a trick. By the end of the night the two have already had a lover's quarrel and hold hands during a nightmare breakfast with Katherine and her fellow actors in a coffee shop. As they part, Mark says to Gabe, "You know I think it's good how it turned out. We got the hard part over with."

The charm of *Trick* is that it has the innocence, optimism, and exuberance of the musical comedies Gabe dreams of writing but which, at the beginning of the story, he can't really write because he has never experienced romantic love. Perry (Steve Hayes), a true show queen, asks Gabe whether one of his songs really "captures that feeling about a really great kiss?" At the end, when a choir and orchestra blast out Gabe's tune, "Enter You," we realize that his new romance has given him the inspiration he needs. If this light, joyful comedy has any idea in its pretty head, it seems to be that sex should be part of a loving, intimate relationship, but it isn't clear what kind of relationship Gabe and Mark will have. Perhaps, like Eric in *Edge of Seventeen,* Gabe has finally found a gay friend as well as a sexual partner. The most touching moment in the film is the reconciliation of two middle-aged lovers whose relationship has temporarily gone on the skids. The embrace of these two non-buff men, which clearly moves Gabe and Mark, is the film's only acknowledgment that not all gay men are under twenty-five (the night I first saw *Trick,* the theater was filled with gay men over forty). The only sour taste *Trick* leaves is its nasty treatment of women: dreadful Katherine, Gabe's roommate's bimbos, a dour lesbian, and (a vicarious insult) a vicious drag queen. Is this all Greenwich Village has to offer?

If *Trick* is about potential tricks becoming friends and, perhaps, lovers, *Broadway Damage* (1997; screenplay and direction, Victor Mignatti) shows us two best friends becoming lovers. Robert (Aaron Williams), fresh out of NYU, is another aspiring songwriter looking for inspiration. (It is assumed here, as in *Trick* and *Edge of Seventeen,* that falling in love is the key to writing good songs. Lorenz Hart, Cole Porter, and Stephen Sondheim would find that premise a bit silly, I think.) In true show-queen fashion, Robert is an avid reader of *The Sondheim Review.* Bespectacled and sporting a haircut that went out with the Beatles (this is the ultimate bad-haircut film), Robert is nice-looking, but no fantasy. Robert's best friend, and the object of his unrequited affection, is Marc (Michael Shawn Lucas), a would-be actor who is more of a romantic than he is willing to admit. Marc shares a flat with this film's over-the-top fag hag, Cynthia (Mara Hobel), a zaftig rich girl from Long Island prone to fits of panic and self-hatred. Why do these men have no gay friends? Do the women in these films exist to show that gay men are superior to straight women?

Romantic gay men are also superior to cynics. Marc falls in love with David (Broadway musical leading man Hugh Panaro), a gorgeous songwriter-singer who lives in the next building. David sends out dangerously mixed signals. On the one hand, he is the world-wise skeptic, berating the "cheesy sentiment" of musicals; on the other hand, when the lights are out he can sound like the cheesiest ballad: "We could fall in love for tonight. Just for tonight. Let's be lovers," he says, a line he is obviously not using for the first time. This moment is shot with Marc and David looking into a mirror, which underscores the narcissism and fantasy underlying the dialogue. Marc, who believes that "life should be more like a Broadway musical," buys as honest sentiment the cheese that David proffers. The morning after their first blissful night, what does Marc put on the stereo but a Sondheim song, "You Must Meet My Wife." Eventually, Marc discovers that David is a liar, a cad, a hustler, and a thief. Meanwhile Robert, pining for Marc, has been spurned by a cute guy his age and suffered, horror of horrors, a night with a man over forty. Eventually Robert decides to "lay his heart on the line" and writes and sings a love song for Marc. "That was beautiful," Marc responds. "What was it?"

"The grand gesture," Robert replies. It works, and Robert and Marc tentatively begin a romantic relationship. When Cynthia asks them if they're a couple, they can only respond, "Maybe. We're not sure." What would it take to be sure? Are we to see their caution as a positive sign after Marc's disastrous affair with David? *Broadway Damage* is another romance with a qualified ending.

The enjoyable *I Think I Do* (1997; screenplay and direction, Brian Sloan) is one gay romance that presents its central relationship in terms of marriage. The wedding weekend of Matt and Carol (Jamie Harold and Lauren Vélez) is also a reunion of their college friends, many of whom hope for a rekindling of their college romances of five years before. In an act of perversity or political correctness, the bride and groom have chosen as maid of honor Bob (Alexis Arquette), the one openly gay member of the group, now a successful writer of television soap opera, who arrives at the festivities with his boyfriend, gorgeous soap star Sterling Scott (Tuc Watkins, stealing the film). What better catch than a handsome television star who wants to settle down into a cozy domestic partnership? Throughout the film, no one bats an eye at the possibility of a wedding for Bob and Sterling—except Brendan (Christian Maelen), Bob's college roommate and object of unrequited love. Brendan, who has finally come to terms with his sexuality, comes to the wedding in hopes of finally picking up with Bob, whom he violently spurned years before. This little romantic triangle—a quadrangle if you add Sarah (Marianne Hagan), who hopes to rekindle a romance with Brendan—plays out amid a confused tangle of reunions and sexual misadventures. *I Think I Do* comes down foursquare for coupledom for straights and gays.

"LINEN SPORTS JACKETS ARE CASUAL. FUCKING SOMEBODY IS NOT CASUAL."

My younger friends seem to fall into two groups: those who live in coupled relationships and socialize with other couples, and those who depend on a close-knit circle of friends for emotional support while seeking sex in less intimate liaisons. Recent films like *The Broken Hearts Club* and the series *Queer as Folk* offer such a close circle of gay friends—a gay family—as an alternative to the romantic couple, though neither shows unattached gay men as content with their lot.

There's only one couple at the end of writer-director Greg Berlanti's *The Broken Hearts Club* (2000), and half of that couple, Howie (Matt

McGrath), is the most neurotic of the film's group of West Hollywood gay friends. (Of course, Howie is studying to be a psychologist.) Howie is full of "issues," many of which center on his own relationship. He is too uptight to "express any physical affection outside the bedroom" and can't see beyond his own hang-ups to understand or appreciate his erstwhile boyfriend, Marshall (Justin Theroux). "It would be nice," Marshall says, "if your attraction to me had anything to do with me"—a common refrain in this movie. When we first meet Howie and Marshall, they have supposedly broken up, but they still sleep and socialize together. Howie can't admit he loves and needs Marshall (who, like most of the men in the film, is stunning). When Marshall moves on and starts dating other men, Howie eventually comes to appreciate what he has lost. In the final scene, Howie and Marshall are back together and Howie is once again nagging Marshall, who shuts him up with a kiss. As in great 1930s romantic comedies about divorced couples who get back together (*His Girl Friday, The Philadelphia Story*), we are convinced that this couple has negotiated their way to a real relationship.

Jack (John Mahoney), the owner of the restaurant that is the place of employment and hangout for the characters, has been in a relationship for twenty years with "the Purple Guy" (Robert Arce), so called because he always wears purple. As much as the young men love and revere Jack, who is their surrogate father, they can't understand his relationship with a partner who isn't outgoing or, more important to them, physically attractive. At Jack's funeral, the Purple Guy gives a moving eulogy that makes the young men understand the love and devotion that sustained the relationship, though they don't seem capable of having such relationships themselves. Their idol, after all, is Cole (Dean Cain), who is the best-looking of the group, but who "has no soul." Nonetheless, he is the role model for his friends. When we first see Cole, he is using an old audition monologue, part of which he has written on his hand, to end an affair. "You are worse than all the muscle boys combined," the recipient of this performance screams. "At least they don't presume to want a relationship." This young man is foolish enough to insist that "fucking somebody is not casual." It is to Cole, until he finds someone even better-looking and more straight-acting than he—a closeted movie star—to break his heart.

The central romantic relationship in the film is between Dennis (Timothy Olyphant) and the "newbie," Kevin (Andrew Keegan). Dennis is a twenty-eight-year-old aspiring photographer. He is obviously independently wealthy. He owns a beautiful West Hollywood home, drives an SUV, and is able to move to Europe at the end of the film to "find [his] photographer's eye." Dennis longs to grow out of the cycle of casual sex. He throws one gorgeous young man out of his bed on his birthday because, he says, "I'm tired of sex with people who only care what I look like and make up the rest." After this moment of virtue, Dennis goes into his kitchen and finds Kevin, who has just had sex with Cole. Kevin is new to the gay scene and has reservations about the behavior of Dennis and his friends: "You're a bunch of bitter, jaded fags," Kevin says. Inevitably, Dennis and Kevin become friends, then lovers. After they have sex, Dennis realizes that he has a lot of growing up to do to be worthy of someone like Kevin: "I'm twenty-eight years old, and the only thing I'm good at is being gay." As in classic Hollywood heterosexual fantasies, maturity is equated with stable relationships. Even Dennis's decision to go off to Europe and develop his photographic skills is linked to his desire for a mature relationship: "It's the only way I'll have something to give back to someone." Kevin vows to be there when Dennis returns, suggesting the possibility of a relationship in the future after they both have matured sufficiently.

What the men in this film have in place of stable romantic relationships is their group of close friends, their support group. As Terrence McNally's play (later made into a film) *Love! Valour! Compassion!*[16] celebrated the intense friendships of a group of New York men who formed a kind of intentional family, so *The Broken Hearts Club* celebrates this circle of Los Angeles friends for whom being gay is the tie that binds. "Why be friends with a group of people just because you're all gay," Kevin asks Dennis, but in this comedy of manners, Kevin comes to see this hyper-articulate group as his university in coming out. Not only does he have sex with two of the group; he shares their hairdresser, takes a job at Jack's, where most of them work, and eventually dresses and accesorizes like Dennis. In his book *Gay Men's Friendships: Invincible Communities,* Peter M. Nardi observes, "Friendship is a personal process as well as a social one, and it's at this intersection, where self and community are reproduced among gay men, that the power of friendship can be palpably experienced."[17] Andrew's integration into the group and his socialization as a gay man through this circle of friends is a textbook example of the kind of process Nardi describes.

This group of friends, like all intentional families, may have its drawbacks. "We make each other miserable," one of the group proclaims, but they also make each other laugh. Like most families, the group can hold its members back more than move them forward—Dennis realizes he has to get away for a while to grow—but the circle of friends is more important than the romantic relationships individual members may have. Yet there's still the ideal of a loving relationship for this "bunch of 10's looking for an 11."

Dirty Old Men

When I was a teenager, at a time when the media offered no gay romantic models, middle-aged movie stars were extremely popular. A graying Cary Grant threatened Doris Day's virginity in *That Touch of Mink* (1962) and saved Eva Marie Saint from Mount Rushmore in *North by Northwest* (1959). A middle-aged James Stewart destroyed Kim Novak in Alfred Hitchcock's masterpiece, *Vertigo,* (1958) and took on an aging John Wayne in *The Man Who Shot Liberty Valance* (1962). In his fifties, Fred Astaire danced his way through *Funny Face* (1957) and *Daddy Long Legs* (1955). Clearly there was a large audience of women who found these middle-aged men sexy and men who found them suitable role models. In the fifties, eternal youth was not the goal of young Americans, and adolescence was a miserable phase one got out of as soon as possible. Now we occasionally have celebrations of aging masculinity like Clint Eastwood, Donald Sutherland, James Garner, and Tommy Lee Jones going into space in *Space Cowboys* (2000). Those daring codgers were straight, of course, and out to prove that their libido and the organs connected to it still worked well and often. Now that I'm middle-aged, I long to see a gay version of *Space Cowboys.*

In *Trick,* Gabe has a heavyset, middle-aged gay friend, Perry, who reconciles with his heavyset, balding lover in one of the film's most touching scenes. In *Broadway Damage,* Robert spends the night with a sweet forty-something man who grieves over the loss of his friends to AIDS. *Billy's Hollywood Screen Kiss* (1998; screenplay and direction, Tommy O'Haver) presents three generations of gay men, but the forty-something is unrequitedly smitten with the twenty-something hero, and the sixty-something is a grand old queen and a bit of a dirty old man. The film of Terrence McNally's *Love! Valour! Compassion!* (1997; screenplay, Terrence McNally; direction, Joe Mantello) has a few men over forty, most of whom pine over men half their age. These films are at least acknowledgments that there are gay men over twenty-five, but it is clear that few gay filmmakers are interested in making movies about us.[18] If we are to believe those filmmakers who do, gay men past the buff years are dirty old men obsessed with young straight men. This is not to say that *Gods and Monsters* and *Love and Death on Long Island* aren't excellent films, but it would be nice to see older gay men cast in something besides variations on *Death in Venice,* meditations on mortality.

"I KNOW A REAL MAN LIKE YOU WOULD BREAK MY NECK IF I SO MUCH AS LAID A FINGER ON HIM."

In *Gods and Monsters* (1998; screenplay and direction, Bill Condon), based on Christopher Bram's fine novel, *Father of Frankenstein,* it is the mid-1950s and James Whale (Ian McKellen), the director of two classic Frankenstein films, is recuperating from a stroke in his Hollywood home, tended by his dour, disapproving maid, Hanna (Lynn Redgrave). Whale's stroke has left him unable to control the mass of memories and sensations stored in his brain. While Whale's brain may be a muddle, his libido is intact. When an ambitious college student comes by to interview him, Whale makes him remove an article of clothing for each question he asks. Whale then turns his attention to his hunky new yardman, Clay Boone (Brendan Fraser). Clay, a rather lost young man, lives in a trailer and spends his nights in a local bar picking up whatever women he can for sex without any commitment. The female bartender he has been sleeping with tells him, "You're not marriage material. You're not even boyfriend material. You're just a kid." Boone does seem strangely unmoored, filled with anger, but also gentle. He is flattered that the director of *Frankenstein* pays attention to him, even more flattered when Whale wants him to model for drawings, but he goes homophobic when Whale reminisces about the orgiastic gay parties he used to host.

Despite his intolerance of Whale's more ribald reminiscences, Clay keeps returning to Whale's house. He admires and cares for the old man, and is grateful for his interest. On his last night alive, Whale is haunted by visions of his first love, a young soldier he fought with in World War I. Alone together Whale shows Clay the scribblings that are Whale's attempts at drawing the young man. "It's all gone for me now," the former artist, designer, and director cries. In response, Clay stands nude before Whale, in a gesture of trust and an attempt to become Whale's muse—to rekindle his creativity. A despondent Whale uses Clay's gesture as the opening gambit in a bid to goad Clay into killing him, but Clay, alas, is not the murderous Hollywood rough trade Whale is hoping for. "I am not your monster," Clay cries. "You're a bloody pussycat," Whale scoffs at the weeping young man. Forgiving to the end, Clay tucks Whale into bed as the old man takes on the role of the mad, dying King Lear. "Pray you, undo this button," he says to the loyal if confused Clay. Later that night, Whale drowns himself in his pool. He leaves Clay his original sketch of Frankenstein's monster, which, years later, Clay proudly shows his son, who doesn't appreciate Whale's film or the importance of the director to his father. On the back of the sketch, Whale has written the monster's question, "Friend?"

What develops in *Gods and Monsters* is not a romance but a friendship between two lonely men who find comfort in each other's company. In their last conversation, Whale asks, "Do you believe people come into our lives for a purpose?" Clay's purpose is to lovingly ease Whale toward death. "I didn't do this," Clay tells Hanna when they discover Whales's suicide, but in the director's dreams, Clay as the monster leads him to join his first lover in death in the trenches. At the end of the film, we see Clay outside his home walking around in the rain like Frankenstein's monster, a reminder of his relationship with Whale.

"THE DISCOVERY OF BEAUTY WHERE NO ONE THOUGHT OF LOOKING FOR IT."

If James Whale is more than half in love with easeful death, Giles De'Ath (John Hurt), in *Love and Death on Long Island* (1997; screenplay and direction, Richard Kwietniowski), finds a reason to live in the vision of a handsome young movie actor. Giles is a British novelist who has managed to keep the twentieth century at bay. Ignorant of technology and popular culture, Giles takes pride in wearing the mantle of the pure artist; his novels are read only by the cognoscenti, and he would not deign to have his works turned into film. Recently widowed, and, like Whale, cared for by a doting housekeeper, he has also avoided contemplating or experiencing his homosexuality. Caught in the rain without his keys, Giles ventures into a cinema where a film version of an E. M. Forster novel is playing but, unfamiliar with modern multiplexes, ventures into the wrong auditorium where he finds himself watching a horrible teen-exploitation film called *Hotpants College II,* which appalls him until Ronnie Bostock (Jason Priestley) appears on the screen, inspiring infatuation and hurling Giles into the world of contemporary trash culture. Like the most smitten adolescent fan, he starts buying teen magazines and cutting out pictures of Ronnie for his scrapbook. After careful viewing of the videos of Ronnie Bostock's awful films, Giles lectures on "the discovery of beauty where no one thought of looking for it." Giles's perception of Ronnie is partly erotic, partly aesthetic. He connects an image of Ronnie's character, covered in ketchup languidly lying on a soda-shop counter with Henry Wallis's famous painting, *The Death of Chatterton.* "It [his perception of beauty in Ronnie] has brought me into contact with everything I have never been," Giles tells a puzzled audience, but the beauty is contained in a callow young man starring in truly dreadful mindless trash. When his agent suggests he is in need of a trip, Giles flies off to Long Island, where, according to a fan magazine, Ronnie Bostock lives. Living in a cheap motel and eating at a greasy spoon, Giles goes looking for Ronnie's home. Through a cleverly managed supermarket encounter with Ronnie's girlfriend, Audrey (Fiona Loewi), he finds himself face-to-face with his new idol.

Audrey quickly catches on to Giles's real motivation for his attempts to guide Ronnie's career to a higher plane and spirits Ronnie away. Before he leaves, Giles meets Ronnie in a coffee shop and confesses his love, offering to devote himself to Ronnie's career, to be the older lover to Ronnie's ephebe, and finally admitting "how completely, how desperately, I love you." This foolish, futile gesture is Giles's coming to life as well as his coming out. At the end of the film, we see Giles heading back to the airport with his dark glasses on. Ronnie may be the same nice, vapid actor at the end, but Giles has been transformed by this quixotic unrequited romance.

What do such movies mean to a gay man the age of James Whale and Giles De'Ath? In his post-stroke deteriorating mental state, Whale sees beautiful young men as part of a lost past. All he can do when Clay displays his body is try to make him simultaneously part of that past and a monster who will kill him. We are barraged with images of beautiful if bland young men, a bevy of Ronnie Bostocks, reminders of our lost youth, of what we cannot have and perhaps don't even want. Would a young gay man today respond as kindly to Whale's confusion or Giles's plea for love, or would their naked avowals be food for mockery? Those of us who can proudly sing "I'm Still Here" have no role models in gay cinema, no middle-aged stars still considered sexy. Even the thirty-ish men on *Queer as Folk* think a forty-year-old is ancient. If Cary Grant could age gracefully and elegantly and continue to be a romantic lead into his sixties, perhaps there is hope.

Chapter Eight

BLACK AND WHITE

"Ennobling Love"

In the first episode of Alan Ball's HBO series, *Six Feet Under,* closeted David (Michael C. Hall) is secretly in a relationship with a black police-man, Keith (Mathew St. Patrick). When Keith appears at David's father's viewing, David introduces him as his friend. "You have a friend who is a cop?" David's mother (Frances Conroy) asks, as if there is something shocking in the class discrepancy involved in the friendship of an under-taker and a policeman. Later, David's teenage sister, Claire (Lauren Am-brose), asks her other brother Nate (Peter Krause), "David has a friend who's a cop?" as if such a relationship were the apex of unhip. No one mentions that Keith is black. We are told that David spends a lot of time with his lover's family but is closeted in his own home. Toward the end of the episode, David and Keith, who is much less neurotic than the white people on the series, kiss passionately. (Cable television, which builds its audience on its willingness to break taboos—"Showtime—No limits"—is much less skittish about gay men kissing than Hollywood film or network television.) What Ball's script doesn't mention is that there are difficulties in being a gay policeman in most American towns and cities, and there are particular problems associated with being gay and black, which a growing number of African American gay organizations are try-ing to address. I don't mean to suggest that black homophobia is any more virulent than white homophobia—only that it exists and that, as Henry Louis Gates observes, "Disapproval of homosexuality has been a

characteristic of much of the black nationalist ideology that has reap-
peared in the aftermath of the civil rights era."[1]

The only major film to touch upon the issues of race and homophobia is *Philadelphia* (1993; screenplay, Ron Nyswaner; direction, Jonathan
Demme), in which homophobic attorney Joe Miller (Denzel Washington) takes on the suit of Andy Beckett (Tom Hanks), a gay attorney with
AIDS, against the law firm that unjustly fired him. "These people [ho-
mosexuals] make me sick," he tells his buddies at a bar, "but a law has
been broken." However, the film is careful to separate Joe Miller's homophobia from his African American identity. He is a homophobe because
normal all-American guys like him are homophobes. His pals at the bar,
who also make homophobic comments, are white, as are the senior partners at Andy's law firm. To his horror, Joe is propositioned by a handsome
young black man—black gay men do exist in this film, but they live in a
world apart from the white gay men. There are few black faces other than
Washington's at the costume party Tom Hanks's Andy Beckett throws for
himself. His lover may be a handsome Spaniard (or are we to believe An-
tonio Banderas's Miguel is Latino?), but his friends are all-white. This is,
for many gay men, their situation in many American cities: an all white
enclave in an urban center in which the majority is nonwhite. There are
no people of color in the Pittsburgh gay scene depicted in Showtimes's
Queer as Folk.

Joe Miller's "normality" and health are contrasted with Andy Beckett's
progressive debilitation, as if heterosexuality and blackness represent
strength, and homosexuality and whiteness mean weakness and disease;
for, to some extent, *Philadelphia* buys into the concept it purports to attack: that gay men bring AIDS on themselves. Like many Hollywood
products, the film also presents the black man as superior to his white
counterpart.

In his 1948 essay "Come Back to the Raft Ag'in, Huck Honey!," Leslie
Fiedler observed the motif of love between a white man and a black man
in classic American literature: "Just as the pure love of man and man is in
general set off against the ignoble passion of man for woman, so more
specifically (and more vividly) the dark desire which leads to miscegenation is contrasted with the ennobling love of a white man and a colored
one."[2] We can see the same phenomenon in a series of films about the relationships of white and black men: *The Defiant Ones, The Delta,* and *Parallel Sons.* Each sets a fraught relationship between a white man and a
person of color in a landscape outside the city—the southern backwoods,

the outskirts of Memphis and the Mississippi River, rural upstate New York—echoing what Fiedler calls the pattern of classic American literature, which celebrates "the mutual love of a white man *and a colored*" in a setting as close to "nature undefiled" as the late twentieth century allows. The assumption of these films seems to be that close, eroticized bonding between a white man and a black man can take place only as a temporary idyll outside conventional social institutions, and that it will inevitably have tragic consequences. An element of criminality is involved in all these films, as if moving into biracial homoerotic intimacy inevitably moves one outside the law. "In the myth," Fiedler writes of our literature, "it is typically in the role of outcast, ragged woodsman, or despised sailor ('Call me Ishmael'), or unregenerate boy (Huck, before the prospect of being 'sivilized,' cries out, 'I been there before!') that we turn to the love of the colored man." From Joker in *The Defiant Ones* to Seth in *Parallel Sons,* the white men in these films see themselves as alienated from their environment. The black man offers them, however briefly, a sense of belonging and a sense of revenge against the milieu they hate.

"YOU'RE MARRIED TO ME ALL RIGHT, JOKER, AND HERE'S THE RING."

When he says this, Sidney Poitier's Noah Cullen is not engaging in a commitment ceremony with Tony Curtis's "Joker" Jackson in Stanley Kramer's sermon on male bonding and racial enlightenment, *The Defiant Ones* (1958; screenplay, Harold Jacob Smith); rather, he is reminding Joker that these two fugitives are still chained together as they try to make their escape from a Southern prison. "How can they chain a white man to a black?" one policeman asks the sheriff, who responds, "The warden's got a sense of humor." While the policeman is sure the two will kill each other, Kramer wants to show how under duress a black man and a white man can bond. It would be almost another decade before Kramer could present a sermon on interracial marriage in *Guess Who's Coming to Dinner,* but *The Defiant Ones,* filmed, appropriately, in black-and-white, can easily be read in ways that would have shocked the liberal filmmaker. Unable to create a heterosexual romance, he managed to create a crypto-gay one.

It is to Kramer's credit that there is more to the tension between his two protagonists than race. Noah may bristle at being called "boy" and carry with him a lot of hostility at the white men who have kept him down, but Joker, who comes from a poor background, equally resents having to pay deference to men who have more money and power than he. Throughout the film, Joker needs to be cared for by Noah. The white man is a fast talker, but his body is constantly under attack: He becomes infected from lacerations caused by the chain, is threatened with potential lynching after he has darkened his skin, and is shot by a young boy when he tries to return to Noah after the chains have been cut. The black man is placed in the role of protector and caregiver, which is, as David Savran points out, "a position long reserved for African Americans in the 'white imaginary.'"[3] On their first day running, the two men dive into a clay pit to avoid being spotted. When they try to scramble out independently, they keep pulling each other back in. It is only when Joker climbs onto Noah's shoulders that they manage to climb out. This moment is typical Stanley Kramer symbolism, less heavy-handed and potentially funny than the black man's putting mud on the white man's face so he isn't easily spotted in the dark.

On their first night together, the two men sleep on a hillside. When Joker wakes up, he has a moment of panic when he realizes that he has slept huddled against Noah with his arms around him. Was this just to keep warm? Kramer may have wanted this moment to be nonsexual, but such a reading is more difficult now. Later, the men arrive at the cabin of an attractive woman (Cara Williams) and her son. After helping the men break the chain that has joined them, the woman immediately takes a romantic interest in Joker and makes plans to run away with him to New Orleans. When he realizes that she has sent Noah to his certain death in a swamp full of quicksand, Joker throws her aside and runs to be in the swamp with Noah. As in the western, a man chooses the outdoors rather than the domestic space, the unacknowledged eroticized male bond rather than heterosexuality, freedom rather than love and fatherhood. The men are no longer chained together, but another strong bond has been forged. Does Kramer want his audience to believe that these men give up their freedom to stay together out of a sense of racial harmony? Only one interpretation makes sense of the characters' motivation. In the final sequence, Noah has his arms around a wounded Joker, shot by the son of the women he fled, and is singing as the sheriff comes to recapture them. What more do we need to see?

As the film progresses, the other characters are less important as agents who would put the two men back in prison than as obstacles to their relationship. Even the woman, ostensibly there to keep the proceedings properly heterosexual, becomes overly aggressive (by 1950s standards), predatory, and indifferent to the fate of one of the protagonists. At the end, Joker says to Noah, "We gave them a hell of a run for it, didn't we?" Their adventure, like those of most of the eroticized interracial couples I have found, is temporary, of necessity outside of conventional society, here represented by the prison.

SIDNEY POITIER'S SON

Tony Curtis's Joker didn't become smitten with just *any* African American; he left the eager blond woman to be with Sidney Poitier, who quickly became a symbol of the Acceptable Black Man, appearing in a series of movies between 1958 and 1967 in which he became more and more idealized. In John Guare's play *Six Degrees of Separation* (1990; film version, 1993; direction, Fred Schepisi), a young homeless black man cons his way into the homes of wealthy, nominally liberal, middle-aged New Yorkers by claiming to be the son of Sidney Poitier, who is to them "the barrier breaker of the fifties and sixties."[4] Poitier still represents for these people the black man who can "come to dinner." Within a few minutes of entering the Kittredge household, "Paul Poitier" has performed a number of the functions of the Acceptable Black. He has been wounded (supposedly) by a fellow African American, thus distancing himself from "the other," he has entertained with manufactured anecdotes and plagiarized platitudes, and he has served by cooking up a meal. Above all, he has allowed his hosts to indulge themselves in feelings of liberal complacency. When Paul brings a white hustler, an unacceptable sign of homosexuality, into the Kittredges' home, his hosts panic. The Acceptable Black is no longer acceptable; the naked hustler only a "thing." The Kittredges don't understand that hiring a white hustler is a turn-on for Paul because it is the ultimate sign of the ex-hustler's new power and prestige. What moves Paul from the streets of Boston to the homes of the rich is not only his chosen name but his sexuality. Paul's gayness may have isolated him in an African American community, but it was his entrée into Trent Conway's apartment, where he offered sex in exchange for the information on Trent's rich friends that ultimately gained him access to the Kittredges. But his sexuality also alienates his hosts and ultimately gets him arrested.

Paul's welcome into the Kittredge home and his betrayal of his hosts' trust are presented as anecdotes, flashbacks narrated by the Kittredges. Throughout, he exists only as a memory of a traumatic and/or liberating experience for the whites he encounters. He has no voice of his own. For Trent Conway he is a black male Eliza Doolittle: "I'll make you the most eagerly sought-after young man in the East."[5] For Rick, a young, heretofore straight actor, he is a romantic idyll and the black man as stud—"We took a carriage ride in the park and he asked me if he could fuck me and he did and it was fantastic"[6]—and an experience so unsettling to Rick's concept of himself that he commits suicide. Paul is, throughout the character's reminiscences, the embodiment of the racial and sexual fantasies of the characters who narrate his part in their lives. At the end, he suffers the fate of black men like Sidney Poitier's Noah; he is arrested and disappears without a trace into the criminal justice system. Paul's only crime is not being Sidney Poitier's son—not being the black man his white sponsors could accept.

"SORRY. I'M JUST PLAYING."

The first and last shots of writer-director Ira Sachs's *The Delta* (1996) are of Minh Nguyen (Thang Chan), a gay, half-Vietnamese, half–African American man, woefully out of place in either culture, riding his motorbike down a highway. The rest of the film is a flashback to the days preceding this moment, during which Minh has a brief affair with a white teenager, Lincoln Bloom (Shayne Gray), and a lethal encounter with an African American man. Minh's motorbike is a figure for the aimless movement, often hostile relationships that aren't really connections, and meaningless, often violent actions that we see in *The Delta*.

Lincoln Bloom, Minh's seventeen-year-old weekend lover and alter ego, is a true member of generation X. Lincoln lives with his father in the suburbs of Memphis. On the surface he is a good-looking, quiet, proper southern boy; underneath he is all sexual confusion. Lincoln excuses himself from the Sunday family dinner to retire to the bathroom to masturbate. He leaves his friends and girlfriend—granted, a tedious lot—to pick up men in a local cruising spot. It would take more reflection than Lincoln is capable of for him to integrate his sexuality with the life he is expected to lead. Nor is he clear on the possibility of an authentic, as opposed to a performed, relationship. "Tell me you love me. Tell me you can't live without me," he commands his girlfriend. "Sorry, I'm just playing. Didn't mean it." At the cruising spot, he has a brief sexual encounter with Minh in his car. Later, Lincoln runs into Minh again in the hall of a porn-video emporium. It is unclear what motivates Lincoln to take Minh off to his father's boat for the weekend—sex, loneliness, curiosity about someone so different, or attraction to potential danger in this volatile young man. Yet for a moment, in the morning, as the two young men bathe in the Mississippi River, a tenuous, temporary emotional connection is made. Minh wants a real connection, a friend. Above all, Minh, filled with anger, particularly against the African American father who won't acknowledge his existence, wants to make an impression: "If I hurt you, you will remember. I want you to remember." Can the vacuous Lincoln feel enough to be hurt?

Their overnight boat trip down the Mississippi takes Lincoln into alien territory, populated mostly by African Americans. He and Minh walk to a black-owned bar, where Minh purchases illegal fireworks. When a black policeman tries to arrest them for setting off the fireworks, Minh forces Lincoln to run. Frightened and exhausted, Lincoln beats Minh and leaves him. Lincoln is not emotionally equipped to deal with such chaos and the potential for public exposure of his affair with this racial and social "other." After leaving Minh and returning the boat, he drives to his girlfriend's house and seduces her: "I love you. I really do," he says, though his words of love are qualified by despair: "I'll do anything you want. I don't care." Is Lincoln having sex with her as a means of establishing an alibi for his weekend tryst before he faces his furious father, or is it a confused young man's attempt to return to "normality"? Only his beating of Minh springs from an outpouring of genuine emotion, but sex seems the only connection he is capable of.

The final third of the film follows Minh the day Lincoln leaves him beaten in the woods. He goes back to the apartment he shares with a gay Vietnamese man, but Minh, half-black, doesn't totally belong in that world even though he speaks the language. After being berated by the wife of the owner of a Vietnamese bar for not paying his debts, he goes to another bar, where he picks up a black man whom he takes to Lincoln's father's boat and kills, an act that can be seen as symbolic of Minh's wish to kill his father and as an act of revenge against Lincoln, who also spurned him. Is this the first man Minh has killed? Before killing the man, Minh tells him, "I play with people. I talk. I say nice things. But inside I nothing." This is as much an expression of Lincoln's feelings as his own. Lincoln isn't above recycling Minh's words: He recounts to his girlfriend a dream he supposedly had about her that is actually a paraphrase of a dream Minh had—or fabricated—about *him*. At the end, as at the beginning, we see Minh driving down a road on his motorbike. However many men he has killed, the experience seems to have had no effect on him, neither excitement nor release, any more than Minh has had any effect on Lincoln.

This slow-moving, dark, black-and-white film, with much improvised dialogue, is disturbing precisely because of the aimlessness and lack of affect of its young characters. Early in the film, Lincoln gets picked up by an older man and taken to a motel where the man asks to be beaten. Lincoln just looks at him blankly, then calmly puts on his clothes and leaves. Even Minh's status as a racial, cultural, and sexual outsider, a casualty of America's racism and imperial adventures (and of Vietnamese racism as well), is less a political statement than a figure for universal alienation. So are Lincoln's travels through gay cruising spots and peep shows more a figure for disconnection than for sexual identity. The pointless improvised dialogue of the scenes of teenagers wandering around looking for something to do is purposely tedious. Yet writer-director Sachs seems to be aiming for wider resonances. The name of his protagonist—Lincoln Bloom—ironically evokes both the president who freed the slaves and James Joyce's Leopold Bloom, the Irish Jew whose nocturnal wanderings through Dublin are leavened with ironic references to past, more coherent civilizations. Movement, though constant in *The Delta,* is even more random than it is in *Ulysses.* There are echoes of *Huckleberry Finn* in the boat trip down the river, but they too only provide ironic counterpoint. For all this, *The Delta* is a profoundly disturbing film.

"ALL THIS NIGGER SHIT. YOU DON'T EVEN KNOW ONE, DO YOU?"

Race is, as it is not for Lincoln Bloom, a passionate concern for young Seth (Gabriel Mann) in John G. Young's *Parallel Sons* (1995), another narrative of a volatile relationship between a white teenager and a person of color. Living in a small town in upstate New York in which "everyone is fucking interchangeable," blond Seth stands out with his dreadlocks, rap music, and urban black clothing. His room looks like that of a highly political black undergraduate. What could be more rebellious in a conservative, all-white town? A talented artist, Seth works in a diner and lives at home with his father and younger sister, whom he adores, but he dreams of going to art school in New York City. His only escape seems to be liquor. His father, a local gun dealer, has no understanding of Seth's dreams—"What are you going to do with a college degree in painting?" he asks. Seth's one friend, Marty (Josh Hopkins), content with his life and his one job possibility as a corrections officer, sees Seth as an oddball affecting "nigger shit" to get attention. Kristen (Heather Gottlieb), the most rebellious girl in the town, fantasizes a relationship with Seth, but he violently spurns her sexual overtures. Marty and Kristen would see Seth as even more of an oddball if they knew of the sexual fantasies that are intertwined with his racial identification: Gay boys would be even more alien in this small town than blacks. Above all, Seth wants to escape from this town.

Enter Knowledge Johnson (Lawrence Mason), a young black escapee from a prison hospital, who tries to rob the local café but is too weak from a gunshot wound and collapses on the floor. Seth picks him up, hides him in a cabin in the woods, and nurses him back to health. As a gay black man, Knowledge too feels alienated: "In my hood, man, if you're black and a fag, you're just a fag." Now dependent on a white man and desperate to avoid prison, Knowledge is at first hostile toward this white "nigger wannabe." Seth, however, is fascinated. There's a beautiful moment when Seth washes the naked body of his unconscious charge and for the first time touches and explores a black man's body, checking his fingers to see if the color comes off. Seth's feelings for Knowledge are more than erotic fantasy: He's willing to risk his life to save Knowledge. The film chronicles the development of a relationship between Seth and Knowledge—first the development of a friendship, then love. How important is it to Seth's racial/sexual fantasy that the relationship begins with Knowledge totally dependent on Seth?

After Seth has killed the town's sheriff to protect Knowledge and in the process has trapped his friend in a more desperate chase, the two begin a tragic journey to cross the border into Canada, pursued by Seth's father, on a vigilante mission to destroy his son's relationship, and by the local police. When Seth breaks his leg, Knowledge must care for him. On their last night of freedom, the two finally have sex.

The tragic ending of *Parallel Sons* grows inevitably out of the action. There is no escape for men like Knowledge in a culture that ascribes to them the worst possible motives. He will be unjustly blamed for the killing of the sheriff. Nor is there the possibility of escape for Seth, who has written or tattooed on his arm the word CONVICTED. "I don't want to be here anymore," he says to Francine (Maureen Shannon), the owner of the diner where he works. There seems to be only one way out.

Parallel Sons opens with the accidental shooting of a black boy, Knowledge's son, and ends with another senseless death. As Knowledge was trapped in his neighborhood, where his sexuality would never be accepted, so Seth is trapped in his. Race and class might separate these men, but each is an alien in his own culture. As Knowledge touches Seth for the first time, Seth tells the story of two events that happened when he was thirteen. A boy camping with his family disappeared and, despite a massive search effort, was never found. "It was like all of a sudden this place people thought was beautiful turned into a monster that could swallow you up." A couple of weeks later, Seth's father caught him experimenting sexually with two male friends, one of whom was Kyle, who later hanged himself with his Superman blanket: "Dad said if I was ever bad again like that, something like what happened to that kid could happen to me." And indeed it does. The primary visual irony of *Parallel Sons* is that such a tragic tale of entrapment could take place in such a beautiful location. As the two young men try to walk to Canada, they pass through lovely mountain scenery without a sign of civilization. Here, briefly, they can feel free, before civilization destroys their relationship, another temporary idyll, which is all these works allow their black and white lovers.

As Leslie Fiedler says:

> Our dark-skinned beloved will take us in, we assure ourselves, when we have been cut off, or have cut ourselves off, from all others, without rancor or the insult of forgiveness. He will fold us in his arms . . . And yet we cannot ever really forget our guilt; the stories that embody the myth dramatize as if compulsively the role of the colored man as the victim.[7]

At the end of *The Defiant Ones,* Noah, who could have gotten away, is going back to prison for his loyalty to Joker. An innocent black man is dead at the end of *The Delta.* At the end of *Parallel Sons,* Knowledge is sitting in a police car watching as Seth's body is carried into an ambulance. He will go back to prison, lost in the warehouse for urban black men. His entrapment is far from over, while Seth may have been spared a miserable existence in a place he hated. For a brief moment, in as close to "Nature undefiled" as one can get in the late twentieth century, a black man and a white man had a moment of tenderness that is far more fulfilling than the anxiety-ridden bonding of straight white men we see in films like *Deliverance* and *The Deer Hunter.*

Coda

ASSIMILATION

In Alan Ball's television series, *Six Feet Under,* the two sons represent conflicting expressions of confused masculinity. Nate left home as a young man to find himself. Now, at thirty-five, he is a self-confessed failure who has never decided what he wants to do with his life and has never had a relationship that lasted more than two months. His father's death makes him aware that life may pass him by altogether if he doesn't start making positive decisions. Despite his absence and confusion, or because of it, he is the apple of his mother's eye. Perhaps his mother is devoted to him because Nate is, like the feckless sons in *Death of a Salesman* and *Cat on a Hot Tin Roof,* beautiful. His younger brother, David, has tried to be the good boy, working in his father's undertaking business and living next door to his parents. Like many closeted people, David is blind to the fact that his family has already figured out his secret. David's closeted state is consistent with the way in which he tries to control all his emotions. The beauty of *Six Feet Under,* broadcast opposite Showtime's vision of life in a gay ghetto, *Queer as Folk,* is that gayness is included in a wide spectrum of human experience. Both brothers see themselves as failures and unhappy, and David's sexuality is merely one part of his personality, as homosexuality is merely one possible avenue for sexual and emotional expression. There is no ghetto here. Gay people are part of the human landscape, and gay men can be seen in comparison with straight men rather than as separate beings. The problem for David and Nate is to figure out how to be mature men after their father, their role model, has died. Sexuality and masculinity are untied here. By the end of the first season of *Six Feet Under,* there was a close, loving bond between straight and gay brother. In a world without a patriarch, men can thrive professionally and personally and women like Nate and David's mother who defined themselves by their marriage can find themselves anew.

In the 2001 film *The Deep End* (screenplay and direction, Scott McGehee and David Siegel), the father, a naval officer, is literally and figuratively "at sea," a metaphor for his inability to understand the changes taking place in his own family. Throughout the film, enacting her own version of "Don't ask, don't tell" his wife goes to great lengths to conceal from him knowledge of their son's homosexuality, the greatest threat to the patriarchal order he represents. Corpses are hidden and vicious blackmailers are confronted, so to suppress the knowledge. Nonetheless, in *The Deep End,* patriarchy poisons homosexual and heterosexual relationships alike; "straight-looking and -acting" older gay men are as capable as straight men of being violent and tyrannical to their lovers. Like Laura in *Tea and Sympathy,* the heroine of *The Deep End,* Margaret Hall (Tilda Swinton), becomes defender of the weak and sensitive against the strong and brutal, and as devoted to Alek (Goran Visnjic), the sad young man who tries to defy his ruthless partner in blackmail (perhaps his sexual partner as well), as to her own son. While the alpha males get their comeuppance, sensitive men are embraced by a strong, protective, motherly woman. Few American films offer as powerful a challenge to traditional American gender roles.

At the same time, there is a warning implicit in Margaret's compulsion to hide all traces of her son's homosexuality. In the era of George W. Bush, homosexuality is again supposed to be tacit. "I'm a 'Don't ask, don't tell' fella," W. said in one of his presidential debates, and his unquestioning support of the military's attempt to silence, if not eliminate, homosexuality, has spread to public discourse.

The events of September 11, 2001 may herald significant changes in American culture. The destruction of those two phallic symbols and the maiming of the seat of the American military might have brought us to a state of prolonged military conflict and public fear. As we watched repeatedly images that eerily echo dozens of movies, from *Die Hard* to *Godzilla,* identity politics, a luxury of peacetime, seem to recede into the distance, a vestige of the late twentieth century. Nothing would please more some of the conservatives now in power in Washington. As we are attacked by a foe who believe women should be kept uneducated and servile and gay men should be tortured and killed, it seems crucial to hold onto and fight for the gains women and gay people have made. Two nights after the horrible attacks, the two kingpins of American funda-mentalist Christianity, Jerry Falwell and Pat Robertson, interpreted the assault as God's punishment on a nation that allows the American Civil Liberties Union, abortion, and homosexuals, thus showing themselves as kin to the Taliban. As military forces began moving into Afghanistan, the Pentagon announced that during the conflict, enforcement of the ridicu-lous, cruel "Don't Ask, Don't Tell" policy would be at the discretion of commanding officers, implying that those who disregard the "Don't Tell" part of the policy might not be thrown out until after the conflict is re-solved and their wartime usefulness is ended.

It may be difficult to think seriously about movies right now, but as flags hang from almost every business and residence, it is important to understand the light and dark sides of our national mythology, as it has been disseminated by Hollywood. How prescient was it that on Septem-ber 9, HBO began airing a miniseries celebrating wartime male bonding, entitled *Band of Brothers?* Let's hope that the loving brotherhood of gay and straight men depicted in *Six Feet Under* can be part of twenty-first century America.

Durham and Baltimore
September, 2001

NOTES

FOREWORD

1. Susan Jeffords, *Hard Bodies: Hollywood Masculinity in the Reagan Era* (New Brunswick, N.J.: Rutgers University Press, 1994), 11.
2. Ibid.
3. Robert Bly, *Iron John: A Book About Men* (New York: Vintage, 1992), 1–2.
4. Quoted in Charles Kaiser, *The Gay Metropolis: 1940–1996* (Boston: Houghton Mifflin, 1997), 277.
5. Ron danced briefly with the touring company of the Joffrey Ballet. When the press focused on his profession, he was moved to the ensemble of the main company. I saw a performance of his at the New York City Center during the presidential campaign. The women around me were obviously there to see young Ron. He was generally in the back row of the ensemble and seen only fleetingly in the foreground; my neighbors were quite frustrated. Ron stood out only because he was taller than his fellow dancers.
6. Bret Easton Ellis, *American Psycho* (New York: Vintage, 1991), 384.
7. Mark Doty, *Firebird: A Memoir* (New York: HarperCollins, 1999), 56.
8. Ibid., 102.
9. Michael Kimmel, *Manhood in America: A Cultural History* (New York: Free Press, 1996), 7.
10. Ibid., ix.
11. Robert Anderson, *Tea and Sympathy* (New York: Random House, 1953), 39. For a fuller discussion of *Tea and Sympathy,* see my own *Still Acting Gay: Male Homosexuality in Modern Drama* (New York: St. Martin's Press, 2000), 116–20.
12. Jeffords, *Hard Bodies.*
13. Susan Bordo, *The Male Body: A New Look at Men in Public and in Private* (New York: Farrar, Straus & Giroux, 1999), 55.
14. Alexander Doty, *Flaming Classics: Queering the Film Canon* (New York: Routledge, 2000), 1.
15. Steven Cohan, "Queering the Deal: On the Road with Hope and Crosby," in *Out Takes: Essays on Queer Theory and Film,* ed. Ellis Hanson (Durham, N.C.: Duke University Press, 1999), 23–45.
16. Ellis Hanson, "Introduction," in *Out Takes,* 5.
17. Patrick E. Horrigan, *Widescreen Dreams: Growing Up Gay at the Movies* (Madison: University of Wisconsin Press, 1999), xx.
18. Doty, *Flaming Classics,* 11.
19. Quoted in Don Graham, *No Name on the Bullet: A Biography of Audie Murphy* (New York: Viking, 1989), 198.
20. Ibid., 119–20.

21. Peter Biskind, *Seeing Is Believing: How Hollywood Taught Us to Stop Worrying and Love the Fifties* (New York: Henry Holt, 2000), 315.
22. Susan Faludi, *Stiffed: The Betrayal of the American Man* (New York: Morrow, 1999), 376.
23. Graham, *No Name on the Bullet,* 124.
24. Ibid., 210.
25. Angus McLaren, *The Trials of Masculinity: Policing Sexual Boundaries, 1870–1930* (Chicago: University of Chicago Press, 1997), 33.
26. Quoted in Steven Cohan, *Masked Men: Masculinity and the Movies in the Fifties* (Bloomington: Indiana University Press, 1997), 34.
27. Audie Murphy, *To Hell and Back* (New York: H. Holt, 1949), 10.
28. Biskind, *Seeing Is Believing,* 256.
29. Cohan, *Masked Men,* 8–9.
30. There are a few collections of Clum's writing, the most notable of which is *Tombstone's Epitaph,* ed. Douglas D. Martin (Albuquerque: University of New Mexico Press, 1951).
31. Douglas Firth Anderson, "Staging Civilization: John P. Clum, Romantic Protestantism, and the Southwest, 1871–1886," paper proposal for the Western History Association, 2001.

CHAPTER 1

1. Gary Taylor, *Castration: An Abbreviated History of Western Manhood* (New York: Routledge, 2000), 3.
2. Ibid., 9.
3. Bordo, *The Male Body,* 89.
4. Ibid., 90–91.
5. Peter Lehman, *Running Scared: Masculinity and the Representation of the Male Body* (Philadelphia: Temple University Press, 1993), 28.
6. Ibid., 5.
7. Bordo, *The Male Body,* 175.
8. Ibid., 81.
9. Steve Slagle, "Gorgeous George," Professional Wrestling Online Museum. (www.wrestlingmuseum.com).
10. James Gilligan, *Violence: Reflections on a National Epidemic* (New York: Vintage, 1997), 231.
11. Ibid., 47.
12. Ibid., 83.
13. Quoted in David Savran, *Taking It Like a Man: White Masculinity, Masochism, and Contemporary American Culture* (Princeton: Princeton University Press, 1998), 178.
14. A New Breed of Gay Men (http://Home.clara.net/pb/newbreed.htm).
15. The Gay Site of Amateur Wrestling: Wrestling for Gay Guys (http://home.snafu.de/mitch/gw_intro.html).
16. Savran, *Taking It Like a Man,* 185.
17. Ibid., 38.
18. Bordo, *The Male Body,* 103.

CHAPTER 2

1. Faludi, *Stiffed,* 225.

2. Howard Lindsay and Russel Crouse, *Life with Father,* in *Sixteen Famous American Plays,* ed. Bennett A. Cert and Van H. Cartmell (New York: Modern Library, 1942), 1015. Further quotations from *Life with Father* are also from this edition.
3. Ibid., 1011.
4. Ibid., 983.
5. Ibid., 1012.
6. Philip Green, *Cracks in the Pedestal: Ideology and Gender in Hollywood* (Amherst: University of Massachusetts Press, 1998), 61.
7. R. W. Connell, *Masculinities* (Berkeley: University of California Press, 1995), 77.
8. Arthur Miller, *The Crucible* (New York: Penguin, 1978), 23. Further quotations from *The Crucible* are also from this edition.
9. Ibid., 54.
10. Ibid., 137.
11. Ibid., 137.
12. Ibid., 143.
13. David Mamet, *Oleanna* (New York: Pantheon, 1992), 76. Further quotes from *Oleanna* are also from this edition. The ellipses in the quotes are Mamet's.
14. Ibid., 1.
15. Ibid., 3.
16. Ibid., 65.
17. Ibid., 79.
18. Ibid., 80.
19. Ibid., 68–69.
20. Ibid., 80.
21. Sally Robinson, *Marked Men: White Masculinity in Crisis* (New York: Columbia University Press, 2000), 86.
22. George Kelly, *Craig's Wife* (Boston: Little, Brown, 1926), p. 2). Further quotations from *Craig's Wife* are also from this edition.
23. Ibid., 5.
24. Ibid., 16–17.
25. Ibid., 18.
26. Ibid., 60.
27. Lindsay and Crouse, *Life with Father,* 1004.
28. Kelly, *Craig's Wife,* 63.
29. Foster Hirsch, *George Kelly* (Boston: Twayne, 1975), 28.
30. Ibid., 15.
31. Kelly, *Craig's Wife,* 113.
32. Ibid., 126.
33. Ibid., 141.
34. Ibid., 140.
35. Ibid. 169.
36. Ibid., 174.
37. Doty, *Flaming Classics,* 108.
38. Elia Kazan, who directed *A Streetcar Named Desire, Cat on a Hot Tin Roof,* and *Sweet Bird of Youth,* was an alumnus of the Group Theatre, the seedbed of the American version of Stanislavskian realism known as the Method. Kazan gave Williams his greatest hits, not only by being a brilliant director by cannily knowing what his audience would accept and admire as "art." Harold Clurman, who directed *Orpheus Descending,* was one of the founders of the Group Theatre and the person who did the most to bring Stanislavskian theories to the United States. Other alumni of the Group Theatre, including Lee Strasberg, Stella Adler, and Sanford Meisner, defined the acting style (which might be called psychological realism)

that dominated American theater through the 1940s and '50s. Though Williams's own impulse was toward a more poetic, less realistic theater, directors, actors, critics, and audiences pushed his work more into psychological realism. When, in the 1960s, emboldened by the work of absurdist playwrights, Williams moved further from realism, critics excoriated him.

39. For another discussion of this subject, see my essay, "The Sacrificial Stud and the Fugitive Female in *Suddenly Last Summer, Orpheus Descending,* and *Sweet Bird of Youth,*" in *The Cambridge Companion to Tennessee Williams,* ed. Matthew C. Roudané (Cambridge: Cambridge University Press, 1997), 128–46.

40. Tennessee Williams, *Orpheus Descending* in *The Rose Tatoo and Other Plays* (New York: Penguin, 1976), 286. Further quotations from this play are also from this edition.

41. Ibid., 275.

42. Val stole a watch from Carol Cutrere's cousin Bertie, who lives with someone named Jackie. Jackie can, of course, be a female name, but given that Williams pairs Jackie with Bertie, one cannot help but think that this might be a male couple, like the offstage Jack Straw and Peter Ochello in *Cat on a Hot Tin Roof.* Val could have stolen Bertie's watch anywhere, but intimate circumstances would make the theft easier. Hence a hint that Val has had sex with Bertie and that Val, during the wild years he is eager to renounce, was not fussy about the gender of his sexual partners.

In *The Fugitive Kind,* Val's entertaining is clearly more sexual than musical. In the opening scene, he tells a New Orleans judge about a party at which he was supposed to provide the entertainment. Later, Carol (Joanne Woodward) slaps Val on the ass while saying, "You were providing the entertainment" (at a party she attended).

43. *Orpheus Descending,* 286.

44. Ibid., 326.

45. Ibid., 328.

46. Ibid., 278.

47. Ibid., 313.

48. Ibid., 246.

49. Ibid., 263.

50. Ibid., 251.

51. Ibid., 251.

52. Ibid., 268.

53. Ibid., 294.

54. See Stanley Edgar Hyman, "Some Trends in the Novel," *College English* 20 (October 1958), 2.

55. *Orpheus Descending,* 252.

56. Ibid., 279.

57. Ibid., 343.

58. Ibid., 347.

59. Ibid., 347.

60. Ibid., 283.

61. Williams's offstage homosexuals, Allan Grey in *A Streetcar Named Desire,* Skipper, Jack Straw, and Peter Ochello in *Cat on a Hot Tin Roof,* and Sebastian Venable in *Suddenly Last Summer,* are dead. His gigolos, Chance Wayne and Val Xavier, figures for homosexuals, die violent deaths. In his more sexually explicit short fiction, his homosexuals die violent or painful deaths. The sexual outlaw is a martyr-saint in Williams's works.

62. In Peter Hall's respectful film version, a great improvement over the Lumet mess, Kevin Anderson plays a Val clearly visiting from the Midwest. In a performance obviously influenced by the Brando-Clift-Dean style of acting, but more economical, Anderson manages to hold his own against Vanessa Redgrave's diva turn as Lady.

63. Donovan plays the protagonist in the British film *Hollow Reed* (1996, screenplay, Paula Milne; direction, Angela Pope), a gay, divorced father who fights successfully for custody

of his son, who is being abused by his ex-wife's boyfriend. This well-made, well-acted melo-drama presents gay domesticity as superior to a fraught heterosexual household. The gay man has a sweet, beautiful, sexy lover (Ian Hart), while the ex-wife (Joely Richardson) ends up with a brute (Jason Flemyng). The supply of cute, sweet gay men must be greater in England than the supply of sensitive straight men.

64. Green, *Cracks in the Pedestal,* 139–40.

CHAPTER 3

1. *The New York Times* (online), January 24, 2001.
2. Virginia Wright Wexman, *Creating the Couple: Love, Marriage, and Hollywood Performance* (Princeton: Princeton University Press, 1993), 84.
3. Barbara Ehrenreich, *The Hearts of Men: American Dreams and the Flight from Commitment* (Garden City, N.Y.: Anchor Press/Doubleday, 1983), 17.
4. Kimmel, *Manhood in America,* 236.
5. Tennessee Williams, *A Streetcar Named Desire,* in *The Theatre of Tennessee Williams,* vol. 1, (New York: New Directions, 1971), 354.
6. Cohan, *Masked Men,* 255.
7. Quoted in Ibid.
8. Ehrenreich, *The Hearts of Men,* 24.
9. Robert Anderson, *Tea and Sympathy,* in *Famous American Plays of the 1950s* (New York: Dell, 1962), 311.
10. Faludi, *Stiffed,* 266.
11. Gary Wills, *John Wayne's America* (New York: Simon & Shuster, 1997), 157.
12. Wexman, *Creating the Couple,* 69.
13. A number of extended discussions of the relationship of masculinity, homoeroticism, and homosexuality in *Red River* have been written. See Cohan, *Masked Men,* 204–20; Joan Mellen, *Big Bad Wolves: Masculinity and the American Film* (New York: Pantheon, 1977), 175–79; and Wills, *John Wayne's America,* 138–48.
14. Wills, *John Wayne's America,* 156.
15. Quoted in Ibid., 13.
16. Carla J. McDonough, *Staging Masculinity: Male Identity in Contemporary American Drama* (Jefferson, N.C.: McFarland, 1997), 15.
17. Mark Simpson, *Male Impersonators: Men Performing Masculinity* (New York: Routledge, 1994), 212–13.
18. Faludi, *Stiffed,* 36.
19. Don Shewey, *Sam Shepard* (New York: Da Capo, 1997), 5.
20. Robert Warshow, *The Immediate Experience: Movies, Comics, Theatre & Other Aspects of Popular Culture* (Garden City, N.Y.: Doubleday, 1962), 150.
21. Rick Lyman, "Watching Movies with Woody Allen: Coming Back to 'Shane,'" *The New York Times* (online), August 3, 2001.
22. Warshow, *The Immediate Experience,* 150.
23. Kimmel, *Manhood in America,* 252.
24. Arthur Miller, *Death of a Salesman* (New York: Viking Penguin, 1976), 53. Further quota-tions from *Death of a Salesman* are also from this edition.
25. Ibid., 47–48.
26. Ibid., 51.
27. Ibid., 48.
28. Ibid., 49.

29. Ibid., 85.
30. Ibid., 85.
31. Kimmel, *Manhood in America,* 103.
32. Miller, *Death of a Salesman,* 86.
33. Ibid., 44.
34. Ibid., 138.
35. Robert J. Corber, *Homosexuality in Cold War America: Resistance and the Crisis of Masculinity* (Durham, NC: Duke University Press, 1997), 42.
36. *Death of a Salesman,* 135.
37. Ibid., 22.
38. Ibid., 23.
39. Ehrenreich, *The Hearts of Men,* 20.
40. Quoted in Ehreenreich, *The Hearts of Men,* 18.
41. Miller, *Death of a Salesman,* 138.
42. Sam Shepard, *Buried Child* (New York: Dramatists Play Service, 1997 [rev. ed.]), 71.
43. An extended discussion of Shepard's debt to the western can be found in my essay "'True-to-Life-Westerns': The Classic Western and Shepard's Family Sagas," in *The Cambridge Companion to Sam Shepard,* ed. Matthew C. Roudané (Cambridge: Cambridge University Press, 2002), 171–88.
44. Lynda Hart, *Sam Shepard's Metaphorical Stages* (New York: Greenwood Press, 1987), 105.
45. Tennessee Williams, *Cat on a Hot Tin Roof,* in *The Theatre of Tennessee Williams,* Volume 3. (New York: New Directions, 1971), 58. Further quotations from the play are also from this edition.
46. Ibid., p. 58.
47. Ibid., p. 115.
48. "'There was a tremendous amount of homosexuality among the hoboes,' one of Dr. Henry's subjects told him from firsthand knowledge, 'and generally a great deal of affection.'" John Loughery, *The Other Side of Silence: Men's Lives and Gay Identities: A Twentieth Century History* (New York: Henry Holt, 1999), 97.
49. Corber, *Homosexuality in Cold War America,* 120.
50. *Cat on a Hot Tin Roof,* 81.
51. A young academic, anything but macho, lamented to me, "It's so hard being a gay man. I have to spend hours at the gym." When I asked why, he looked at me like I was crazy. Hard, buff bodies are essential for young gay men to feel that they are attractive.

CHAPTER 4

1. Leslie Fiedler, "Come Back to the Raft Ag'in, Huck Honey," in *A New Fiedler Reader* (Amherst, N.Y.: Prometheus Books, 1999), 7. Further quotations from this essay are also from this edition. The essay in a controversial early attempt to read the racial dynamics and the homoeroticism of classic American literature.
2. Ibid., 5.
3. Ibid., 9.
4. Savran, *Taking It Like a Man,* 38.
5. I discuss these works in my essay, "The Sacrificial Stud and the Fugitive Female in *Suddenly Last Summer, Orpheus Descending,* and *Sweet Bird of Youth,*" in *The Cambridge Companion to Tennessee Williams,* 128–46.
6. Robinson, *Marked Men,* 6–7.
7. Neither Robin Wood (*Hollywood from Vietnam to Reagan*) nor Susan Jeffords (*The Remasculinization of America: Gender and the Vietnam War*) thinks it worth mentioning,

though it was made in the midst of the war. I certainly can see the film of *Deliverance* as a Vietnam War parable—American men travel into alien territory and face what amounts to a guerilla war in which they can't tell who among the "others" they encounter is the enemy. While some survive, they can hardly be called winners, and their conflict leaves them with a profound sense of guilt and loss. If that isn't a parable of Vietnam, I don't know what is!

8. Robinson, *Marked Men,* 166–67.
9. Richard A. Kaye, "Losing His Religion: Saint Sebastian as Contemporary Gay Martyr," *Outlooks: Lesbian and Gay Sexualities and Visual Cultures,* ed. Peter Horne and Reina Lewis (London: Routledge, 1996), 87.
10. Ibid., 89.
11. Robinson, *Marked Men,* 176.
12. Robin Wood, *Hollywood from Vietnam to Reagan* (New York: Columbia University Press, 1986), 291. Wood wants to read the film as offering a bisexual triangle in Mike, Linda, Nick. I see the film as homoerotic, but not believing in the possibility of any relationship.
13. Ibid.
14. The telefilm presents Shepard as an innocent victim. We will never know if there was any truth to McKinney's testimony, though it is the classic alibi for fag bashing, which used to do the trick in getting bashers exonerated by homophobic judges and juries.

CHAPTER 5

1. W. R. Burnett, *Little Caesar* (New York: Dial Press, 1929). The opening scenes establishing the friendship of Rico and Joe are not in the novel on which the film is based. From the very beginning of the novel, Rico thinks that Joe, a successful ballroom dancer who offers a respectable "front" for the gang's activities, is soft and untrustworthy: "He'll turn yellow some day. A man don't take money for dancing." Rico is right. Joe eventually does confess, leading to a manhunt for Rico. The parallel of Rico's rise and fall with Joe's rise is not in the novel; neither is Rico's death behind the billboard.
2. Mellen, *Big Bad Wolves,* 80.
3. Jonathan Munby, *Public Enemies, Public Heroes: Screening the Gangster from* Little Caesar *to* Touch of Evil (Chicago: University of Chicago Press, 1999), 47–48.
4. See my book *Something for the Boys: Musical Theater and Gay Culture* (New York: St. Martin's Press, 1999), 94–100, for a discussion of the way in which Astaire's masculinity was defined against a series of homosexual stereotypes.
5. Jack Shadoian, *Dreams and Dead Ends: The American Gangster/Crime Film* (Cambridge, M.A.: MIT Press, 1977), 29.
6. Burnett, *Little Caesar,* 68. In Burnett's novel, Ramon Otero, a Mexican American, has a girlfriend but worships Rico: "He is a great man like Pancho Villa and I love him with a great love. I would not shoot Rico if he shot me first." It is Otero who robbed gas stations with Rico in Ohio, not Joe. The bed scene I discuss is not presented with any erotic overtones in the novel (194–95).
7. Shadoian, *Dreams and Dead Ends,* 30.
8. Warshow, *The Immediate Experience,* 63.
9. Clifford Odets, *Golden Boy,* in *Six Plays by Clifford Odets* (New York: Grove Press, 1979), 242. Further quotations are also from this edition.
10. Burnett, *Little Caesar,* 4.
11. Odets, *Golden Boy,* 242.
12. Edward Murray, *Clifford Odets: The Thirties and After* (New York: Ungar, 1968), 68.
13. Gabriel Miller, *Clifford Odets* (New York: Continuum, 1989), 74.

14. Odets, *Golden Boy,* 273.
15. Ibid., 273.
16. Ibid., 260.
17. Ibid., 261.
18. Ibid., 231.
19. Ibid., 262.
20. Murray, *Clifford Odets,* 63.
21. Odets, *Golden Boy,* 224.
22. Ibid., 261.
23. Ibid., 269.
24. Ibid., 224.
25. Ibid., 256.
26. Ibid., 271.
27. Ibid., 271.
28. Ibid., 271.
29. Margaret Brenman-Gibson, *Clifford Odets: American Playwright: The Years from 1906 to 1940* (New York: Atheneum, 1981), 469.
30. Odets, *Golden Boy,* 271.
31. Ibid., 280.
32. Dyer, *The Matter of Images,* 52–72.
33. Ibid., 52.
34. Frank Krutnik, *In a Lonely Street: Film Noir, Genre, Masculinity* (London: Routledge, 1991), 25.
35. Mellen, *Big Bad Wolves,* 153.
36. James F. Maxfield, *The Fatal Woman: Sources of Anxiety in American* Film Noir, *1941–1991* (Madison, N.J.: Fairleigh Dickinson University Press, 1996), 23.
37. See my discussion of *The Green Bay Tree* in *Still Acting Gay,* 78–84.
38. Dyer, *The Matter of Images,* 65. Robert J. Corber, in *Homosexuality in Cold War America* agrees:

    > In film noir, the gay male characters are linked iconographically to the femme fatale who lures the hero to his ruin. Like her, they are fastidious about their appearance, wear expensive, well-tailored clothes, and are identified with luxurious surroundings (10).

39. Dashiell Hammett, *The Maltese Falcon* (New York: Knopf, 1930), 84. In the novel, Spade slaps Cairo "savagely," yet Spade's savagery isn't questioned.
40. *Encarta World English Dictionary* (New York: St. Martin's Press, 1999), 798. For a discussion of the word "gunsel" as it relates to Wilmer in *The Maltese Falcon,* see Vito Russo, *The Celluloid Closet: Homosexuality in the Movies* (New York: Harper & Row, 1981), 46–47.
41. "The boy lay on his back on the sofa [Spade has knocked him out], a small figure that was—except for its breathing—altogether corpselike to the eye. Joel Cairo sat beside the boy, bending over him, rubbing his cheeks and wrists, smoothing his hair back from his forehead, whispering to him, and peering anxiously down at his white, still face" (Hammet, *The Maltese Falcon,* 229). Throughout the ensuing scene in the hotel room, Cairo keeps whispering in the boy's ear until the boy finally punches him. "Cairo cries out as a woman might have cried and drew back to the very end of the sofa" (243).
42. James Naremore, *More Than Night: Film Noir and Its Contexts* (Berkeley: University of California Press, 1998), 222.
43. With his accent, fair complexion, and German colleagues, it is hinted that Ballin is a Nazi sympathizer. Like his Führer, he wants to rule the world.

    It was not uncommon for plays and films to connect Nazis to all forms of depravity, including homosexuality. John Loughery notes:

One of the best ways to characterize Nazis before the war, writers and cartoonists found out, was to equate it with sexual perversion. Bolsheviks were a threat to be fought by every means necessary, but they represented an enemy seen as masculine—dour, determined, pragmatic. National Socialism, with its florid pageantry, its leader's histrionics (not to say hysterics), its cult of blond youth, and its self-conscious joy in male bonding, lent itself to a different approach. The Nazi was not only an anti-Semite and a bully; he was that lowest of men, the sexual degenerate. (*The Other Side of Silence*, 107)

This association was exacerbated by the Night of the Long Knives in 1934. Clifford Odets may have led the way, though Odets, characteristically, made his gay Nazis relatively sympathetic. In Odets's *Till the Day I Die* (1935), written as a companion piece for the Broadway production of *Waiting for Lefty*, homosexual desire is read as the redeeming feature of two Nazi characters.

44. John Kobal, "The Time, the Place and the Girl: Rita Hayworth," *Focus on Film* 10 (1972), 17.
45. Dyer, *The Matter of Images*, 70.
46. Sean French, *Patrick Hamilton: A Life* (London: Faber & Faber, 1993), 199.
47. Arthur Laurents, *Original Story By: A Memoir of Broadway and Hollywood* (New York: Knopf, 2000), 127.
48. Robin Wood, *Hitchcock's Films Revisited* (New York: Columbia University Press, 1989), 351.
49. D. A. Miller, "Anal *Rope*," in *Inside/Out: Lesbian Theories, Gay Theories*, ed. Diana Fuss (New York: Routledge, 1991), 125.
50. Richard Dyer, "Resistance Through Charisma: Rita Hayworth and *Gilda*," in *Women in Film Noir*, ed. E. Ann Kaplan (London: British Film Institute, 1978), 94.
51. Laurents, *Original Story By*, 130–31.
52. Alfred Hitchcock and Arthur Laurents had wanted Cary Grant for Rupert and Montgomery Clift for Brandon. According to Laurents, Hitchcock told him that Grant and Clift turned down the film because the sexuality of the characters might turn a harsh light on the actors' sexuality (*Original Story By*, 131).
53. Corber, *Homosexuality in Cold War America*, 64–65.
54. Loughery, *The Other Side of Silence*, 111.
55. John Logan, introduction to *Never the Sinner* (Woodstock, N.Y.: Overlook Press, 1999), 13–14. Logan's play, first produced in Chicago in 1985 and since produced in New York, London, and elsewhere, romanticizes the Leopold-Loeb relationship.
56. Anthony Minghella, *The Talented Mr. Ripley: A Screenplay* (New York: Hyperion, 1999), 130. Further quotations from the screenplay are from this edition. There are some discrepancies between the published screenplay and the cut of the film available on DVD (Paramount, 2000). Most of the cuts made after the published version went to press are in sections of dialogue that are overtly gay. While the film makes no secret of Ripley's sexuality or his affair with Peter, these are presented as cautiously as they would be in a film of the 1940s. Often, too, Matt Damon seems to improvise approximate versions of Minghella's lines.
57. Minghella, *The Talented Mr. Ripley*, 54.
58. Ibid., xii.
59. Patricia Highsmith, *The Talented Mr. Ripley* (New York: Vintage, 1992), 81. Further quotations from the novel are also from this edition.
60. Ibid., 81.
61. Ibid., 79.
62. Ibid., 89.
63. Ibid., 92.
64. Ibid., 100.

65. Ibid., 142.
66. Ibid., 147.
67. Ibid., 152.
68. Ibid., 192.
69. Ibid., 274.
70. Ibid., 34.
71. Ibid., 249.
72. Phyllis Nagy, *The Talented Mr. Ripley* (London: Methuen, 1999), 35. In 1998, the British playwright Phyllis Nagy wrote a stage adaptation of *The Talented Mr. Ripley* that is much more Nagy than Highsmith. In Nagy's version, Tom is openly gay from the beginning, and somewhat Nietzschean. In one scene, he cuts his hand in front of Dickie to show how he can transcend pain and blood: "Pain is an asset. Vulnerability is what your enemies exploit." At the end, he is trying to revel in his isolation, but is still haunted by the voices that mock and diminish him.
73. Minghella, introduction to *The Talented Mr. Ripley,* xiii.
74. Ibid., xiii.
75. Ibid., 11.
76. Ibid., 44.
77. Ibid., 104.
78. Ibid., 35.
79. Ibid., 56.
80. Ibid., 58.
81. Ibid., 106.
82. Ibid., 129–30.

CHAPTER 6

1. Brooks had actually written one of the era's more sympathetic treatments of homosexuals in the 1940s in his 1945 novel, *The Brick Foxhole,* an urban nightmare in which the homosexual is the victim in a well-meaning, "liberal"-for-its-time, depiction of homosexuals and attack on violent homophobia. The novel concerns a gay bashing by military men during World War II.

   When *The Brick Foxhole* was turned into a film, *Crossfire* (screenplay, John Paxton; direction, Edward Dmytryk), in 1947, the soldiers were veterans of the war who no longer know where to direct their anger and penchant for violence. Monty Crawford (Robert Ryan) here kills a Jew, Joseph Samuels (Sam Levene). The police captain (a pipe-smoking Robert Young) is an Irish Catholic whose grandfather was murdered by anti-Catholics. *Crossfire* is a fine example of the sort of Hollywood liberalism that would soon be quashed by anti-Communist hysteria. It is a somewhat preachy sermon against bigotry, though the primary target of bigotry in the novel, homosexuality, is erased, sort of.
2. Vito Russo, *The Celluloid Closet,* 259.
3. On his DVD commentary, Taylor says, "Personally I don't think the two have a shot in hell of making it as a couple."
4. Paul Burston, "Just a Gigolo?: Narcissism, Nellyism, and the 'New Man' Theme," in *A Queer Romance: Lesbians, Gay Men, and Popular Culture,* ed. Paul Burston and Colin Richardson (London: Routledge, 1995), 215.
5. Burston, "Just a Gigolo," 114.
6. Lehman, *Running Scared,* 18.

7. Hyper-romantic Canadian films like *Lilies, Being at Home with Claude,* and *L'Escorte* are in-fused with an operatic sense of irrational passion and fatal love. I greatly admire the daring of these works.

CHAPTER 7

1. Played by Ben Weber, who plays the cute but not gorgeous gay man in *The Broken Hearts Club,* miserable because he's not as beautiful as his buddies.
2. Showtime's *Queer as Folk* is the American version of the successful British series. Though the characters are more fully fleshed out in Showtime's continuing series than they were in the much shorter British original, and the setting has been changed from Manchester, England, to Pittsburgh (the series is actually filmed in Toronto, which is more picturesque than Pittsburgh and much more of a gay mecca), something is missing, mainly because of some terminally bland casting. The weak link is Gale Harold's charmless, one-note Brian, a far cry from his raffish prototype, Aidan Gillen's Stuart, on the British series.
3. James Harvey, *Romantic Comedy in Hollywood: From Lubitsch to Sturges* (New York: Da Capo Press, 1998), 433–34.
4. After a series of box-office failures (though the films, including *Sylvia Scarlett* and *Bringing Up Baby,* are now considered classics), Hepburn had Philip Barry tailor a Broadway vehicle for her with her close collaboration. *The Philadelphia Story* was a huge hit. The film version gave her career new life. James Harvey points out that "everyone recognized that the character of Tracy Lord, aristocratic and beautiful and arrogant, was 'about' Hepburn herself. Even about her career problems" (Harvey, *Romantic Comedy in Hollywood,* 408).
5 Stanley Cavell, *Pursuits of Happiness: The Hollywood Comedy of Remarriage* (Cambridge, MA.: Harvard University Press, 1981), p. 145.
6. David Ehrenstein, *Open Secret: Gay Hollywood 1928 - 1988* (New York: William Morrow, 1998), 30. Grant lived a relatively openly gay life during his first decade in Hollywood, sharing a house with Randolph Scott, engaging in gay society. There were brief marriages during this period, but Scott seemed his primary relationship. During World War II, he became more cautious.
7. The 2001 comedy *Bridget Jones's Diary* offers a contemporary variation on *The Philadelphia Story*—and on *Pride and Prejudice* and a few other classic romances. Bridget must choose between two men, a sexy cad (Hugh Grant) and a socially awkward honest man (Colin Firth playing his Darcy again—he played Darcy on a British television version of *Pride and Prejudice*.). She ends up with the man she knew as a child, who is also the man she hasn't been sleeping with.
8. Bordo, *The Male Body,* p. 160.
9. In one of the film's few glimmers of wit, son Sam asks Robert if he is a faggot. When Robert and Abbie ask him if he knows what "faggot" means, Sam answers, "It's when two boys kiss. And go to the opera."
10. Other than *The Living End,* discussed in chapter 6, I do not discuss the many depictions of gay relationships made during the time when the AIDS epidemic was devastating the gay community (1981–1995). Particularly noteworthy were *Parting Glances* (1986; screenplay and direction, Bill Sherwood) and *Longtime Companion* (1990; screenplay, Craig Lucas; direction, Norman René). I discuss many of these works in *Still Acting Gay, Something for the Boys,* and in my essay, "'And Once I Had It All': AIDS Narratives and Memories of an American Dream," in *Writing AIDS: Gay Literature, Language, and Analysis,* eds. Timothy F. Murphy and Suzanne Poirier (New York: Columbia University Press, 1993), 200–224.

11. Does one, then, have an obligation to proclaim one's sexuality to the world at large? Actually, heterosexuals proclaim their sexuality all the time, particularly to allay any suspicion that they might be gay. I think that those of us in long-term relationships have the right to the same respect and legal protection for our private lives as coupled heterosexuals. For it not to be an issue, we have to live as if our life choices are as valid as heterosexuals'. To hide them is to suggest that they are indeed shameful.

12. *Defying Gravity* was filmed in Los Angeles, hardly a place lacking in gay nightspots. Cute Griff is more likely to join up with the guys in *The Broken Hearts Club* than remain isolated from gay friends.

13. One can say the same thing of *Defying Gravity*. In his confusion, Griff is hurtful to just about everyone who cares about him.

14. Wexman, *Creating the Couple*, x.

15. Wexman, *Creating the Couple*, 5.

16. I discuss this play at length in *Still Acting Gay*, 261–280.

17. Peter M. Nardi, *Gay Men's Friendships: Invincible Communities* (Chicago: University of Chicago Press, 1999), 7.

18. Middle-aged gay men can be the subject of farce, as in *The Birdcage* (screenplay, Elaine May; direction, Mike Nichols), the 1996 American film version of the French stage and film farce *La Cage aux Folles*.

CHAPTER 8

1. Henry Louis Gates, "Backlash?" in *Dangerous Liaisons: Blacks, Gays, and the Struggle for Equality*, ed. Eric Brandt (New York: The New Press, 1999), 29.

2. Leslie Fiedler, "Come Back to the Raft Ag'in, Huck Honey," in *A New Fiedler Reader* (Amherst, N.Y.: Prometheus Books, 1999), 8. Further references to Fiedler's essay are from this edition.

3. David Savran, *Taking It Like a Man: White Masculinity, Masochism, and Contemporary American Culture* (Princeton, N.J.: Princeton University Press, 1998), 251.

4. John Guare, *Six Degrees of Separation* (New York: Vintage, 1990), 25. Further references are from this edition.

5. Ibid., 79.

6. Ibid., 91

7. Fiedler, 11.

INDEX OF TITLES

Unless otherwise noted, these are film titles. All of the plays I discuss in depth have also been made into films.

INDEX OF NAMES